THIS PLACE A STRANGER

Caitlin Press Inc.
8100 Alderwood Road,
Halfmoon Bay, BC V0N 1Y1
www.caitlin-press.com
Edited by Vici Johnstone, Rebecca Hendry, Kathleen Fraser and Andrea Routley
Cover image: Dudarev Mikhail Shutterstock_120401317
Printed in Canada

Caitlin Press Inc. acknowledges financial support from the Government of Canada through the Canada Book Fund and the Canada Council for the Arts, and from the Province of British Columbia through the British Columbia Arts Council and the Book Publisher's Tax Credit.

Library and Archives Canada Cataloguing in Publication

This place a stranger : Canadian women travelling alone / Vici Johnstone.
ISBN 978-1-927575-73-4 (pbk.)

    1. Travelers' writings, Canadian (English). 2. Women authors, Canadian (English)—Travel. 3. Women travelers—Canada. I. Johnstone, Vici, 1959-, editor
II. Title.
PR1309.T73T45 2015   910.4
C2015-900931-6

THIS PLACE A
Stranger

CANADIAN WOMEN
TRAVELLING ALONE

edited by VICI JOHNSTONE

CAITLIN PRESS

CONTENTS

VICI JOHNSTONE

INTRODUCTION

VICI JOHNSTONE

I am large
I contain multitudes.
—Walt Whitman

I have been fortunate in my life and career to have had many opportunities to travel, sometimes with a companion, but more often than not, alone. I have seen the Blue Mosque in Istanbul, hiked to a monastery in Metéora. I swam in the Black Sea, ate in the Carnivore restaurant in Nairobi and spent aimless hours in museums, castles and art galleries. Last year, I spent a warm spring day on Signal Hill in St John's, Newfoundland, watching an iceberg implode, and in that same season, I drove countless hours through the expansive and diverse terrain that is my own home province of BC.

When I bought Caitlin Press, I knew that the years to come would be busy and that my commitment to rebuilding the press would keep me fairly close to home, at least on the continent. So, as publisher, my first decison was to take a holiday abroad before putting nose to grindstone. It was hardly high adventure, but I booked a flight to Cancun and from there I took a cab to a small resort in Tulum's Reserva de le Biósfera Sian Ka'an.

It was June and the end of the season in Tulum, so the buses, which would normally shuttle tourists to the ruins and into town had ceased running for the season. After settling in to my hut on the beach, I decided to explore. I walked to the viewpoint at the end of the peninsula where I stood for hours photographing the brown pelicans swirling and dancing in the final throws of the windstorm. I was so fascinated by their grace and agility that I wasn't aware that a man had come up behind me until I felt his breath on the back of my neck and his body pressing into mine. Instinctively, I thrust my elbow backward into his stomach and then turned abruptly to face him. His look of shock turned to dismay and then what appeared to be shame. He disappeared as quickly and quietly as he had surfaced.

Unnerved, I tucked the camera into my bag and hurried back to the tavern in the little village that I had passed earlier. When the waiter came I ordered a bowl of soup to calm my nerves. I pulled out my book and began to read but after a few moments I had the sense that someone was watching me. Expecting the worst (that the man from the peninsula had followed me), I stood up and looked over the sign that advertised fresh tortillas and cold Mexican beer. A small child, perhaps two years of age was looking at me, and when she realised she had caught my attention, she smiled and ducked below the sign. A few seconds later she popped up, squealed and hid again. I laughed and sat down thinking the game was over, but she was clearly entertained by me and we continued to play peek-a-boo for another ten minutes. Eventually, her mother came. She smiled at me as she scooped up her adventurous daughter and left me to finish my lunch.

A few minutes later the waiter returned to my table with my soup. He explained that they were shutting down for the season and had to empty out the fridge and bar. He wondered if I would like a glass of wine and some fresh ceviche to accompany my lunch. Of course I said yes.

On my walk back to the resort, I thought about the little girl and the stark contrast between her and my earlier experience with the man who had taken advantage of my distraction. I wondered what asumption that man had made when he saw a white woman travelling alone. Would he have approached me in such a way if I had been travelling with a man or even a group of friends? I also wondered about the young girl, and her fascination with me. Was I an exotic foreigner or was I appproachable because I was alone? Would I have played with the girl if I had been travelling with a companion? It occurred to me that in some ways they were both trying to engage with me, and the fact that I was a visitor had made me an object of interest. But, that is the thing about travelling alone, isn't it? The very act involves engagement, sometimes welcome, sometimes not. We are not just benign observers and neither are we invisible.

When I began to review the submissions for this anthology, I was pleasantly surprised to discover that we had received nearly two hundred stories from across the country. I spent many days as an armchair traveller reading these stories of adventure, tragedy and discovery. The authors had travelled the entire globe it seemed, from northern Canada to East Africa, South Asia and more. It was clear that each woman experienced travel in a different way, and that her socio-economic background and purpose for travel heavily influenced that experience. But these stories shared a common thread: they explored how we move through the world when we are out of our comfort zones, and how being alone heightens both our awareness and our vulnerability.

The idea for this anthology was born from a comment I received from a group of women travellers I encountered on one of my trips. They told me I was "brave" to travel on my own, and that they would never have the "courage." I did not think of the man in Tulum in this moment, but was instead struck by what a loss this was for these women. I received many stories of gender-based violence, and some of them are included here. After all, it is impossible to ignore the cultural realities at home and in the world that make women more vulnerable to such violence. But it is also a tragedy to let such fears prevent us from engaging with new people and places. When we travel alone, without a familiar companion to reflect back to us a familiar self, we are strangers— to ourselves and to those around us. The following stories illustrate the many ways, for better or worse, such experiences can change us, reveal us, open a world of understanding.

I hope you enjoy these stories. And I also hope that you are inspired by the strength and insight of these women.

WHAT ARE YOU MOST AFRAID OF?

YVONNE BLOMER

L eaving or not coming back. Leaving or not wanting to come back. I feel I should raise my right hand, my left on my passport, say, "Hi, my name is Yvonne, I'm a mom and I love to travel ... by myself."

It is impossible to divide the self from the self. The self is integrated so I am here and I am home. I am sad to leave and I am excited. I would never not come home while at the same time the thought moves through the passages of my mind.

What is travel?

In my twenties and thirties it was two years in Japan, three months cycling in Southeast Asia, cycling in Mexico for two weeks; it was living in England for a year, hiking in Spain; it was cycling in Northern France, driving to Wales, or touring Cyprus. It was research trips to Dublin, to Ravenna and Bologna, Italy, with a newborn son tied to my chest (making me an easy target for a pickpocketing Gypsy mom with a babe on her hip).

These days, when I travel on my own—and many, if not most, of the aforementioned travels were with my husband—it is to do research, tour a new book or attend a conference, festival or professional development workshop. It makes me sound so very adult, that travel is now for business, but remember my admission—I love to travel—so I often go out of my way to find a reason to pop down to Seattle on the Clipper ferry, to go to Toronto or further afield, to Lithuania. I also, of course, travel with my family—camping trips, beach holidays, visits to lakes, and autumnal cabins with wood fires and loons or crows just outside the window. Family holidays are different from time away on my own. Time away on my own allows a different self to emerge.

To travel solo means not only to enter a new place physically but also to delve into my interior places. As a woman, it also allows me to explore my strengths and fears, to check in on how or whether things have changed for women. Are we safer in the world unaccompanied or not? Do we feel safer? Must every decision take into account the risk? My frustrating ability to get turned around and lost in a heartbeat is paired to my desire and determination to get out there and explore the winding hillsides of Wales by bike, or the wending cobbled streets of Lithuania on foot. These desires are paired with a knowledge of risk. In Wales I cycled to Merthyr Tydfil, stayed in a questionable B & B with a depressed female owner and in the evening walked out to find dinner. I did not feel safe, so returned and made do with what I carried. I did not see the castle in the moonlight because the people walking the streets around me, and the vibe of the city itself, made me too uncomfortable. In Vilnius I travelled alone but was on a literary seminar with a group.

My son was six when I left him and his dad to go to Lithuania for two long weeks. My son has special needs: he has a dual diagnosis of Prader-Willi syndrome and autism. Let me just fess up at the beginning—those two weeks were long for all three of us. Long and luxuriant sometimes, long and filled with the deep ache for the little boy I'd left behind. We would Skype, but when he looked at my face on his dad's computer screen, it was clear that this conduit, this mediated connection, was not going to work, was perhaps worse than not seeing me.

What do you gain as a woman and a mother when you travel alone?

I fly Victoria to Calgary to Frankfurt to Lithuania. Half the time I wonder, who would leave their beautiful son? This thought fills my mind like a fog as I'm settling the lump down my throat, the seat belt across my lap. "What if the big one comes while I'm away?" I ask my husband every time I leave. His answer is always the same: "You come home to us." The big one, the earthquake we are expecting on the west coast of Canada, is an open but fixed possibility that holds the potential of anything that could go wrong and thus far has not.

Seconds later and in sync with the *why leave* is that euphoric race down the runway right before takeoff, and the leaping realization: I am on my own. It will go fast, I tell myself. It will be great. Bonding time for the boys. Lithuania, writing time, dare I think *freedom*? In the airplane on my own, my body is my own. This life, tied as it is to those two creatures—boy and man—is also my own. Such great guilt and spasms of relief as I lean my forehead on the window to watch clouds swallow Vancouver Island, then Calgary, as I pull out a book or a notebook, as I look at my guidebook and imagine the hours in Frankfurt and how I will, solo, fill them.

I arrive in Vilnius late on Saturday night unsure which day I've lost—Thursday or Friday? I am, to my utter delight, fetched from the airport along with a woman who flew in from Boston, and we are driven through the windy and confusing streets of the Old Town of Vilnius to our separate apartments by Ursule and her friend. As we navigate the narrow streets, bodies spill from nightclubs, hollering and gleeful. The woman from Boston is let off first, atop a hill at a very red building with large windows. That is about all I can take in as I peer up in the dark, peer down toward what might be the city. Then we drive deeper into the city, down narrower cobbled alleys and park, blocking the street. I'm guided through a dark archway, into a dark courtyard, up a flight of darkened stairs to where we jiggle a key in a dark door, then enter a sprawling apartment.

"There is a food store across the main street," Ursule points. She then gives me a map, a hug goodnight, tests the key a few times with me. I close the door behind her and voila. Silence. Space. Solitude.

Does everyone crave this as I do?

Excited, peckish, thirsty, how will I sleep? I try the key in the lock several more times. It must be near midnight. I don shoes and a light jacket and head to the main street, walking briskly through the darkened archway, left on the darkened and quiet street, to the busier and bustling late-night street. I can see the small grocery store and cross to it. I am full of anticipation for this rare city, and I want to get out in it so I can sleep knowing I've arrived.

What is worse, hazy-eyed and in the wrong time zone, the dark quiet street or the busy chaotic drunken revellers with a language and culture you do not understand?

I walk through the revellers to the store, buy bread, milk, coffee, wine, water, cookies, apples and cheese and walk back. The key works and I relax into my solace knowing there is nowhere and nothing I have to do on Sunday except find my way to a specific pub/café by evening for the welcome. I perch on the wide windowsill, drink the water and the moon, drink the distant peaked church roofs, the gravel courtyard and crumbling dark buildings around it. The Internet does not work, so that is one thing I'll have to deal with tomorrow. For now, my husband cannot know I've arrived safely. I am restless and exhausted. I'm wired, off-kilter by travel and time. I am reading P.D. James's *Death Comes to Pemberley*, not a brilliant book, but entertainment that distracts me to sleep.

I wake the next morning glad to not be feeling too overwhelmed by what I have done—left my boys and the security of them. In Frankfurt yesterday, tired and quaking a little at being on my own, I noted that I was the only woman in all the world without her blond-haired child as families carried, coerced, settled their small children. I was at once envious and relieved.

In the light of this new place, the birds perched on the sill outside my magnificent windows let their voices trill along with the church bells, the distant cars, bike bells, other voices. Coffee in hand I watch and listen. It is early, too early to go out, so perched there I let my single self come forward, ready to let her footsteps echo down the halls and streets and let her not worry for the shadow self left at home.

So I go out in search of iced coffee after waking at three, sleeping, waking at seven, daydreaming and unpacking. I have called Ursule regarding the Internet. The landlord will come by later; in the meantime, a new city to explore before I return for more sleep.

Backpack slung, I wander to the main street and turn left. It is Sunday-morning quiet and I am in another time zone. I smile as I pass the few morning wanderers. I find where the workshops will be, I find the main shopping street and an iced coffee, Wi-Fi, a quietly shaded table to send a quick message home—I'm here, I miss you.

Everyone in Vilnius seems draped in flowing dresses and loose trousers, in their soft accents: Irish, Italian, Lithuanian and German. It is another kind of music and I try not to look too stupid-happy as I wander. I try to walk with purpose, though at this point I have none.

In the old town, one of the oldest intact medieval cities and a UNESCO heritage sight, I move from ultra-modern shops inside ancient buildings to a sprawling university, where Latin is carved into the entryways for the different disciplines—philosophy, science and medicine. I find church building after church building, a square and vendors selling amber jewelry, wool socks and matryoshka. I find Literatu Street only because I'm determined the map will eventually lead me there. This narrow lane has small plaques along a plastered wall depicting the teeth of a critic, Milosz's profile, sketches of pigeons and a portrait of the writer Ricardas Gavilis, a wooden plaque that says "POETS," then Vytautas Mačernis, a brass handprint, tile photo of two boys and more. This wall of Literatu is backdropped by metal and tiled roofs, the spire of a Russian orthodox church, the wider shopping streets just a slip of a corner away.

Should I dive fully into this solitude? What will the reverse process entail?

3:38 a.m. I'm awoken by wind rattling the giant windows and rain booming through. I scramble out of my books and sheets and close all but one, which I shut and then open from above, so the rain can't come in but I can still hear it. I sit again in the window and watch the sky, the rain in slivered sheets, the bricks alight with lightning. Son and husband will be eating dinner, or getting ready for bed. We talk as I wake and before the boy goes down for the night. These are the hardest times for us—waking and sleeping, that breath of longing feathering across the body just before the brain comes back or lets go. Hence the books in my bed, hence the late-night Skype chats and my son's grunting attempts to reach my hand, take me where he wants me.

The opening ceremony, earlier this evening, was drinks and nibbles and conversation. I found my nonfiction cohort, but few of the poets. A friend from Victoria has just finished the first two-week session; another Canadian will be in both my poetry and CNF classes. There are three Canadians, the rest American. I find that I fall in the middle here, and it makes me feel old and more attracted to solitude. There are twenties and thirties in university doing master's degrees; there are fifties and sixties exploring and pushing their writing; there is me, just newly forty-one. I am anticipating the first workshop. I am awake at four in the morning. I watch the wind and rain and the flash of lightning, then pull myself back to bed.

Is freedom waking in the night and staying up? Joining or shunning the group?

With no one to disturb, the hours of the night are mine. The seminar will mean that on Monday, Wednesday and Friday we are in poetry in the morning and nonfiction in the afternoon. There is also a fiction group and there is a Jewish Lithuania group who tours through the troubled history of Jews in Lithuania every day until most can barely take in any more. On Tuesdays and Thursdays there are walking tours and tours to Trakai Castle outside the city and Paneriai also outside the city. I don't like to miss out, but by the end of every day, sometimes late after dinner, I walk into the solace of my apartment and wonder why I've been away from it all day.

Are you a woman alone or a woman in a pack of women?

Rain again as we walk, small pack of women. Miraculously, we come to Town Hall and think now we can fall into easy conversation because my place is that way, mine that way, mine up that way. We know exactly where we are! But the streets in Vilnius do not line up or meet or add up or have the same name from one block to the next. We look up or out from the conversations we are coiled in and we are on a dark street, out of the hustle and bustle. A man comes out a dark door, from which deep voices spill, and whistles to us as if calling his cat in from the rain. A cathedral bright and familiar in daylight seems ominous. Familiar or not, we cannot tell, its grounds dug up as if bodies have grown bored of the patter of rain and es- caped. Neither street names nor landmarks are known. Then we turn another corner and—Oh yes, one of us says, I know this street. Then two part for home and two let Traku Street lead us to Vokieciu up and along toward Vilnius Street. Late now, but still people about, walking in small groups. Our English words float ahead of us. At a corner, we almost part ways; then I notice a big-screen TV at an outdoor bar—the Olympics are on and it's swimming.

We order drinks and the waitress says, "Lithuania has a young swimmer who is doing really well." So we watch. And she wins. The bar is not busy, but there are a few tables with big groups. Everyone stands up for the national anthem and a beautiful blond young woman of fifteen years steps up to the podium, a gold medal placed around her neck. We sing along, as best we can, the voices so loud, the country small, and everyone knows that girl, or her mother, her aunt or uncle, her farming brother, her politician granddad. Or so I imagine.

Do you understand your place in the hierarchy of education and death?

Vilna, Wilna, Wilno, Vilno. Even in the late seventeenth century, maps of this city showed its name with six different spellings. Plurality is not a new concept. I am a writer and a daydreamer. I am old to some, and young to others. I am a mom, but not visibly, though everyone knows my son exists. The city was made up of Europeans, Jews, Russian Orthodox, Polish, Germans. Napoleon was here, Roman Catholic churches, a synagogue. It wanted to be homogeneous but it never was. The grand duke invited even the pagans to live here. All of these races of men could attend university, so on a tour, when we talk of early days of universities, the guide says all were welcome. In my head I correct him. Women were not. Whether Russian or Jewish, Polish or German, Orthodox or Christian, women were not allowed in the universities. I fold Virginia Woolf's voice over the guide's and I step, lightly, on the grass while he speaks and I walk slowly through the library taking in its beauty and the presence of its female students, books stacked around them, heads ponytailed and bent.

Do you feel safe here?

Now I know that everywhere I look I'm looking at things lost. Jewish gravestones taken to rebuild schools after war, or used for pavement, so that I am walking on them. Hebrew writing shining, pentimento, through whitewash in the old Jewish Quarter, which was cordoned off and all the Jews moved into it before they were moved out of the city. In the museum, black and white photos are too graphic to absorb. I can't get my head around it all, and I begin to retreat into myself again. After days of being drawn into conversations, I can feel the desire to be alone so aloneness has more pull than the new people and the history of this place. I slip away from the group tour and wander aimlessly on my own. I find my new favourite street. It leads up a slight hill and ends in an archway. Just before the archway, which opens to more of the city, a small shop sells postcards and rents out bicycles. I buy a few cards and inquire about the cost of the bikes before wandering back to my place. I store the details of the shop and bikes for later. So nice to have a place here, a space I can talk out loud to myself if I need, or collapse and cry or write or sing, even dance to the patter of rain.

Do you dream when you sleep?

I barely sleep.

A grad student from New York walks me home from a house party at an expat American poet's. The poet is a writer who has been living in Vilnius for some years. He has known Robert Bringhurst since the sixties and knows Jan Zwicky as well. Once home, I work on a poem for class, then the boys Skype me. It's near or past midnight. My little boy is getting bigger and bigger, even though I'm not there. He smiles, curious and sleepy, having just woken up. He looks almost perplexed to see me there. I can see the fine hairs on his arms. Such anticipation in everything—the pulse in his neck that I can see, his soft hair and blue eyes—not as good as to hold and breathe him in. His dad tells me we got the At Home Program, funding for kids with special needs. We've proven he lacks the skills for independence.

By the time Nazi Germany arrived in Lithuania, they had perfected their cull. The Jews, mentally handicapped, aged, ill were the first to be killed in those first weeks of occupation. Next were all the lefties, the different. The only one left of my family would have been my husband. I am preparing myself for Paneriai. The question rises about history and knowledge. Of what I can subject myself to and what I cannot of this country's difficult history. How to bring myself to visit one of the killing grounds?

And so I do not sleep but greet a beautiful day—the sun filtered by threads of breeze. I'm in my windowsill again. I can see the trail of an airplane in the sky. Orange tile roofs, wisps of clouds, the crumbling brick building beside mine in the courtyard below, trees, laundry, flower garden with orange daisies and hydrangeas not yet in full bloom. Our morning lecture has been cancelled and I am thrilled. Up late and restless all night—worrying the poem, worrying the soft beads of thought that circle my son. The image of him on the computer screen before bed is a trap for my dreamless mommy self.

In Monday's non-fiction class we are editing a long piece, in detail, all very seriously and dedicatedly, when the writer pipes in and tells us it was just an exercise, not to take it seriously. Some of it was made up. The metaphor we are discussing is an accident; nothing was intended. I understand the need for the writer to have a defence mechanism, an out, but feel like I've wasted my time. There is an underlying arrogance here, an inability to take the work seriously. I have left my family to be here and I take it very seriously. There is a contract between a writer and her or his reader, and the writer has just broken it. I walk away, walk home. I harbour thoughts of escape. I think I could cycle to the Baltic and skip a day of this. I think, I am a little fed up after a week away, with myself or with the others, with being invisible because of my age, or too visible, with being the smart one in class, or the dummy, the quiet one, the old one. Tired of all these woven threads, of the garments of life. Longing for the strength that comes in knowing no one, or travelling with one you know all too well.

So gradually, bit by bit, a little rebellion begins to take place.

I am invited to the expat poet's again along with an American prof/writer, the New York grad student who is staying there and my poetry instructor. The two other Canadians have invited me to join them for dinner, which will be my escape plan, my excuse for leaving early. I am not sure how I feel, but I am the only woman invited and I feel cautious, vulnerable, though why I cannot say, and I feel exposed. Our host is very sociable, his house unusual with many storeys and steep staircases, a small deck perches practically off the roof, overlooking what was the Jewish quarter. All his walls have narrow, packed bookshelves. I'm in a skirt and the men follow me up the ladder to the rooftop patio. Self-conscious, female, exposed, I speak loudly to be heard. Our host looks forward to the arrival of many Americans each summer in his adopted city where he can talk art and literature, give walking tours, speak fluidly in his native tongue. When I say I have to go, and the three men follow me, he is deeply disappointed. I email him later to apologize, and he replies that he understands the need for solitude. We are all on working holidays, we all are writers, and perhaps everyone feels vulnerable.

Then, and again, I do not sleep—overstimulated by the evening and conversations, by the wind and rain, the thunder, lightning, hungry in the night, I wake and sit in my window and snack and write a love poem to my husband. Rarely on these solo trips do I miss my husband; always he is usurped by the small body of the boy we have made. So I am surprised in the middle hours to miss him, to write to him by lightning and by rain, these two elements that seem to reside in my blood and my skin:

> What to say? Everywhere I miss you,
> so I am fractured and I am whole.
> In the funnel of ear, my voice;
> in the chamber of vein, your song.

In some ways life is easier here. It is a between world where I study/eat/write/socialize/sleep. Simplified down to these elements, in some ways, this is harder.

What do you think you need, want?

I need to grow teeth. Need to let go of that fear of missing out and that focus on want.

Today our walking tour takes us up out of Old Vilnius to the market across the river. We begin to cohere as a group. Begin to easily pull together and apart. To connect and separate and connect. The Polish bread man winks as he passes me a heavy-grained loaf and I feel momentarily native. After the market, we walk through the old shtetl where a house has recently burned, and people peer through curtains. I look down, walk quietly and alone to seem less invasive, then wait for two women from the US, both Jewish, to go for lunch. After lunch we separate and I speed past skyscrapers and back over the river into the ancient town. We cohere and yet I'm feeling a need for solace in the second week. Missing my son and husband, who are camping, so beyond my reach. Without them, I want to be truly on my own. The days are full—from workshop to lunch to workshop to evening reading to dinner to home with barely any time to contemplate, wander and write. What to pull back from, what to pull close to?

Is this just skipping school?

I wander back up my favourite street where the arch leads out of the old city and stop at the small store to rent a bike. I do this after poetry class; after lunch I disappear. I text my classmates and say I'll be going to a nearby bar for beer at six and then I get on my granny bike, with back-pedal brakes, and learn the shape of the city from its bike paths and rivers—the Neris and the Vilnia. Every day I learn something new—human beings everywhere, but today I coast past them all and learn again the perfection of the bicycle. This machine mediates my passage through Vilnius and reconnects me to myself. I do not have to smile or stop to speak to anyone, but when I stop to people-watch on a grassy slope I do smile, give directions and watch families with young children learning to ride. I feel calm and content, unhurried, silent.

I cycle past the familiar parts of Old Vilnius from across the river, then cross toward the city on a pedestrian bridge and follow the bike paths the long way round to Stikliu and Zydu streets, stop at the Italian deli for wheat beer and pedal back to the shop. I run home for a shower and meet the gang for beer and fried bread. I feel less and more of everything—less grouchy, more in myself.

What are you most afraid of?

I'm afraid of the rain. It is raining so hard in the morning that I decide not to go to Paneriai, then decide to go. After, I write this:

I Confess We Ate Chocolate
(after Theodor Adorno)

First, the bus driver kept getting lost and those on it began to wonder from what edge, into what ditch, we would
drop. Rain; let me speak of rain in the Baltic. Rain filled
the narrow pitted roads, hung from trees while branches
scraped the bus's roof and slaughtered peace, leaving cracks
in all our frail judgements. When we arrived at the pristine
compound in the middle of the wood and rain we stood,
umbrella to umbrella. We loved our guide, her Austrian accent and suit, her brown hair and meagre raincoat. We were
not in Austria but in the complicated village of Paneriai
outside Vilnius where the Russians dug pits to hide muni-
tions, and the Germans used them for other things. (Have I
mentioned the hot coffee and rich rye bread, the currants
I'd eaten that morning? How each seedy berry bled a story,
grown from fields once graves?) She talked and we followed (Jews and Catholics, some with their German heritage on their faces, some from New York or other places on
this earth). She led us to the edge of a pit, a sloped saucer,
green with grass. She led us there to speak of numbers, of
the half-starved men brought to sort through things, of the
villagers who came as if to market to find new (used) shoes
and clothes. Came in rain. In the small museum and the
rain we read everything. Like crows we pecked down to the
marrow of some bitter carrion. Like wolves. We combed
for (hope) the story. The Japanese official who issued vi-
sas, the music and poetry of the captives. We were wet and
huddled as a group. Then each of us, alone, walked onto the
bus. Silence rode us back to the city. In our wet socks and
our silence we shared shards of dark chocolate.

We follow this trip with a lecture titled "Lessons from Holocaust in
a Never Again World" by Simon Wiesenthal. He has riddles for the
occasion: "When can you tell a new day has dawned? When rich man/

poor man or black woman/white woman are not distinguishable." I like what he has to say. I think again about everyone being welcomed to the university in Lithuania in the past and of being a woman, and of having a child with special needs. I am a white woman. Does that matter? Do the labels matter beyond the experiences they give us—white, woman, mother, daughter, sister, wife, writer, teacher, forty-year-old, traveller? We all have experiences, like markers or secret cards in the hands we've been dealt. These cards are our wild cards; they give us an edge in how we see things, cards that shift us from average to unique.

I have a child with special needs and one of the Canadians is gay. He writes about being a mama's boy and then over dinner, when we are discussing my son, he uses a teasing tone about raising a mama's boy. This is too complicated. Were we ordering food or eating? Did I try to explain what I was saying or did I suddenly go pale? What am I most afraid of? Being judged and found lacking. You can't explain the wild cards. They are beyond simple catchphrases. Special needs. Gay. Holocaust. Genocide. Wiesenthal says, "When we hear holocaust is a lie, hope is lost." He says, "Too much talk of holocaust leads to indifference." He says, "Once you name what happened in Rwanda as genocide, that language opens a whole series of consequences." When I say "special needs" anything can be imagined. If I say "autism" most imagine a silent, awkward genius. I am the wild card. I leave the table.

I am a mother alone in a city. I have a son with special needs. I've left him behind.

Mothers are not supposed to leave. Only bad mothers do, we know this from fairy tales. Over dinner, when my Canadian friend and I misunderstand each other, I leave as fast as I can because this wild card is beyond description, because I'm all done being the mother without the son. But the next day, he pins me down, leads me out to lunch and wants to talk it through. He understands that the language he used and the one I used were referring to different things, so they waved as they passed each other, our two understandings of mother-son/son-mother, and he could not bear it. Perhaps he was a mama's boy, or perhaps not. Perhaps I am a boy's mama.

I want to disappear. I'm afraid I will disappear. I'm afraid of the endless night and I want the night to last.

Things are winding up. Now we are in metaphor and now we are in image. Three smells, three sights, three sounds, three tactile experiences, three tastes of Vilnius:

This is not a city of scents but coffee is on the air, and cologne blended lightly with cigarettes so that I long for the smell of my baby's buttery-soft hair. Smoke—puffed and ambient and in my hair. Damp stone in the stairwell. Somewhere a cat, its pee.

Pink heart-shaped lock on the lovers' bridge. The others dull and rusted, but not the pink one. Woman in a skin-tight blue suit and three-inch heels, white-blond hair. Her ankles as she walks never turn or quiver. Babies, babies, babies. We try to find the girl babies in among the blue-clad pudgy bald boys. Then note—pink socks may be a hint.

The he-ya and clap of sports announcers, whoosh of ball on air. Tandem, two men and the echoing, piercing ring of their bicycle bell. Dong-dong-dong of church bells at odd times—9:37, 2:23, and the bells ring while all other sound stills and I perch, birdlike, on my sill. Slam of a door, thunder like the advance of a Russian army.

Step, swoosh, slide over wet brick. Run my hand over smooth stucco to brick to damp clay—Miklaus Street and the cold iron of the hostel gate. Texture of sorrow: heavy rain, leaves low with green damp, wet shoelaces, Paneriai.

How a heap of spinach and peas can taste of coconut milk and rain. Cheese-curd soup—cold sensation of cucumber and blended salt-licked milk. Taste salt and tobacco. Smokey coffee on pale lips.

Leaving is preparing for re-entry.

Sometimes a soft click follows, then a horn, waft of bread, dill in everything, clap of rain, orchestra of voices that might be saying "Bellissimo" or something satiny and Lithuanian spilling from Lithuanian lips. I rewind: Vilnius, Frankfurt, Toronto, Calgary, Seattle, a train, a bus, or a taxi. I can't remember. Where do they meet me? I don't know, but there they are, wherever we are. My son is a little cool when I reach for him. He is tired. I'm back but we are not home. We are in Seattle and so the travel does not end. Does it ever? Hotel pool, afternoon nap, carousel and the market before a ferry to Victoria. You could live like this forever … from port to port, from hotel to apartment, from tour bus to hot afternoon in the shade and energy only to watch the clouds and follow the voices as they pass. Here it is English and I marvel at the American "a," at the scent of French fries and the soft skin of this little boy.

I have been gone just over two weeks. It will take time to soften and allow these two males back in, to find the place where we three are whole and one and where I am whole within. Like fish gills, I imagine, how the skin there is both open and closed; things can enter and escape, but not everything.

GRINGATISTA

NADINE PEDERSEN

Note: As Chiapas continues to be a low-intensity war zone, names of people and places have been changed to preserve their anonymity.

I grew up in a family of travellers. Not the kind that shop along the Champs-Élysées or book all-inclusive tropical vacations, but the kind that tend to find themselves off the beaten path, blindly bush-whacking toward the top of a precipice. My childhood home was cluttered with unusual artifacts—a camel-hump lamp, caribou-bone snow goggles, poisonous arrows. Travel, as I understood it then, was a way to appreciate the wonders of our vast world, and also a way to figure out one's own place within it. It was also not without risk. My grandfather contracted rabies in India; my dad, amoebic dysentery in Afghanistan; my mom, encephalitis in Southeast Asia. Not all of my relatives got off so lucky, either. Branches of the family tree end rather abruptly with phrases like "lost exploring in the Northern Territory of Australia." There is also a family claim to us somehow being distantly related to Henry Hudson, that overly determined explorer whose men mutinied and cast him adrift in the wintry ex-panse of Hudson Bay.

Still, with the need to travel apparently rooted more deeply than common sense in my DNA, I took every chance I could to travel for cheap, or free, whenever opportunities presented themselves. By the age of twenty, I had managed to participate in student exchanges, a bursary program and work opportunities that took me across Can-ada, to Japan and Hong Kong, and through Western Europe. Along the way, I experienced my share of misfortunes: having my passport stolen on the way to Macau; being groped on a commuter train in Tokyo; being groped at a concert in Yokohama; being groped, repeatedly, on the streets of Lisbon; being stalked in Dijon; even being held captive overnight by a crazed fellow traveller in the Algarve.

Except for the stolen passport—which was clearly the result of my own stupidity—each of these incidents filled me with indignation. Two of the men immediately felt the lash of my anger when I spun around and used karate on them—one running off in panic, the other crashing to the ground with an expression of surprise on his face. But no matter how these encounters ended, they always added to the pile of anger that had been building up in me for years: a slash heap of injustices, made up of subtle and sometimes not-so-subtle reminders that I could never move through the world as freely as my twin brother simply because I was born a woman.

After the liberating experience of hitchhiking in France dressed in accidental drag—the French being so unaccustomed to seeing women dressed in overalls and combat boots that they just assumed they were stopping to pick up *un mec*—I briefly considered keeping my hair short and getting a breast reduction. In the end, though, I decided that I liked my boobs too much, so rejected this idea, and instead let the slash pile of anger combust into a roaring determination to continue going out in the world as I was and not let anything get in the way. Which helps explain how, at the age of twenty-two, I found myself hiking alone in the Mexican jungle.

———

On January 1, 1994—the day NAFTA went into effect—several thousand Indigenous guerillas materialized out of the Mexican jungle, overtook seven towns in the state of Chiapas, declared war on the government and presented a list of demands that included, among other things, the right to health care, education and democracy. After six decades of one-party rule, the Mexican government was having none of this *mierda*. It dispatched the army to crush this uprising. For two weeks, fierce fighting broke out between the Mexican military and the Zapatista Army of National Liberation (EZLN). Then Samuel Ruiz, a local bishop, negotiated a ceasefire and agreed to mediate peace talks between the two sides, and the Zapatistas retreated back into the jungle.

In the normal course of events, this would have signalled the end of the revolution: the EZLN would have fallen off the front pages of newspapers and faded into historical obscurity. Instead, the Zapatistas became even more famous, thanks to the emerging popularity of the Internet and to the poetic communiqués of their spokesperson, Sub-comandante Marcos.

A year later, when the government broke the ceasefire and sent troops into the jungle to quash the EZLN—and the army attacked the Zapatistas' civilian support base while they were at it—Mexico faced a wave of international condemnation. And when a local human rights centre then asked for human rights observers to go into affected villages and report back on what was happening, people from around the world volunteered, myself among them.

If the Zapatista revolution was bad for the peso, it ended up being great for left-wing tourism, as I discovered when I arrived in San Cristóbal de las Casas in July 1997. Around the town square, entrepreneurs sold T-shirts featuring the familiar pipe-smoking, balaclava-covered face of Subcomandante Marcos alongside shirts emblazoned with portraits of Che Guevara and Bob Marley. The children who swarmed tourists in the town square yelling "¡*Chicle, chicle!*" ("Gum, gum!") sometimes also sold little dolls wearing black ski masks. The cafés were full of punks and hippies; the streets, beggars and policemen. One day, I met an American who was going into the jungle with a group of his comrades to build a solidarity camp.

"What are you going to do there?" I asked.

"We're going to show our solidarity to the Zapatistas."

"How?"

"By going into the jungle and building a camp," he repeated, obviously annoyed that I didn't *get* it.

As for me, I was experiencing the first ripples of doubt that perhaps I wasn't as cut out for my volunteer mission as I had thought. Although I had breezed my way through the screening process back in Canada, now that I was actually in Chiapas, in a room full of people being trained as human rights observers, all of whom spoke the language far more fluently than I did, I realized that I actually spoke Spanish with the fluidity of a three-year-old. Sure, I might have been able to order beer in a restaurant, or haggle over the price of a blanket in the market, but was I really prepared to confront members of the Mexican military if they contravened the conditions of the ceasefire? Or take down the testimony of villagers and accurately report back any human rights abuses? Maybe not.

Perhaps I wasn't the only one having these doubts because the day I completed my training, a staff person at the human rights centre told me they were assigning me to a remote, half-Zapatista village where a group of international engineers were in the process of building a water system. "That way you'll have lots of company," she said, generously.

———

The trip to San Myron remains the toughest journey of my life. In the company of three Spaniards assigned to neighbouring villages, I left San Cristóbal at 3:30 a.m. the next day. The early start was to avoid questions at the military checkpoint on the way out of town, which—rather conveniently for drug runners, paramilitary groups and human rights observers—wasn't manned in the wee hours of the morning. Twenty-seven hours later, after a hellish bus ride, followed by a hellish night spent trying to sleep in a hammock, followed by an even more hellish six-hour hike up into the mountains on a trail that was so muddy in places the puddles reached above the top of my gumboots—I arrived in San Myron, dehydrated and sore from where the nylon straps of my army-surplus backpack had dug into my shoulders.

The village was composed of two rows of houses scattered over half a kilometre. While some of the buildings had corrugated metal roofs and walls made out of milled planks, many of the buildings were constructed from rough pieces of wood lashed together with cord. Smoke from cooking fires billowed through the banana-leaf thatched roofs. About half a kilometre away, the wooden barracks of a military base stood out from the landscape like teeth.

As my guide and I neared the civilian peace camp, all I could think was, W*ater, food, sleep. Water, food, sleep.* But, alas, the last of these three things was not to be. Arriving at camp, I was greeted by an Italian woman named Sofia, the wife of one of the engineers, who told me that I'd arrived just in time for the fiesta! The engineers were just finishing the water system! They would be leaving the next day! With the human rights observer I was replacing!

As Sofia spoke even less Spanish than I did (though far more expressively than I ever could), I kept hoping that I had misunderstood her. But no, this really turned out to be the situation. The first half of the night passed in a haze of guitar and marimba music, the rest with me shivering in my hammock listening to the snoring of one of the engineers. Back in San Cristóbal I had understood that it would be so warm at night, I wouldn't need a sleeping bag. In reality, this high up in the mountains, the temperatures plummeted after dark. *If I got this simple fact wrong,* I fretted as I clenched my teeth together to stop them from chattering, *what else have I misunderstood?*

In the morning, I blearily followed Sofia around as she gave me a crash course on how to cook over the fire, do dishes in a bucket and store food in bags hanging from the rafters so that the insects couldn't get at it. Then she and the other foreigners picked up their backpacks and walked out of the village. I watched as they disappeared, one by one, into a cornfield.

———

The civilian peace camp consisted of three buildings that descended, in Goldilocks-like progression, from big to small. My hammock was strung up in the community centre, a one-room building that housed an assortment of communal objects: musical instruments, a sewing machine, tools, a table and chairs, and an almost-empty medicine cabinet. Luckily for me, it also contained gear left behind by earlier human rights observers, including a pair of red long underwear and an only slightly manky sleeping bag.

Next door, in the cooking hut, a waist-high wooden platform covered in hardened ash supported the fire. Cooking pots and food bags hung from the smoke-blackened ceiling. Near the door stood two buckets for fetching water, doing the dishes, and dousing the fire.

The smallest hut was the bathing shack, where the night before I'd stood with puckering flesh as a hose from the newly completed water system spurted cold water over my body at irregular intervals.

Just down the hill, a contender for the world's worst outhouse leaned precariously to one side near a well full of brackish water.

And that was it: home for the next two weeks.

———

Shortly after the engineers left, a geyser of water exploded out of the trench in front of the community centre with a loud *pop*. Once my heart started beating again, I realized that a joint in the newly completed water system had burst—an event that would be repeated almost daily at different places around the village. A woman rushed over to try and fix it and I joined her. After twenty minutes of muddy struggle, with the help of a man and some kids, we managed to clamp the hose back in place.

The woman smiled at me shyly, wiped her muddy hand on her dress and extended it toward me. "*Bi na bil Rosa*," she said in the local Tzeltal language. "*Bi na bil?*"

I shook her hand and replied in Spanish, "Nadine. It's nice to meet you, Rosa."

———

That afternoon, I was in the kitchen struggling to relight the fire when a man in a white cowboy hat appeared at the door. Introducing himself as Augusto, he explained that he was on his way to a fiesta in a neighbouring village and had come by to borrow a guitar. We chatted for a few minutes, during which time a frown deepened across his forehead.

Finally, he said, "*You* were sent here a*lone*?"

"Yes," I said, explaining that the human rights centre had thought the other foreigners would still be here.

"But ... but ... you don't speak very good Spanish!"

"That's true ..."

"And you're *alone*," he repeated slowly.

"That's right."

Augusto shook his head, as if he couldn't comprehend how this situation could possibly have happened. Then he got the fire ablaze and promised he would return the next day with some kindling. After he left, I poked at the fire with a stick, wishing it could burn up the parts of me that were feeling more and more deficient.

———

I probably would never have become a human rights observer if, in grade eight, I hadn't developed a crush on an exchange student named Eduardo. I don't think Eduardo ever noticed that I existed, but my fantasies of striking up a conversation with him propelled me to the library, where I borrowed a cassette tape to learn how to speak Spanish. For hours, I would sit in my room, repeating useful conversation starters like this one:

"*¿De dónde es Usted?*"
"*Soy de Jerez.*"
"*¿De Jerez? ¡Jerez es el pueblo donde hacen el vino de Jerez!*"

(Which translates to, "Where are you from?" "I'm from Jerez." "You're from Jerez? Jerez is the place where they make sherry wine!")

Although my affections for Eduardo soon waned, my passion for the Spanish language did not. I started studying Spanish in school and ended up skipping a grade after writing a story about a Canadian teenager who meets a handsome Hispanic man on a bus who, it turns out, is an illegal immigrant from Cuba. After he shares with her the details of his harrowing journey from the Communist nation to Vancouver, she helps him sort out his refugee status and it all ends happily ever after.

As this story implies, aside from being an incurable romantic, around this time I had also started to develop an interest in global issues, thanks in part to a social studies teacher who sent me to various youth conferences. By the time I was in university, I knew that neoliberalism was sending the world to hell in a handbasket. Applying to be an observer in a Zapatista village was something I needed to do as an act of solidarity.

———

After dinner, Gabriel, the village *responsable,* officially welcomed me to San Myron. A stocky man with greying hair, Gabriel spoke slowly and carried himself with quiet authority. Being rather self-absorbed, it hadn't occurred to me until after my encounter with Augusto that if I was upset the engineers had left almost immediately after my arrival, this was probably nothing compared to how the villagers felt about having me as the sole buffer between them and the one thousand soldiers next door. Now, looking at the villagers' faces, I felt myself awakening to the reality I had hiked into: I didn't speak the language well enough, I didn't have the proper gear, I couldn't even start a fire by myself—and yet I thought I was somehow qualified to help these people? *Was I crazy?*

Maybe. Yet at the same time, I hadn't left for Mexico expecting to be with other observers. And while I had definitely been overconfident in my language skills and overly optimistic about the suitability of my gear, and, okay, while I had believed I was a more proficient outdoorswoman than I was proving to be, I did actually have a pretty good idea of what I had signed up for. I'd interviewed other observers before leaving Canada; I'd read as much about Chiapas as I could before I left; hell, I'd even read newspaper reports while I was in San Cristóbal describing violence throughout the region, and I had trained to be a human rights observer anyway—because beneath my flickering moments of self-doubt, I had felt that ultimately I could handle it. And in that moment, as the villagers appraised me, I decided that despite my shortcomings, I'd probably been right all along: I could handle it. Whatever "it" was.

Besides, given the circumstances, there was no other choice.

Speaking with that odd temporary fluency that normally only happens when you're drunk, I thanked the villagers for welcoming me, introduced myself and swore that I would do my very best to protect them. The villagers, who represented the Zapatista half of the village, seemed to appreciate this, nodding in agreement as I spoke. They introduced themselves, pointed to their homes and told me I was welcome to wander wherever I liked in the village, but warned me not to speak with the *priístas,* who had solar panels and white flags in front of their houses. For a while, they hung out talking among themselves in Tzeltal, but gradually they drifted away beneath a star-packed sky to the flickering lights of their houses.

I went inside the community centre and got ready for bed. After pulling on the long underwear, I considered the spiderweb-like sac of my hammock with loathing and decided I couldn't spend another night in it. I spread the sleeping bag out on the table and gingerly got in. The table was a bit too short, but it didn't matter: that night I had the best sleep I'd had in days.

———

A montage of the week that followed would look like this: woman tries to light fire but mostly manages to get ash all over her face; flinches when she reaches into food bag and gets bitten by ants; burns breakfast; shrieks when she discovers thumb-size cockroach in her toiletry bag; burns lunch; gets caught, repeatedly, in sudden tropical deluges; develops pitiful addiction to Maria cookies which she buys, guiltily, from the village store; burns dinner; eats more cookies.

Slowly, though, I fell into a routine dictated by the rhythms of nature. Without electricity, I woke when the sun first rose in the east and went to bed shortly after it set in the west. I learned how to coax fire from banana leaves with slow, deep breaths and when to cycle back to my hearth throughout the day to keep the fire burning. I watched the rain fall, the sun warm the earth, the mist rise; listened to roosters crow in the morning and insects thrum at night. Every once in a while a helicopter would fly over a nearby mountain to the army base, and I would wander over to the east end of the village to see what was happening, usually noting a change of troops in the logbook. Aside from this, though, I hardly even noticed the military and gradually started to relax.

———

One day the *Santa Cruz,* a sacred Catholic cross, passed through San Myron on its journey around the highlands. The entire village emptied as people went to greet the priest carrying it. I was about to follow the procession back to the village when an old man grabbed my arm. He had only two teeth and his face was so lined it looked like a topographic map, all hills and valleys. His eyes were lit up with a kind of God fire, and he spoke urgently in a mixture of Spanish and Tzeltal.

"Word of God [*something something*]," he mumbled, "now divided [*something, something, something*]. Before there were baptisms, marriages, [*something, something*]. Now it's bad. Beautiful dresses, beautiful faces, but their hearts? No!"

I knew he was talking about the political division in the village. In February 1995, when the Mexican military tried to crush the EZLN, they also targeted its civilian support base. The people of San Myron had fled as the military came into the village, ransacked their houses, stole their animals and destroyed their crops. At some point (either during the military attack or sometime before, it was never clear to me which) about half of the three hundred villagers fled to the town of Ocosingo. During the attack, the other villagers ran into the jungle, where they hid out for twenty days. When the Catholic diocese renegotiated a ceasefire, all of the villagers returned. Those who had been to Ocosingo hung white flags in front of their houses in the universal sign of truce, while those who had fled into the jungle remained stanchly pro-Zapatista. The Mexican government, led by the Institutional Revolutionary Party, or PRI, rewarded the "priístas" for their submission by giving them solar panels to power their radios; the Zapatistas, meanwhile, became the sole beneficiaries of taps from the water system the engineers had built just prior to my arrival. It was a community divided. Even in church, the Zapatistas sat in the front, the priístas in the back. Now, one of the village elders was trying to explain to me that the conflict had changed their very hearts.

With surprising vigour for a man who walked barefoot and thought he was likely eighty-nine years old, Miguel led me to his house, where he told me that he expected Jesus would return in the year 2000 and solve the poor people's problems. In the meantime, he supported the Zapatista revolution because the life of the Indigenous farmer was too hard. As he spoke, his wife served us coffee, potatoes, squash and *pozol*, a porridge made out of fermented corn paste that looked and tasted like it was made from chalk.

"We have no money to buy things," said Miguel, as he watched me sip the pozol. "We just have corn. We do not buy soft drinks.

We do not buy milk. When there is nothing else, there is pozol. Pozol at noon and pozol in the evening. This is how we survived in the jungle. This is how we have always survived: pozol."

That night, there was a fiesta in the village to celebrate the holy cross. Although I had been vegetarian for years, when one of the villagers offered me some chicken to eat, I ate it with new-found gratitude. It was delicious. It tasted just like … chicken.

There wasn't much for me to do in the village except cook, eat and clean, so I spent much of my time slowly reading a book of legends about the wild-woman archetype titled *Women Who Run with the Wolves*. Meanwhile, my actual life could be summarized as *Woman Who Runs from Cockroaches*, or *Woman Who Chases Chickens*, or perhaps, more depressingly, *Woman Who Desperately Tries to Make Friends and Fails*.

It's not that I lacked for company. Every few days, a human rights observer from a nearby village would show up for a visit. Children would sometimes drop by the camp to draw. Women would bring me tortillas and eggs. In the evening, men would gather outside the camp and talk. Sometimes a woman named Alicia, who had gone to school for a few years and spoke Spanish, would invite me to help her shell beans, or Gabriel, the responsable, would come by and we'd look at a globe of the world together and talk. But mostly the villagers were busy living their lives and didn't have time for the *gringa* in their midst. Besides which, by then, foreigners had been cycling through San Myron for two years, so I wasn't a novelty, let alone good entertainment.

Further complicating things, during my training, the human rights centre had gone over a long list of things observers weren't supposed to do: teach, play doctor, give stuff away, flirt—so I was terrified of making a cultural misstep, especially as the villagers would ask for medicine or inquire if I needed my mosquito netting after I left the village.

But the greatest challenge was that I had absolutely no idea how to relate to the women. I'd been a tomboy my entire life and had deliberately avoided learning domestic skills—like how to cook or sew beyond the basics—out of fear that if I knew how to do these things then I would somehow get stuck caring for babies and baking casseroles, instead of being out in the world doing *stuff.* Consequently, language barriers aside, I had no idea what to talk to the women about, most of whom married before reaching twenty and whose lives did revolve around making food and caring for kids.

One day, a group of young women sat outside my dormitory sewing, whispering in each other's ears and giggling.

"Are you sewing dresses for the upcoming festival?" I asked, sitting down on the bench across from them.

"What?" said one of them, in a way that didn't exactly encourage conversation.

"Are you sewing dresses for the festival next week?"

"Yes." She bowed her head and concentrated on where the needle was entering and exiting the fabric.

"Do you use a pattern or is it all from your head?"

"From the head."

Silence for a few minutes. Then I took another stab at conversation: "How many hours does it take you to make a dress?"

"All day."

"Just one day? That's pretty fast."

"Hmm."

Finally Diana, one of the women who spoke the most Spanish in the village, took pity on me and said, "*Lakshi.*"

The other women nodded, still not looking at me.

"Do you know what *lakshi* means?" asked Diana.

"No."

"They're scared of you."

"What? They are? But ... but ... *why?*"

"For the same reason they would be scared of any strange animal like a jaguar. And you," she said accusingly, "have eyes like a jaguar."

"Ha, ha," I laughed as if this was the most preposterous thing I'd ever heard. Then I pounced on this new opportunity to make conversation. "Have you ever seen a jaguar?"

"Once," she said, "by a lake, it was—"

But whatever she said next was drowned out by the noise of two helicopters appearing in the southwest and flying to the army base. I got up, grabbed my camera and notebook and went to see what was going on. I was expecting another troop change, but instead I saw columns of black smoke rising into the air. The army barracks were on fire.

———

Whenever life gets particularly stressful—like the day I gave birth to my son and learned he needed almost immediate heart surgery—I'm always grateful that I travelled when I was younger. The experience of not sleeping well, of having to cope with extreme temperatures, of having your body revolt against the weird foods you're ingesting and of having pretty much no idea what's going on most of the time, let alone what's going to happen next—well, in combination, all of these things are a really valuable way to discover your personal stress threshold. And my high-water mark was reached the day the military burned their barracks—even though, in the end, nothing bad happened.

To get a better view of the army base, I climbed up onto the scaffolding of an abandoned house. Beyond the flames, the jungle undulated in the heat. Soldiers were climbing into the helicopters. When the first helicopter rose into the air, instead of flying back the way it came, it flew straight toward the village and then directly over my head, not quite skimming the houses but flying low enough to stir the smoke from the fires, to startle the animals, to wake the babies, to make every heart in San Myron pound with the rhythm of its blades. The next helicopter repeated this performance.

The men returned early from farming their *milpas* and lined up against the wall of the church. No one spoke. The tension was as palpable as the smoke that rolled over the village and settled like an acrid fog over the afternoon.

"What do you think is happening?" I asked Gabriel.

"It appears that the military is burning their houses and leaving."

"What do you think is going to happen next?"

"I don't know." But I could tell from the way he kept his eyes trained on the soldiers that he was nervous and wondering the same thing I was: Would the soldiers leave peacefully? Or would they do something to the village again first?

Every thirty minutes or so a new helicopter would come, load up, and leave. The flames dwindled. The column of smoke shrank. The army was gone.

Given that the villagers seemed to throw parties every few days, I expected there would be a celebration that night, but it was oddly quiet, as if the village had drawn in a collective breath and not yet dared release it.

———

The following morning, likely to make the point that the military hadn't really left, two soldiers walked through the village. They were dressed in civilian clothes, but their broad shoulders and short hair gave them away. Squaring my shoulders, I walked out to confront them, all the while wondering what I would say. When they saw me coming, they started walking more quickly. I picked up the pace and they sped up too. I started walking even faster and they entered into a trot, until our weird game of walking tag ended when they exited the village and then kept right on going—just two guys out for a relaxing speed walk.

That afternoon, two Spanish human rights observers showed up, sweaty and listless from the long hike up to the village. Initially, I was almost giddy to have regular company, but within a couple of days, I couldn't wait to get away from them. I was appalled at how much food they wasted; at how condescending they were when they declined the villagers' invitation to go to church; at how Lucia boasted about shocking the men in another village by bathing in a stream wearing only a long T-shirt; at how she strutted around the village snapping photographs with a big SLR camera that likely cost more than what any of the villagers would make in a year. Seeing the look of pained surprise on Gabriel's face when she told him the value of the camera, she hastened to explain, "People are paid more and things cost more in Spain than they do here." But the damage was done—with her words I felt an abyss open up between the villagers and us.

Of course, what I disliked about Lucia the most was how similar we were. She forced me to recall how, shortly after I arrived, a villager had caught me burning some corn that I was worried was going bad and how embarrassed I'd felt when I saw his reaction of total dismay. Or how I'd socially forced my company on the women sewing outside the camp, despite them clearly not wanting anything to do with me; or how I'd probably spent more on cookies since arriving in San Myron than the villagers spent on groceries in a month. There was no avoiding the embarrassing truth: I was just as much of a twit as Lucia—I just didn't want to admit it.

At least with two other human rights observers now in the village came the freedom to explore. Restless and suddenly desperate for personal space, I decided to hike to the nearby village of Baiyaha, where two of the Spaniards I'd travelled with had been posted.

———

The jungle pulsed with life. It was full of birdcalls and butterflies alighting on vines that twisted from branches where vibrant green moss and flowers competed for space. Everywhere it seemed that plants grew on top of other plants that grew on top of other plants. Of course, it was also mosquito filled and muddy and full spider webs and little burrs attached to my clothes, but I was willing to overlook all this.

I'd heard that, like San Myron, Baiyaha was a divided community, but I didn't realize just how divided it was until I got there and the trail led between two symmetrical rows of rectangular shacks in front of which hung limp white flags. The suburban uniformity of the houses was unlike anything I'd seen anywhere in Mexico. As I walked between the houses, it was also unnaturally quiet.

Finally I saw a man standing outside a house. Feeling not unlike the stranger in a spaghetti western, I approached him. "Excuse me, could you please tell me where the camp is?"

"Below," he said, pointing to a path.

"Thank you." I turned around and saw people looking out at me from inside darkened doorways. Nobody spoke as I walked down the path. A few minutes later, I came to a field where half a dozen soldiers in uniform were clearing bush. Acting as if it were totally normal for me to be strolling past them, I gave them a nod and continued walking for another five minutes. I started noticing that the mud under my feet was becoming increasingly pockmarked with footprints bearing heavy treads. A growing unease settled on me. Could the man in the village have thought I meant the military camp? Was I possibly walking into the very last place on the planet I wanted to be?

I turned around, walked back past the soldiers, back past the villagers shrinking in their doorways and found the man again.

"Excuse me," I said again. "But where is the *civilian peace camp*?"

"Below," he said, pointing to the same path.

"How far below?"

"Fifteen minutes."

"Past the soldiers?"

"Yes."

So I walked past the soldiers a third time, this time feeling quite nauseous, my eyes trained on the muddy path, until I saw a single child's footstep amid the boot prints and finally knew that I was going the right way.

Ten minutes later, I entered paradise. Children approached me, asked me my name and led me to the peace camp. Luis, one of my Spanish friends, greeted me with a hug and guided me to where a stream arched out of a fissure in a cliff into a small pool. Although in keeping with local custom I had to bathe with my skirt on, when I got out of the water I felt cleaner than I had in weeks.

We ate lunch in a community centre decorated with the posters of Zapatista leaders and the lyrics to revolutionary songs, trading stories about the villages. Looking at the sky, I realized that if I wanted to be back in San Myron before dark, I needed to leave soon. Luis gave me a couple of bananas, which, after days of not having even seen fresh fruit, felt like a major gift. One of the villagers then asked me if I wanted some oranges. Using a long stick, he knocked about a dozen down from a tree and handed them to me. I felt my mouth filling with saliva as I thanked him. The oranges were big and green and fragrant, and they weighed down my bag in the most pleasant way—I couldn't wait to get back to San Myron and share them.

Luis accompanied me past the soldiers' field and the weird priísta village, and then I was on my way. Two hours later, I arrived back in San Myron, caked in mud, euphoric and energized.

Augusto spotted me as I walked toward the peace camp. "What did you do today?"

"I went to Baiyaha."

"With who?" he asked.

"By myself."

"Alone?"

"Yes."

"But that's dangerous!"

"Oh," I said, playing dumb. "Really?"

"Yes! It's dangerous because of the jaguars. And what if a snake had bitten you? Or you had fallen? You would have been all alone!"

I nodded. Except for the snakes, I had been conscious of the dangers.

"Or the military!" he continued.

"Yes," I admitted, "I was scared of the military."

"I would have accompanied you!"

"Oh," I said again, feeling a bit bad for having upset him while not regretting my solo walk at all. To my knowledge, nobody had ever told the European men who visited San Myron that they shouldn't hike alone. Nobody stopped when the men of San Myron picked up guitars to go play music in neighbouring villages. I finally understood that when Augusto said "alone," what he really meant was "without a man."

I left San Myron a couple of days later. Before I left, Gabriel told me I was welcome to come back any time, but I already knew it was unlikely I would ever return. Feeling too sad to go around the community and say proper goodbyes to everyone I'd met, especially when I felt most of the villagers wouldn't even care that I was leaving, I said goodbye to the few people I'd felt briefly connected to. Then I hoisted my pack onto my back, followed my guide out of the village and disappeared into a cornfield.

Sips

Three True Tales of Travelling Alone as a Woman in Turkey

CATHERINE OWEN

1. SULTANAHMET

Buying a gift for your lover's wife requires a certain indelicacy of conscience, but I am determined to do so anyway. After all, I am visiting Turkey, the land of their birth, mainly to uncover things about my lover impossible in a Canadian context. This is a trip that requires a kind of propitiation. Thus far, I've only sensed what an anomaly he is, this chilled, taciturn man, proudly ineffable. So different from the men on every corner with their overheated invitations. "Hey lady, sexy girl, be my wife! Marry me! Want to come home?" However, I also know I must be missing something, having only been in Sultanahmet twenty-four hours, the majority of them spent in my hostel, the Daffodil, smoking peach *shisha* from a hookah and munching hard-boiled eggs in the top-floor lounge overlooking the dangerous sea.

The owner, Mahsoud, warned me away from the docks, told me the Sufi dancers weren't worth the ticket price and even that I should watch out for the crooked vendors at the many shish kebab stands.

"They overcharge, especially they see pretty white girl and they think things, you alone, why?"

I can't explain this to them. The reason I have travelled halfway across the world by myself. Such a trip only marks me as wealthy, slutty in their eyes, and no amount of further narrative detail serves to humanize me beyond this serviceable stereotype. So I've been held a kind of hostage at a corner table in the hostel lounge, a room of blue walls, posters of Rumi and Cappadocia. As the hours pass, I read Kerouac and watch the parched quickness of lizards slipping in and out of the rusted roof tiles, wondering how to release myself from Mahsoud's dictates without risking my life when he says to me, poking his head around the top of the stairs,

"You, me, we go for a walkabout, visit my uncle, he be happy, I introduce you?"

I have become weary enough of my surroundings that I am determined to believe him a safe option. Two days and already I am feeling the desperation of the ultra-visible, a constant sense of exposure every time I venture out that has distracted me from why I am here. Perhaps with a man at my side, a business owner, I will diminish to controlled, shadowy proportions again and thus free up some mental space to think of my lover, his wife, how this folie à trois had all unfolded.

However, Mahsoud keeps trying to take me by the hand as we stroll past the tour-bus-ringed environs of Hagia Sophia, the less popular gate to the sewers, the oldest *hammam* in Turkey from which wafts steam, the pile of soft white towels, a glisten of heated flesh. I am unable to let the armour that has settled on me loosen for a moment, men's eyes now following the luck of my chaperone, a homely man who has apparently snagged a white tourist girl.

"Hayir." I smile tightly at him, refusing to grab his hand, testing out one of the few Turkish words I have learned. "Pardon."

"But why?"

"Don't … want a boyfriend."

"O."

Mahsoud seems perplexed, chastened, lets his fingers fall against the slippery fabric of his chinos. "My uncle here, him. Come."

He nods toward a stolid man in an Armani suit, a full head of salt hair, standing in front of the sign for Karim's Persian Carpets, fine importers and distributors. He is smoking a cigar but when he spies Mahsoud, his mouth opens in a blank startle of teeth.

I suddenly feel like a fly drawn by the promise of light, air, into the gluey mesh that passes for family in this tourist town, all relatives doubling as traders, dealers, traps. Mr. K, as he calls himself, purrs toward me, "Please, my dear, like cousins, no?" as he leads me and Mahsoud into the brightly lit showroom, then downstairs, to a corner with a couch, ornate chairs, motioning to his salesgirl to fetch us drinks.

"Coffee, tea, apple tea, what do you prefer, my dear?"

His English is perfect, hardened into a shiny patter.

"O, apple tea, why not," I sigh. (Only later will I come to comprehend the soporific, lulling qualities of this beverage when I finally escape Sultanahmet for a tour of Cappadocia. Every stop the little troop of tourists is taken to—the rug factory, a pottery barn, the glassware manufacturers—we are plied with apple tea prior to the inevitable sales pitch.)

Almost instantly, the girl returns with a tray on which sit three narrow mugs of apple tea, and a few sweet biscuits, placing them on the long teak table in front of the couch where Karim has suggested we sit.

"Mahsoud here, my nephew, he is a fine young business man, is he not, my lady? A real catch, as they say."

Unfortunately, his English skills are not yet superior. But then he doesn't spend half the year in New York as his uncle does.

His finely clipped, well-polished hand comes to a landing on my knee.

"Having fun with the men, my dear?"

I shift forward to take a sip of the false orchard in my cup.

"That's not why I'm here, actually. More a research trip."

"O but young ladies like yourself, hot, special, surely…"

Mahsoud seems to lean into the lascivious tone, wetting his plush lips while Mr. K grins at me as though they share a velvet secret.

It's important to relax, no? I myself have a wife but when I'm away, ahhhhh, I find my pleasures, a girlfriend here, there, sex relaxation is good for the body, no guilt, guilt is no good, my dear.

I think briefly of my lover's lean flesh, of his long, entangled hair, fingers he always wants me to suck, right down to the webbing between the digits. There is nothing relaxing about being with him, though. My body always tenses up at his touch, becomes hard, highly strung. My cries of pleasure sharp, hacking sounds he always hushes, afraid of his wife hearing them, even when she is out of town, far away.

"Can I see some carpets?" I ask, suddenly deciding that the only way to reclaim this unwanted visit to a rug merchant in the guise of family, this undesired overture by a hostel owner under the auspices of a friendly stroll, is to buy my lover's wife a gift here. Yes, I will bring her back a rug, something opulent, a soft gesture of unsaid apology for having fallen in love with, become addicted to in a sense, her elusive, difficult, hypnotic husband.

Mr. K gleams as if I have provided him proof, once again, of the gold lying beneath his charm, patting my thigh. Then he waves his hand toward a boy who has dipped out of what must be the storeroom.

"Bring them to the lady, Hasif, all of them."

Mahsoud slips upstairs, to get his cut, I am sure, his work as an intermediary accomplished, while I take over an hour to select a circular rug, blue and rose, woven with the traditional symbol for Ararat on it, a bold triangle clasped by a vise of mysterious patterns. So many carpets had flown around me, mesmeric, spinning like heavy butterflies from the boy's slight hand, all those tightly packed threads, dyes of berries, charcoal, oyster shells, symbols of women, of water, the scarab beetle, the pomegranate. Each rug containing its own unique flaw, deliberately introduced into the weft to humanize its design.

"Ararat is a good choice, my dear, a lucky one," comments Mr. K as he signs the bill of sale, hand curving over my shoulder, a chaste, fatherly grip now he has been given my credit card number. "It is, after all, where the ark landed at the end of those forty days and nights of flood. And everything that had entered two by two, as it should be, came out, my lady, saved."

2. TAKSIM SQUARE

Looking at Emre, short but concealing a muscled arsenal beneath that button-down shirt, the scent of a practised seducer despite his sloping pupil, an eye lazy as egg white in his face, I am caught between anxiety and the curiosity bred in me from years of being a writer. It's raining or I never would have come here. Not just drizzling (I am after all a Vancouverite and can handle showers with equanimity) but a torrent of wet that slashes the surface of the Bosphorus, driving the bridge fishers home, that cascades over Taksim Square's marquees and the endless blatting of horns. Simit Sarayi is about to close. It is 3:00 a.m. I arrived in the city earlier today to a miscommunication. One contact had thought the other one was picking me up, as I discover much later, and so I was left stranded, straying about the square. At first, content to play gypsy, I spent several hours at a restaurant eating Greek salad and thick wedges of buttery bread, watching the garishly energetic street life, but as it grew dark, worry began to jab. After walking around in circles for some time, I came upon this late-night Internet café and plonked my backpack down for the duration. Now, though, they are closing. "Excuse me, miss, but shut now." The young boy peers sideways at me where I sit scrawling in my journal. "Do you know where I can go to sleep?" I ask him. "Hotel?" he offers, but I already know that, in this area of town, hotels range upwards of 300 a night, my entire budget for this two-week trip. He has no other suggestions.

So I toss down the last of my Nescafé, crumple up the wax paper that clenches one of their pasty buns, crammed with cheese or spinach or jam, heft the damp bag on my shoulder again and push open the door. Once, years ago when I was still in my twenties, on the trail of a poem, I bedded down in a Clark Drive squat, if bedded you could call it as all they were offering was a mat, scrawny blankets, one candle and a night of junkie prowlings for bicycle wheels, syringes, chocolate milk, the kid called Blake constantly telling me to "Chilloutchilloutchillout!" The experience gave me the sense that I can, if needed, tough things through, which I obviously have no choice but to do now, plumping my jacket beneath my head, just under the partial covering of an awning outside the dark café. Four hours until dawn.

"Up, up! Out!" Someone is shaking my arm, yanking at it. I must have fallen asleep for a few minutes. A policeman tugs at my sleeve, pointing for me to get up, move along. "Kanadoleum," is all I think to gasp in my approximate Turkish, as if a northern status condones me dossing down on the pavement. Here, people call Canada "that cold heaven," my Turkish friends told me before I left. Those few days ago how androgynous and innocent I felt, planning to conquer everything, to overcome so much. I didn't know then that as a woman alone, I am viewed only as easy, rich. Justifying, from them, a certain combination of disdain and hunger. The policeman, however, doesn't care that I am Canadian, a woman; he merely wants me to keep going, no other interest in my well-being. He is just concerned, as must be the case in the vacuity of all big cities, that tourists not witness vagabonds. I rise with difficulty, start to walk. How could there be that many cats in this city, everywhere, clinging like *kargas* to drainpipes, the cusps of roofs, skirting the traffic circle, nursing their perilous babies beneath the giant letters of the Levi's sign. My bag is heavy with wet. My feet scrape the pavement as I dawdle toward the core of the square, almost too tired to wonder what I will do next. And then Emre appears, beckoning me from a doorway in that deceptive haven of English—"Excuse me, miss, but do you need some help?" It is my lover Hasan's fault in a sense, I realize again, the reason I am here, for being so different—his slowed beauty, sullen shyness, impossibly quiet longings have failed to prepare me for the more regular gregariousness, crude flirtations and, harder, the insistence masquerading as hospitality. My adolescent fling with a Serb might have allowed me to intuit this, the parents pushing all manner of things, from homemade wine to an antique wedding ring on me. I, from a puritan upbringing where one serving should always be sufficient, had been shocked. But this was long ago. How was I to know the exception is not the norm? Yes, I am cold, tired and drenched. The rain unceasing. "Nowhere is open anymore to get *kahva* or even *su*," he remarks as if casually, strolling beside me, a proffered umbrella floating above our heads. "I have a place, though, comfortable, small, but you can sleep, promise, a pleasure to assist a Canadian, really." Yes, I have told him where I come from, about the miscommunication. My national pride rises, sewn as tightly inside me as the patch is on my pack, and I relent.

Now I look more closely at him in his apartment, a brisk fifteen-minute stroll away from Taksim. His suite is not tastefully furnished. A shoe rack in the front hall of the three-storey walk-up, narrow sofa in the den, a stack of videos—*Barbarella, When Harry Met Sally*—in the sole bookcase. The only knick-knacks I see are a set of matryoshkas, usually slipped one within the other, but here placed in order of ascending height on a whitewashed shelf. "O, a girlfriend gave me those," he tells me, catching my gaze. "A Russian. She lived with me awhile." It is only long after, staying with the lawyer from Beyoglu who takes pity on me, a girl without a place to stay, nearly broke, that I hear of the Natashas, a name that conjures up a cheesy girl group but refers to sex slaves from the Steppes, blond-haired women lured to Turkey by work, kept, sometimes as long as ten years before their bodies are found. If I'd only known this story before, I would have choked up my food allowance for a room, my traveller's cheapness be damned. Instead, my friends back home had only cautioned me to watch my drinks at bars, keep ID on me at all times. And so I pay attention as in the box of his kitchen, Emre pours us tea, hot water slamming over the rim of pale mugs, the tea bags, cinnamon peach, bobbing on top. "Cookies?" he asks, still playing my saviour.

I sit beside him on the couch and sip as though I am sucking up tiny slivers. He won't stop staring at me. "I'm so tired," I begin. "O, I know," he replies cryptically. "Really, I must sleep after this." "We have a bed, we do. You can sleep alone. Promise," he repeats. Jumping up, opening a closet door, he pulls out a sheet and tosses it on the carpet like an affirmation. "You see, I will sleep here." How badly I want to feel secure. To imagine actually being able to rest in this strange man's place. But I know this is impossible, dangerous. And even now he is gawping at me again oddly with his shifty sluggish eye. "You are crazy, no? To come to a stranger's house?" "Well," I play the naïve Canadian of folklore, "back at home we have no locks on our doors. Everyone is to be trusted. In Canada." "Really? What a bonus place to live! How do you like my English. It's good, yes?" I agree. Very good, actually.

But how? I want to ask him how he learned it, where he's from, but he is saying to me in a harder tone, "You must shower now. Shower before bed. Get clean." He opens the closet again, takes out a pair of folded grey pyjamas, shoves them toward me. "Shower, then change into these."

My hand automatically slides to my midsection to check my money belt in which there is lira, a passport. I try for a smile around my rising ire. "O no, I couldn't. So sleepy. Just need that bed." But now his features have suddenly seized into a simmer on the edge of frightening. "But you will make me angry. I am trying to be kind. Come now. I insist." His sharp arms are urging me toward the stark bathroom where he turns on the shower, tests the heat. "See. This feels nice. Just relax. Get clean now." Then he leaves me there. The door doesn't lock. I stand by the spray awhile, the water draining down, clutching the institutional nightwear, certain there is no way I will get naked, not willingly.

A year before this trip, I had first stripped in front of Hasan. "I want to see you," he had nearly whispered, gazing at me from the couch as, slightly disgraced, I had stood, sticking out the small points of my breasts, cupping my pudenda, lusting for him wholly yet incapable of acting. Finally I had moved toward his belt, as though asleep in my desire, releasing his cock and taking it between my lips while he hardly shifted, barely moaned, a contained hunger I could never fathom, never stir him beyond. I exit the barren square of the bathroom, decline once more, phrasing my refusal carefully, afraid of incurring threats. "It's simply not my country's custom." I strain toward a cliché of womanhood. "In Canada, women don't shower at strangers' houses. Not about trust. About, um, shyness, modesty. So can you show me where I can sleep?" He had been staring out the window, a plot of darkness in the wall, facing nothing. He is not to be fooled that easily. "But crazy girls from Canada go to strangers' houses?" he remarks, a sour ridicule in his words. He doesn't insist, though, gesturing instead toward the bedroom. "Sleep in there. On top of the sheets. You are too dirty. I'll be out here then." I peer in, enter. The room is white and red. Teddy bears are strewn on every available surface and the satin duvet is quilted with *Seni Seviyorum*—"I love you."

What kind of a grown man's bedroom is this? A sudden hunkering down of nausea in me, the ache to flee, even if it means throwing myself out the window. Of course I won't rest here, in this creepy saccharine room, would have been better walking the streets. Still, I am anxious about angering him so I lie down, hug myself to protect my money, identity, wondering how much longer I have to wait until it's light. Minutes later, from what seems a great distance, I hear the door swish open over the too-thick pile of carpet and then Emre climbs in beside me, grows against me in the dark.

3. CAPPADOCIA

The hammam on the edge of Goreme displays all the pretensions of being ancient: clay walls, a massive stone dais, cracked mosaic tiles on the floor. In fact, it was built late last year and only opened six months ago according to the brochure I am perusing in the lobby while waiting to be escorted up to the change rooms. "Distressed." The word pops into my mind unbidden. Is that not what my lover does back in Vancouver? Distress furniture, coarsening its grain with steel wool and sandpaper, fretting away paint until the bookcase or table looks like a French chateau find? This *hammam*, I notice, is full of distressed textures, beautiful scars glowing in the melting light.

Only the receptionist speaks English, sufficient English at any rate to take my twenty-five euros for this "invigorating, traditional experience" as the brochure promises. I have been in the Cappadocia region for three days now. On Sunday, I boarded the all-night bus from the Beyoglu district of Istanbul, finding a seat beside an Asian woman who seemed to be trying to crumple herself into the corner. "What do you do?" I asked at some intimately groggy part of the trip. "I'm a nurse," the woman replied as the bus continued down the flat highway, a drive only punctuated by one rest stop at a sprawl of buildings in the middle of nowhere containing a hive of eighties Atari games, pastry vendors and hole-in-the-ground toilets, rows of them, the sinks hung with signs banning foot washing. "Why are you here?" I tried next, and the woman let out a primordial sigh. "Vanishing. Done with it all. On the road, what, five, six weeks. You?" I didn't really know the answer to that question or, more to the point, I knew but had little interest in telling anyone else. "I'm here to better understand my lover, to see where he came from. I'm here because I cannot have him and so I need his land instead." Yes, this was the real reason I had travelled to Turkey nine days before. But what I tell the likely indifferent nurse is, "O, adventure, why else?" smiling transparently as I do so, just another superficial lone female tourist, aren't I, not this lunatic of love.

Strangely, with all the choices for travellers in this district, the nurse ends up a guest in the same B & B as me, a rundown cement

block on the dusty outskirts of the district known deceptively as
Sweet Tulip Hostel. Each room is fitted with only a bed and a dresser,
the seamed walls decorated haphazardly with torn posters of fairy
chimneys and other romanticized icons of the region. The toilets and
showers are outside, thinly partitioned and cold. The first morning, I
spot the nurse in the breakfast room, a space lined with benches on
the roof of the B & B where guests consume hardboiled eggs, Greek
yoghurt and clots of chocolate to the background noise of Turkish
soap operas. She is sitting by herself, slowly sipping her Nescafé. Passing her, I manage a grin. "Going on the tour today?" But the nurse
only glances up like a very old animal—"Not sure"—before dropping her head back down to the Vincent Lam novel she is reading, or
at least pretending to; I never see her turn a page. Going on a tour.
This is the one sane thing I feel sure I have accomplished so far on
this sojourn: finally setting up a logical little series of day trips for
myself out in the country. The cost is somewhat painful but balanced
out by the thought that, at last, I am coming to my senses, not straying
about anymore, but finding an itinerary and sticking to it. The tour is
going to show me a whole array of those fabled fairy chimneys, a ce-
ramics factory, some underground houses, churches, roadside shrines,
cemeteries. Stuff like that. A sensible tourist's ambitions. What I plan
to see will have minimal relation to my lover's experience of growing
up in the downtown core of Istanbul. I will drive him out of my mind
in such fashion, play *flâneur* rather than archaeologist.

And for two whole days, I have done just that. Watched Hasid
spin a pot with his bare hairy hands, drank cups of ubiquitous apple
tea at the rug manufacturers, gazed in a kind of moved disbelief at
those towering rock outcroppings their guide, Evet, had described as
fingers entwined, two camels kissing, a giant face in the desert. The
third day, though, I wake without a schedule and decide to go to the
hammam. Which is where I see the nurse once more.

The attendant leads me to the showers, hands me wooden flip-
flops and a plush white towel and leaves me to undertake my ablu-
tions, followed, if I so desire, by a sauna prior to the scrub and puri-
fication treatment I have paid for. The brochure shows pictures of
naked women, their nipples topped by meringues of suds, reclining

like goddesses on stone beds, but I am determined to keep my swim-suit on, a simple sleek one-piece I only use once a year on a visit to my sister's place in Tofino. I'm relieved to see I'm not the only prude. Of the three women already in the sauna, one is wearing a tank top and shorts; another sports a puffy silver jumpsuit. She looks like the Pillsbury Space Girl, I laugh to myself, presuming the garb must promote weight loss. Indeed, the woman clambers out of the sauna several times while I am sitting on the bench, weighs herself after unzipping the spacesuit to reveal a plump olive body bound at breast and groin with wide bandeaus of cloth and grimacing, shaking her head, opens the door once more to the steam.

She doesn't speak English either, and the only one who does, the third woman, the nurse, is slumped in the corner of the sauna, a white towel swathed around her as if she is broken. Her eyes closed, hands hanging by her sides, even her legs fallen open. Keeping them together must be too much work. I want to shake her now, yell, "Wake up! Why are you here, did you come to another country to die?" Perhaps an extreme reaction, but the nurse's tremendous las-situde is beginning to unnerve me, even feel like a burden. If it was she who had been held captive and not me, would she have been able to summon the strength to resist, break free? Just how deep did this exhausted yielding go?

I open the door from the sauna, leaving the nurse behind me, and enter the hot room, a vaulted realm of raised beds with what looks like a giant sundial in the centre. A scarfed woman gestures that I should lie down, slip off my suit. O god, why had I been raised to value privacy and concealment so highly? At swimming lessons throughout the seventies, my mother shepherding me and my three siblings into separate change rooms, her clucking noises over those women who paraded nude into the showers, shampoo bottles held aloft like torches. "No shame," she would tut, "No shame," as if feeling appalled by one's naked flesh were a cardinal virtue.

What the hell, who knows me here, I finally decide, yanking the straps down and letting the moist suit ball, drop to the tiled floor. The woman stands above my prone body with a cheesecloth, loads it with suds and begins to squeeze. Clouds collapse onto the plains of my flesh and then the kerchiefed lady starts to rub, laughing as she does so. At what? My obvious struggle to let go, relax? Over the pilules of dead skin that are now sloughing off me, curds, tumbleweeds? Death. Sloughing off me. A sudden jubilance. I raise my arms, let my mouth hang open. All that muscular tension falling away. "*Cok guezel*," the woman keeps uttering as she chafes the cloth upon me, and I know at least what this means, from my guidebook to basic Turkish phrases. It means "very beautiful." If it were only my lover saying such things, but no, I would never trust him like this, trust him the way I can a total stranger I am paying to scrub me down, wash me up, release me lighter into the world.

WHAT AM I DOING HERE?

KAMI KANETSUKA

Standing in this chaotic sea of taxis, I am waiting for a man I had a love affair with thirty-five years ago. Unbelievably, I am in Dimapur, Nagaland, a tribal state of former headhunters in the remote North-East Frontier area of India. It had been closed to foreigners since 1951 until now due to political unrest.

I have driven from Kohima, the capital town, in a shared sumo taxi with three young men similar in age to Adi when we first met. When we reached Dimapur I put on some lipstick, borrowed a mobile and called him.

"I will be there in ten minutes," he says.

"I am waiting by Snacks & Snacks," I tell him.

Every cell in my body tingles with nervousness as I anticipate this reunion after so long.

A couple of weeks earlier, on arrival at Dimapur's tinpot airport, I am the only non-Naga on a flight from Kolkata. A policeman wearing denims and a plaid shirt greets me. He writes my details on a scrap of paper and expresses shock that I am travelling alone with no one to meet me—he tells me there is no transportation into town. Mrs. Atula, a contact name I have been given by Mr. Limu at Naga House in Kolkata, is summoned to come and pick me up.

When staying with my friend Maura in Kolkata I found out that Nagaland had just opened for foreign tourism, and believing that I may not return to India, I jumped at the opportunity of an adventure somewhere where the masses have not yet trampled. Maura did not think it was a good idea, telling me she didn't know anyone who had visited there and that it had the reputation for being dangerous.

At the time my long-lost Naga lover was but a distant memory.

While waiting for my ride from the airport I recall what Mr. Limu had said when I asked if I could really visit Nagaland now: "You can go but you are very courageous." A feeling of apprehension arises as I think, "What am I doing here? This could be more travail than travel … " An elegantly dressed young Naga woman who is also waiting for a ride catches my eye and I say, "I've never been here before. I'm alone and I'm not sure where I should go and what I should do." Warmly, this woman introduces herself as Aben and invites me to share a taxi with her the next day to travel to her hometown Kohima.

Mrs. Atula arrives in a rickshaw and is obviously not too happy with having to transport me. We stop halfway to Dimapur where there is one hotel on a deserted road with no shops or restaurants, just a few rickety shacks selling cigarettes and knick knacks. I tell her the hotel isn't suitable and ask to be taken to the centre of town. We reach Dimapur, a dark, oppressive little town (which I later hear is rife with drugs from the golden triangle), where I find a room in the small Brahmaputra Hotel near the train tracks. While walking in town I am aware that I am the only Anglo-Saxon around, and everyone stares. On the tracks vendors sell grubs, frog's legs, snails and unrecognizable meats and vegetables. When a train approaches the vendors jump up with their baskets, returning only after it passes. The only vegetarian meal I can find is noodles with uncooked cabbage on top. Before bed I telephone Aben to confirm that I will travel with her to Kohima the next day.

I join her in the early morning mist and our shared taxi climbs the winding road of the Naga Hills. On arrival in the centre of Kohima I inquire about rooms in several shabby hotels but nobody seems to want the lone foreigner. Aben mentions that her mother rents rooms to Indians from elsewhere working in Nagaland and says maybe she will help me. I am taken to the family home where I find the Lanuakum family are the aristocracy of Nagaland, with a beautiful home, servants and two cars. I can stay in the adjoining building and have my evening meal with the family. I have struck gold—Achila, Aben's mother, grows flowers and vegetables on their ample land. My dinner is an abundance of freshly picked vegetables with rice and dahl.

Each morning Achila, who works in education, gets driven to work. On my first day I am dropped off at the exquisite museum, which houses traditional clothing and artifacts from the sixteen tribes who once wore finely woven garments with bones and feathers in their necklaces, headdresses and ears. In one showcase there are five human skulls hanging from branches of a tree, presumably from long ago. I also view a showcase with medical instruments, a suit and a bust. It is of Dr. Imkongliba, the first medical doctor in Nagaland, who was assassinated in 1961. I recall Adi telling me the sad story of his father.

That evening at dinner I mention to Achila that I had met Dr. Imkongliba's son when he was studying in Darjeeling and casually say, "I wonder if he still lives in Nagaland." It appears that Achila is from the same Ao tribe and comes from Mokokchung, where Adi lived. "If he is here I will find him," says Achila. The next evening when I come to dinner, she proudly announces, "I've found your friend, he is the cousin of one of my friends. He will call you at 8:30 tomorrow night." This inexplicable piece of magic throws me into a turmoil of emotions, as I am unsure that I want to hear this voice from the past.

My mind rewinds to our time together in 1975. I had left my small daughter with my former husband and was on the road on an extended trip in Nepal and India. I had gone to a school dance for graduating students at St. Joseph's College in Darjeeling with Gary, a young Californian man. As the only western woman there, the students never allowed me to leave the dance floor.

After, with a group of students, Gary and I went for tea in a café. Having been in India for some time I was quite aware of the immaturity of many of these young men who have gleaned their ideas about Western women from third-rate American films showing sexy scantily clad unknown actresses readily popping into bed. These movies somehow made their way to small Indian movie theatres, creating a ridiculous impression of western women. In response, I was always cautious of how I dressed and behaved and recall on this occasion wearing a long black flower-embroidered Mexican dress down to my ankles, which revealed nothing.

I was, however, seated opposite a handsome Tibetan-looking young man with long black hair and almond-shaped eyes. Immediately I felt an aura of worldliness about this man opposite me, who seemed altogether different from the other young men. When our eyes met, the attraction was instantaneous and magnetic. Even at this first meeting where we exchanged a little of our life histories, he seemed to have a genuine interest in who I was. We both knew that we would like to get together more.

Adi told me that he was going home to Nagaland in two weeks. "Let's meet tomorrow," he said, "and I will bring you some books so you can see how beautiful my country is. I'm sorry you cannot visit as it is closed to foreigners."

We met the next day and for much of the following two weeks we walked and talked and drank tea and ate *momos* in the small Tibetan restaurants. He was fascinated with my stories about Canada and my small daughter, as I in turn loved to hear about his homeland with the sixteen different tribes, the forested Naga Hills, the traditional villages with bamboo houses on stilts and the morungs, the longhouse dormitories where young men slept between leaving home and marriage.

At the time I was staying in a little guesthouse called the Shamrock, run by an eccentric and feisty Tibetan woman called Mrs. Ongel, who had a reputation for taking everyone under her wing. Her husband had just died and his body was still in the house for the traditional forty-nine days, where the lamas would recite prayers with musical accompaniment. I was unable to visit Adi in the room he rented in a local home, but Mrs. Ongel, who knew Adi, welcomed him to her house.

Our relationship deepened each day and what had started out rather innocently seemed to be moving into another realm. One evening we returned when prayers were being chanted loudly with the shaking and drumming of *damaru*, a double-headed hand drum. As we entered the room we started to kiss passionately and moved to the bed. By this time a tremendous sexual tension had risen and there was a need to feel each other's bodies and experience the depths of intimacy, which we managed to slip into easily. From that day we experienced the joys of lovemaking with gentleness and blissful sex. Aware that we would be separated soon made every moment precious. When the parting came we both shed tears and his gift to me was a finely woven red, blue and black silk shawl from his Ao tribe.

We corresponded frequently and I always felt a thrill writing to his address, Sunrise View, Mokokchung, knowing it was a place I could go to only in my imagination. Several years later I was in India for a Buddhist meditation retreat and I went to visit Adi in Shillong, Meghalaya, where he was working and studying. I arrived with a mild case of malaria but Adi found me a place to stay and made sure I was getting what I needed. Although he was still attentive I could feel a change and a kind of guardedness and realized that he had a girlfriend in this town. He also questioned me about why I did Buddhist meditation and I sensed that he, as a Christian, did not approve.

When I recovered he arranged for us to go on a trip to Kaziranga National Park to ride on elephants and see the one-horned rhinoceroses. We had a fun time and relived a little of our first attraction but the passion was gone. We were more like good friends, and it was obvious our lives were never destined to take the same path. As I knew he had a girlfriend and he wanted to marry and have children, it was time to end our relationship. The writing stopped. I threw away his letters and never expected to see him again.

But now I am faced with the very real possibility that I will see him again, and I'm not sure how I feel about it. After dinner I have been in the habit of sitting with the father of my host family, Lanu, to watch TV before going to bed. On the night of the call we are watching a football match between Manchester United and Liverpool. While Lanu keeps switching to cricket and back I feel irritated and uneasy about receiving this call on a mobile in a room with no privacy. I am also transported back to England in the '50s—the last time I watched football was with my parents as a teenager. And just like a teenager I wonder if he will really call.

The call comes and I have difficulty understanding Adi. "Oh my god, I can't believe you are here," he says. Excitedly, he slurs his words and I wonder if he has been drinking. He tells me he is married and still lives in Mokokchung. I hear him say, "I remember your sexy eyes and wild hair." For a moment I remember his strong body, high cheekbones, full lips and gentle hands. He invites me to Dimapur where he will be going on business in two days, but instinctively I know I don't want to meet him. I had planned to continue on to Mokokchung, then leave for Jorhat, Assam, to fly back to Kolkata. Since we are both leaving in two days it is possible that our taxis will pass each other on the road like ships in the night.

The Lanaukum family have arranged another homestay for me with relatives in Mokokchung. With the Aier family I visit traditional villages in the countryside where I experience glimpses of how I had imagined Nagaland. In the cool mist I wander around bamboo houses on stilts, go to homes where the women weave shawls and skirts, see the long wooden drums that alert the villagers of danger and totem poles depicting tigers and mythical animals. I do not know where Sunrise View is but somehow I feel Adi everywhere.

My departure approaches and I go to buy an advance sumo ticket for Jorhat, two hours away by road. I am told that both vehicles are broken and I cannot leave the way I had planned. When I tell the family of my dilemma, they tell me that the alternative way to Jorhat is to return to Dimapur where I can take the train. Conveniently, Mogren, the father of my new host family, is driving to Kohima that afternoon, and from there I could travel to Dimapur the next day. I must make a decision immediately if I want to go with him. I phone Adi and he is overjoyed that I will be coming. I recall Mr. Limu's remark about being courageous going to Nagaland, although I am sure this is not what he had in mind.

A still slim and wiry Adi arrives to meet me in Dimapur. "Thank god, we are both still alive," he says as he takes both my hands. At fifty-eight he is still relatively young but I am shocked by his appearance. His front teeth are reddened and broken from chewing pan and betel nut and his eyesight is poor despite his glasses, causing him to walk cautiously. His once beautiful hair is shorn and dyed black. It may also be shocking for him to see his old lover with a well-worn face and the once wild hair short and greying.

Adi takes me back to his tiny stuffy room full of mosquitoes, which he jokingly calls his "Calcutta slum." There is a single bed, a table with two chairs and in the corner a small double burner stove. He tells me he lost most of his money going into politics. I offer to take him for dinner but he insists on cooking noodles and vegetables on his stove, all the time knocking back rum.

I suggest checking into the Brahmaputra Hotel and he offers to go elsewhere and give me his dark dank room, which is in a sleazy part of town. There is no lock on the door and I tell him I would not feel safe alone. While discussing where I should stay, a mini-typhoon erupts with paper and garbage flying everywhere. This turns to thunder and heavy rain. Nobody is going anywhere.

Night falls and we share his little bed, I in my sleeping bag lying one way and he the other. There is no desire or physical contact. Cocooned by a mosquito net the mosquitoes buzz outside while Adi snores loudly inside. I lie there unable to sleep, pondering our changed lives, while glimpses of the past when our bodies sang to each other linger in and out like ghosts or flashbacks in an old movie. In Darjeeling we were both in our prime but now I feel like I am in bed with a stranger. The past seems like another world—what has life done to us both?

The next morning I am irritable but Adi tries to humour me. Until he starts to lecture me. "I can't believe you are not Christian," he says.

I know that 90 percent of Nagas are Christian because of the Baptist Missionaries of the late 1800s and Billy Graham coming to preach in the 1970s. By now I am feeling weary of being an alien because of my different beliefs. Adi and I bicker like some old married couple when discussing religion and way of life. There is more ease when we talk about old times and between us we seem to remember much of the time we had together when each other's company was such a delight.

I make Adi check the train times for Jorhat and he plans to travel on the train with me, as it leaves at 3 a.m., a time he says is unsafe for me to travel alone. When we walk to the station it is pitch dark and I am glad that I am not alone. I have always had a bit of a fear of train stations and Dimapur is a typical Indian station, with sleeping bodies on the platform covered by white cloths like they are laid out in a morgue.

But Adi buys the tickets for a train that does not travel directly to Jorhat, as he has an ulterior motive. We have to get off at some small village and travel the rest of the way by bus. While on the bus he says, "There is a Christian ashram a little way ahead where you can stay the night and they will take care of you." I believe he feels it is his duty to try and convert me. I tell him "No, I'm going to Jorhat, where I can easily find a small hotel for the night." Truth is, I can't wait to be in a relatively modern city where I can wander alone, blending in with the crowds in a city used to seeing people like me.

We travel to Jorhat where we have our last breakfast together. We part on the main road with a little hug. This time we will never meet again. As I wander the town and reflect, I can see clearly now that some love affairs are best left while they are still burning and the pleasant memories remain. Romantic love is so often fleeting and does not have a happy ending, although for me some tiny heart connection does remain.

Since the '60s India was a place I had returned to many times and I have had many adventures. To mark my seventieth birthday I had made this farewell trip to India, resulting in this unexpected visit to Nagaland. If there had been tourist infrastructure in place and if I had travelled with a companion, I probably would not have stayed with families but would have visited the one remote tribe that still follows the old traditions and refuses to be converted. All this was meant to happen, as if by some strange twist of fate everything conspired to create a different ending to a love story that started exactly half my life ago.

THE OTHER SIDE OF FREEDOM

YAMUNA FLAHERTY

With a convincing look on her face, the woman perched at the front door insists that I sit inside and smoke, protecting me from the interested eyes of the men gathered in small vulturous groups on the street corners. The refreshing sea breeze and the spectacle of the busy local street are far more compelling than the double lines of dirty plastic chairs where I am told to sit. In one corner a desk is stacked with unused pipes—spare hoses hanging in a precarious jumble atop an unused fan. She is right. A woman smoking *shisha*, and a *hawaja* (foreigner) at that, attracts too much unwanted attention.

This is not cosmopolitan Cairo after all; I am in Sudan.

I bring a book with me—partly because I want to read it but mostly because it's a strategy to occupy my eyes from meeting the astonished gaze of other customers. Light from a tiny window near the ceiling glints off the bald head of the man preparing my pipe. His face has a noble quality to it and he seems to take his work very seriously, though I cannot discern his opinion about a woman preparing to engage in a decidedly masculine activity. I sense he is curious about my reasons for being in this port city since it rarely sees casual travellers pass through its seafoam-scented streets. Nonetheless, he does as any self-respecting man would do in public—he makes no inquiries that give his interest visibility.

Before I can change my mind he abruptly places a water pipe at my feet, wraps the mouthpiece in aluminum foil and hands me the hose. I have ample years of shisha smoking under my belt from the Mediterranean joints I frequent back home, but I am rarely the one who gets a pipe started. The sheer force of inhalation needed to get it going is enormous for my untrained lungs and always results in a dizzy spell. This time I must go it alone, and such a simple task feels like an evaluation of my mastery in front of this curious crowd. I calmly hold the hose in my left hand and expertly shift the coals with my right, my newly purchased brass bangles clanging together while I attempt to appear as cool·as possible. The onlookers are throwing sideways glances my way and at each other as they survey my next movement. With puckered lips I suck the foil-covered hose, and the nerve-calming sound of water gurgles as the tobacco cools and rises to my lips with sweet familiarity. Exhaling a respectable volume of smoke, I keep my eyes fixed on the page I am using as my decoy, aware that every man here is watching me or pretending not to. I too am pretending not to watch them watch me.

I feel like retching as my body finds the balance between the heady *shisha toofah* and the sickly-sweet coffee. Didn't I say "*zucar shuaya?*" Apparently this is what is meant by less sugar. I'll have to try "no sugar" next time and see if that procures my desired taste. Men of all different dress and social stature are pouring in. I feel like I am in the equivalent of a Cuban cigar lounge with far plainer trimmings. Some have typical African features and others look more Arab; some dress in traditional *jalabiya* and others in plain Western clothes; most of them play with their mobile phones. Perhaps they too require a decoy of some kind to hide their embarrassment. At this point the entire line of chairs across from me is filled with intrigued patrons while I sit alone on the other side, save for a single man in the corner who hasn't looked up from his pipe since I arrived. He must legitimately be here for the shisha and orders a second pipe. I out-smoke all of them but him.

Nausea from the tobacco fills me. My head is spinning, my attention caught by a television set in the corner spewing unfamiliar rhythms of rapid, lively beats, quite unlike the gentle, sophisticated croons of Sudanese music. The screen is filled with dizzying images of women thrusting their hips to meet their clapping hands and scenes of couples in verdant hills frenzied with passion. This most certainly wasn't the country I was in. The Sudanese are a mild-mannered bunch who display their enthusiasm by snapping their fingers and shrugging their shoulders. Hips, cleavage and even ankles are a no-go zone. For the past week I have done everything in my power to deny that I have a figure, preferring to respectfully shroud it in head-to-toe *jalabiya*. It dawns on me that this *shisha* bar may in fact be a hotbed of sinful activity, from smoking to ogling the half-naked girls in Ethiopian music videos. To set the record straight, the men of Sudan have been very decent in my presence—except for that one who got away with a firm hand on my backside while posing for a photo! Still, the complete lack of ladies on the streets has been unsettling and reminds me that I am out of my element here. I cannot help but reflect on the vast cultural and gender differences I'm encountering and I'm sure the locals are also whispering about how we female *hawaja* are able to roam as we please. I begin to wonder if I am as crazy as I seem.

Only I know that my heart is forever intertwined with this land.

Half a year earlier I began my trip in Israel. It was during the afternoon of a bomb scare in the Tel Aviv Central Bus Station that I met a black man with a bicycle and inquired about an escape route. Adam told me he was from Darfur and taught English to other refugees. I had heard that there were many displaced persons from various East African countries seeking asylum here, and this was confirmed by the volume of homeless Africans who lived in Levinsky Park just across the street. My penchant for unusual experiences prompted me to boldly ask if I would be able to visit his class. He seemed as enthusiastic as I to introduce a real native speaker to his students. That evening, in a dilapidated courtyard obscured by laundry drying on a line, I was introduced to a handful of refugees from Darfur who had escaped genocide only to find themselves in a windowless, fluorescent-lit room in Tel Aviv, where Adam also slept.

There I bravely stood in front of twenty young men who were utterly stunned at the sight of me. I introduced myself and told them about the impressive journey I was about to begin. In a week's time I would start walking the Israel National Trail with an organization promoting peace. We would begin in Eilat at the southernmost tip and walk until we reached Jerusalem. It would be a staggering six weeks filled with campfire songs, exciting new friendships and astonishing views. I encouraged each student to introduce themselves despite their apparent shyness. Every now and again they would break out in nervous laughter and talk amongst themselves in indistinct languages. Each one was respectful and cautious when speaking, and they flashed the whitest sets of teeth I had ever seen. I looked at each of their faces and wondered what stories they hid. Had they seen their parents murdered before them or lost their own children before fleeing? And how did they come this far? I learned that all of them had crossed the desert by foot, lived in intolerable conditions in Egypt and then took the risk to cross the Sinai to come to Israel. Unfortunately, they had not found the welcome they had hoped for but were not allowed to leave. No one else wanted them. Suddenly my incredible trip began to feel like a mockery of the punishing journey they had made for peace and security. At the end of the class, each man personally thanked me with a handshake and begged me to return. When the last student had departed, I sat in a warm chair in the first row and burst into tears. Adam sat beside me and put his hand on my shoulder. "I know," he said, looking at the floor. "I know." For the following four months these people would become my family and my world. I learned of their plight, their resilience in very uncertain conditions, and I unexpectedly fell into a very uncertain love.

His name was Taher and he had eyes like black moons filled with a sorrow that was too overwhelming to comprehend. I sensed his feelings for me growing over the months, but we had never been alone. When he finally invited me to his house, I felt like a crook accepting. I had yet to tell the class that I had bought a ticket to Istanbul departing a mere two weeks later. How could I consummate our affections knowing that I would leave him? Something pressed me onwards. Taher possessed a rare humility, uncanny sparkle and innocence in spite of the tragedy he had endured. A naïve part of me believed that by loving this man I would be able to cleanse him of all his suffering. I would act like a defibrillator, jump-starting his shattered heart and bringing it back to a life where the slate was wiped clean. I would create a space where he could release all that he had carried through the merciless deserts between the home of his heart and the place he sought refuge. It was a selfish saviour complex complicated by real feelings. The world I lived in was one of freedom, independence and possibility, and I knew his was of survival, anxiety and uncertainty. In a matter of time I would be on the road again, wandering wherever I pleased for nothing but pleasure. And him? He would continue to live in a country that did not validate his search for asylum; he'd participate in large-scale protests and finally be stripped of any meagre existence he had managed to cultivate by being placed in a detention centre with other refugees. This was the only sliver of time in which our two worlds could interlace. Perhaps it was this sense of urgency that camouflaged the inevitable pain awaiting. We surrendered to our fate.

Until our final night I had never seen Taher cry. He had lost much in his life, and even this he could not keep. Like the tide drawing inwards, collecting in fervour, the force of his tears struck like a tsunami whose origin was the bowels of the earth. His pain kindled mine and soon we were both shedding a tidal wave of helpless tears. Until now I had not realized just how immature my belief was that I could continue unaffected by this encounter. Taher had offered me his whole world in a grain of desert sand and it was the sincerity with which he gave this humble gift that crumbled my soul. His circumstances afforded him a deep gratitude for simplicity and I envied how uncomplicated his heart was. He assured me that even if he married someone else, he would build a room in his home in Darfur just for my visits. I didn't dare protest such a harmless dream even if we both knew the uncertainty of life. I imagined us aged and wrinkled like two characters in a novel meeting years after our brief, youthful love affair. I saw him wearing a long tunic, standing tall and proud in his village with his naked toes sunken in the sand. In his smile I'd see the young man I had loved and everything would be in its perfect place. However, in this moment everything felt sickly wrong. The world was unreasonable if a good-natured, peace-loving gentleman couldn't even dream about the bright future he deserved. As my taxi began its journey away from him, I turned to wave but couldn't make out his face. The contours of his black silhouette bled into the expanse of an equally black sky. His clean and pressed white shirt remained the last visible speck of him as we hurtled through the gritty streets of south Tel Aviv.

Now here I sit smoking a water pipe in the very country that robbed Taher of everything, this act being my own silent protest of the inequity of this world. I wrestle with a nagging guilt. I have been travelling for leisure as long as he has been a refugee. I've prized my liberty and the vast experience it has granted me, yet I'm imprisoned by the shame I feel for not using this privilege to emancipate others from the injustice they suffer. I'm burdened by the price of my indulgence, and any exhilaration I felt is deflated by the despair of his exile. I have to get out of here.

It is impossible to enjoy my freedom when someone I love is a prisoner.

Without regarding the aroused attention of all the other smokers when I stand, I raise my eyebrows to the bald guy in a gesture that signals I am ready to pay. I make a move to the entrance, inhaling a breath of air perfumed with salt and exhaust fumes. So this is what it feels like to be different, to be pointed out and measured. It is a paradox to wish for anonymity and invisibility in this country when Taher only wishes to be recognized for who he is anywhere.

With the sweet flavour of apple tobacco lingering on my lips, I hear the haunting echo of the muezzin calling all pious Muslims to their carpets. Taher's perseverance has taught me that faith is the strongest pillar of the self, and so I close my eyes and let my prayer be like two giant arms embracing him and welcoming him home. I step out into the street; the sun floods my unadjusted eyes. I hear the acceleration of a rickshaw behind me, and laughter in the distance, as I keep my gaze firmly fixed on my destination and my head held high. With rattled nerves I sail into the shabby hotel lobby on the wings of my gentle intoxication, turning back to inspect the scene once I am safely on the other side. From this distance, the dingy cement box I spent the last hour in looks pretty average—hardly the lair from which I could change the world. Rather, it is the world that is changing me and this is where it all starts.

LONESOME THELMA

LORI GARRISON

The captain said the bird's name was Lonesome Thelma.

The captain was a grey man with grey eyes and grey cheeks and a grey, thin smile. The only thing not grey about him were his hands, which were chapped red and raw. They were very beautiful, moving with the slow, thick grace only the hands of working men get, an economy of motion as lovely and utilitarian as the opening and closing of a carburetor. He had a little boat, which he ran to and from the point of the harbour to the sea with the help of a slim blond girl and plump dark boy, taking tourists out for money on the promise of whales.

Thelma was an eagle. She lived on the edge of the cove along the black stone that ran through the narrow channel like a finger pointing out to the open ocean. Her head was white and her breast was the colour of a brass bar rail. When she stretched out her wings she cast a shadow and when she drifted lazily over the boat her shadow fell in the shape of a cross over the face of the captain, over the hull of the ship, over the reflective, rippling surface of the water.

"Ah, Lonesome Thelma!" the captain cried, pointing up at her. Thelma, he explained, was a rather unusual bird. Eagles mate for life, settling into a territory in pairs, but if Thelma had a mate and a nest and nestlings, no one had even seen them. She returned to the bay year after year from her winter hunting grounds alone and stayed alone. It was possible she once had a mate and he had died, but eagles will almost always take another mate if theirs is killed. Male eagles had been seen from time to time attempting to court the lovely Ms. Thelma. They always went away disappointed.

"Personally, I think she likes it that way—clever old girl. Her own life on her own time," the captain said, reaching behind his chair to produce a rusty bucket. The bucket was full of little fish, their eyes dull and glassy as beads in death. Thelma, seemingly at the call of her name, had begun to wheel about the boat. As she drifted closer the captain threw a fish high over his head. It rose sharply and then arched down rapidly toward the water. Thelma folded her wings like a pair of jackknives against the brass of her body and fell like an arrow, snatching it up in the yellow talons of her feet before unfurling herself to let the sea breeze propel her upward again.

The tourists oohed and awed and clapped, as if Thelma were a circus performer and not an animal. The captain smiled. The bird alighted on the rocks and began to tear into the fish, starting at the head, shaking her beak from side to side to rip the meat away like a dog. We passed very close to her and as we did I could see the great, golden emptiness of her eyes was still focused on the boat and the captain even as the muscles in her beak and throat worked dutifully to reduce the fish to bird pellets and a few stray scales. She watched us carefully while she ate, marking the motions of the captain's hands, the passing of the boat, my own eyes following her eyes as I leaned against the railing, silent and still amid the milling tourists.

I watched her until the fog swallowed her, and we went out to the sea proper.

———

When I was twenty, my life fell apart. We're not going to talk about that—that's a different story, a story that has nothing to do with the sea or sea captains or eagles named Thelma, except to say the collapse was total and so was mine. When I was well enough recovered I did the only reasonable thing, which was sell everything I owned, change my phone number, stop talking to my parents, get on a train and move from my sleepy, methamphetamine-addled hometown in Southern Ontario to Ottawa. When that did not immediately put enough distance between myself and the constant, grinding ache in my chest I did the only other reasonable thing and bought a motorcycle.

A 1981 Yamaha Virago. Black and chrome, with a long scratch down the side and a scuff on the gas tank where the middle-aged woman who had owned it before me had driven it once, taken a corner too quickly and dropped the bike along a stretch of gravel road. She'd broken her arm and put the thing up for sale the next day. I bought it for five hundred dollars.

For the same price I could have bought an old beater car, but I didn't want a car. There was something sparse and loose and vaguely suicidal about a motorcycle I found irresistible. A car boxes you in, a bike forces you out. Even today, when I hear the snapping growl of a cruiser ripping by from behind me on the road a shiver of longing passes through me that is not entirely unlike the sexual arousal of seeing a beautiful woman smile at you.

I had the bike for three months before I fell. I dropped it just outside of Kaladar, Ontario, on Highway 7, a sun-baked, cracked asphalt road that runs from Ottawa through to Kingston and on to Toronto. I had been on my way to see Emily, an older woman with whom I was very much in love but who was not in the slightest bit in love with me. A car in front of me came to a sudden stop and I slammed on the brakes, locked up my back wheel and let the bike get away from me. It slid out from under my body like a jackknife unfolding and I hit the gravel still in the saddle.

I showed up at the house of my unrequited lover with bruised ribs, torn blue jeans, scraped thighs, pulled shoulder muscles, and a broken tail light. My helmet was slightly too large and I'd bashed my nose against it when I fell. Blood was spattered across the inside of my visor like violent stars. I arrived like this, tattered and bloody and dusty, but smiling when she answered the door.

She still didn't love me. She had a new boyfriend, in fact.

Two weeks later, I drove out of Ontario for a three-week solo road trip on the East Coast. My unrequited lover said she'd be worried about me if I went, so of course I did. I hadn't planned on going to Cape Breton, but then I hadn't planned on really going anyway; the only thing I planned on was being anywhere that wasn't there.

We did see whales on the tour that morning. Pilot whales. They were long and dark and rose out of the ocean to shoot jets of water from their blowholes like steam from bursting pipes and roll languidly over to show us their fins as if they were aware they were being majestic and entertaining. They seemed to take a showman's pride in our amusement. Seeing them up close—for a land-locked Ontario girl, seeing a whale ranks just below seeing a unicorn and slightly above a leprechaun—left me in a state of Zen-like bliss, utterly calm and yet oddly aware of everything: the salt-smell of the sea, the red cliffs looming over the shore, the tinkling accent of the Japanese tourists. When we docked shortly after eight the sun had come out and the sky was cloudless and very blue and I felt much warmer than I probably was. It had rained almost every day, on and off, in varying intensities, since I had come through Quebec City a week and a half ago. Just seeing the sun had put an extra bounce in my step and, after a short snack of almond butter and white bread sitting with my feet dangling bare and white off the pier, full of this magic feeling from the sun and the whales, I was determined to seize the day and take a hike.

The hike I determined to take was one recommended to me by one of the hands on the boat that morning, who, noting my enthusiasm for marine life, had suggested a trail called Seal Point Cove. It was, he said, not only a challenging and beautiful trail but, at the end where the mountains met the sea there were, ostensibly, seals. Actual, adorable, frolicking, slippery seals that could be observed from the shore. I didn't have a map, but the trail was part of the Highlands National Park hiking system, and I had seen the trail marker on my way in. It was shortly after nine when I parked my bike beneath the slanting boughs of a pine tree, some small shelter for my battered leather seat in case the weather changed, and set out down the trail.

The air was still very fresh from the rain and had a curious, tingly, peaty aroma. I took deep lungfuls of it as I admired the old forest, the slick black trunks of the trees, the thick lichen, the poplar leaves impossibly green and waxy in the diffused light. My boots felt good and steady and firm on my feet and my legs felt strong. That morning I had seen whales. That morning been out to sea. That morning I had seen a bald eagle named Thelma whose loneliness was a great mystery. Now the afternoon, I was on my way to see seals. There was no cell phone and no Internet. No one back home had any idea where I was and the idea that I was out there in a mountain forest alone in the world made me feel light and somehow powerful. No one owned me. I was my own creature. I could do anything I liked. There was still a sharp, stabbing pain in my chest whenever I thought about Emily-who-didn't-love-me, but that was alright. I decided there were two kinds of people in the world; wild things who lived off the land and the road and their wits and felt no pain, and not-wild things, who whimpered and cried and pined away under the weight of living.

I decided I was a wild thing. Everything was good. I could do anything and feel nothing.

Four hours, a washed-out stretch of trail, a thousand bug bites and a moose later, I had lost most of that "I'm a wild thing" feeling. What I was feeling most then was tired and hungry and cranky, because this was taking much longer than I had anticipated. I was sweaty, nearly out of water and developing some half-dozen blisters that felt to be approximately nickle-sized at the moment but were well on their way to quarter country.

Which was why I was rather dismayed to see a sign that read YOU ARE HERE—DISTANCE TO TRAIL HEAD 8KM. There was a rough map cut into the wood and painted in primary colours showing the length of the trail in a loop.

What the fellow on the boat neglected to mention was that the trail is actually sixteen kilometres long and meant to be an overnight hike. The seals, furthermore, were not at the bottom of the trail—they were three more kilometres off-trail where the sea was, far out of sight. It was now four o'clock in the afternoon. I had eaten nothing since my snack that morning but a Nature Valley Crunchy Almond granola bar. There was a blue arrow nailed to a tree, which pointed up the trail, which curled upward into an impossibly steep path laden with loose stones, down which a thin trickle of muddy water was running.

It went on for a very, very long time.

I had come down the bottom of the mountain. I was at sea level.

And now I had to go back up again. For a minute I thought about turning around and going back, but that would be just as far, just as steep, just as hard.

I looked down at my feet. I was wearing an old, battered pair of army boots. They were scuffed and muddy. I had gone in up to my knees crossing a stream and the boots had gotten wet, so when I walked my toes squelched and burped obscenely in my socks. The tongue on the left boot was in tatters, gnawed to ribbons by a friend's border collie puppy. They were pointing toward the trail with its very narrow, steep path up. Moreover, they were pointing forward, not backward. I took the last, long drink out of my water bottle, emptying it. Forward was obviously the direction my feet were meant to go.

Halfway up the trail, I realized I had been wrong earlier. Being a wild thing didn't mean living without pain. Being a wild thing meant accepting pain as part of living.

———

It was nearly eight by the time I arrived back at the hostel. It took me four hours to reach the mountain road again, and when I emerged from the forest I discovered the way I had come out was not the way I had come in. I was disoriented, dehydrated and sun-baked, and could not figure out if I was up the highway or down it from the place I had parked my bike. I stood on the roadside for half an hour with my thumb out, unsuccessfully trying to hitch a ride before a middle-aged couple in a pickup truck with Delaware plates finally took pity on me and pulled over. I explained my trouble to them; like me, they were tourists and as such not sure which way the other trailhead was likely to be, but we picked a direction—back toward the hostel, which seemed most likely since I pulled over at the first Seal Point Cove sign I had seen, although there was the possibility I had simply missed it. I sat in the crew cab trying not to get mud on anything. Fortunately it was the right choice. We found my original trailhead and I managed to get to my bike.

It wasn't until I got back to the hostel and saw myself in a mirror—dust-streaked face and mud-caked, tattered jeans, dirty green bandana wrapped around my greasy, dishevelled hair, a knife with a long, fixed blade in a sheath at my hip—that I realized why it took so long for someone to stop for me, namely that I looked like I might be an escaped serial killer.

Standing beneath the hot pulse of the water, I had never been so grateful for a shower. The water at my feet was nearly black from the dirt washing off my aching back and shoulders. Little bugs like black flies, mosquitoes, moose flies (vicious, voracious cousins of the horse fly) sluiced about amid the soap suds. They were coming out of my hair, where they had become caught and died.

My feet were a raw, tattered mess. My blisters oozed clear, ugly juices like an overripe peach.

I cleaned them up with a medical kit I found in the bathroom cupboard and gingerly slipped into a pair of clean socks.

Clean, I retired to the common room, a simple affair with a battered wooden trolly of paperbacks and a small television set with a VCR I was told worked if you jiggled the plug a bit, and fell into the thin cushions of the couch. Relieved of the duty of being upright and in motion, my body sagged listlessly. I was immensely but satisfyingly tired in the way one can only be when one has completed a difficult physical task.

I took out my book, which was Dostoyevsky's *The Idiot*. A few weeks ago it had been pristine and crisp with newness, but now it was dog-eared from being banged around in my saddlebags and brown from weeks of exposure to the damp East Coast air. The introduction, reference notes and biography were missing where I had torn out pages two or three at a time along roadsides and in campgrounds to use as fire starter. I was on chapter three.

I'm sure that her life is no ordinary one. Her face seems cheerful, but she has suffered terribly, hasn't she?

"Oh," a voice said suddenly. "I've read that."

I looked up. There was a girl—a woman, really—standing there in the entranceway to the common room. She was dressed in expensive-looking blue jeans and a white blouse that showed off the neat cut of her collarbones. She was slim and very pretty, with long, red hair with a light curl to it and high cheeks.

"Never a dull night in Saint Petersburg?" she asked.

"Um, no. No, I guess not."

"You feel better now that you're cleaned up?" she asked, coming forward to sit down on the edge of the couch. "I saw you come in. You looked like hell."

I blushed. "Do I know you?"

"No." She proffered her hand. "I'm Carmen."

"That's a very pretty name," I said, taking her hand. "I'm Jane."

"Thank you," she said. She was looking at me very intently. Her eyes were brown, deep and very dark. Despite what she said and the fact that I knew we had never met before—I would have remembered her, certainly, if I had—I nonetheless felt that I somehow knew her.

"Would you like to go to dinner with me, Jane? The restaurant here is very good."

I blinked, feeling oddly dizzy, and replied that yes, I would like that. Very, very much.

———

Up the road a ways from the hostel was a restaurant. The only one, or so I was told, between there and Sydney, the unofficial capital of Cape Breton, which sits at the northernmost point of the Cabot Trail and connects via ferry to Newfoundland. It was pleasant and warm and had lovely, soft biscuits that broke apart under your tongue and melted like butter. We sat at a plastic table covered with a checkered plastic tablecloth on the patio, which was made of stone, not cement, and looked out over the shore. The tide was out.

The waitress was a middle-aged, curly-haired woman with a matronly smile and flat white shoes like a nurse might wear. She told us her husband was a fisherman and that the lobster and crab on the restaurant's menu had been hauled up from the ocean and into their kitchens that morning by his own two hands. We ordered that and a litre of white wine. The waitress scribbled our order down on a little notepad, took our menus and went away. We sat in silence for a moment. Carmen had her hands folded on the tabletop, one over the other in a little x. Her hands were very fine, long white fingers tipped with perfectly shaped, manicured nails. My own nails were short and ragged. I chewed them when I was nervous, which was often, and they were dirty, partly from the hike but mostly from the week and a half I had already spent on the road. There was a long, ugly cut, only half healed, running diagonally across the back of my left where I had cut myself with a fillet knife a week ago when I had been trout fishing on the Miramichi River.

I lay my palms discreetly in my lap.

"Have you been in Cape Breton long?" I asked when I felt the tension of the silence.

"Not as long as I thought I might have been," Carmen said. She reached across the table with those delicate hands and poured us each a generous glass of wine. "I flew in from Toronto last week to Newfoundland, but when I went to pick up the car I had reserved, it turned out they had booked me a car in Saint John, New Brunswick, not St John's, Newfoundland. Apparently it's a very common mistake."

She paused to take a sip of wine, and I followed her example; I felt so deeply out of my league with this woman, the impossibility of my own scrappy, shabby self having dinner with her, that I imagined my only hope of not making a complete ass of myself was to follow her lead and pray my mimicry of a semi-socialized human being was convincing enough to fool her.

The wine was very cold and tasted faintly of pears. When it hit the back of my tongue it was as if I had swallowed a mouthful of light and I felt better almost immediately.

"Anyways, it wouldn't have been a problem, except there was some kind of a music festival in town and they were out of cars. I'm usually very well-planned for these things, but somehow I hadn't even heard about it and my travel agent never mentioned it. The agent assured me they'd have a car in the next day, but they never called and then it was Sunday and they were closed, so I was stuck in St John's for three days longer than I intended to be. The car never did come in. I managed to get a ride with a friend and I took the ferry over and finally managed to rent a car in Sydney. I stayed there a couple days and then drove down here, but of course because I was behind, the reservation I had made at the hotel was no good. I think I like the hostel better anyways."

"That's quite an adventure," I said. "Although I can think of worse places to be stuck than St John's."

She grinned, lips stretched taut. "Quite. Although it looked like you'd just come back from an adventure yourself when I ran into you this afternoon."

I groaned. "Yes ... there was a bit of an incident at Seal Point Cove ..."

I told her about my gruelling hike, about riding in the rain along the Fiddlehead Highway in New Brunswick, about the roads flooding out in sudden downpours and transport trucks kicking up stones the size of loonies that had hit me and left bruises the size of loonies even through my wet gear and leathers, about sleeping in that same rain in a tent that leaked and dripped into my face, about snorkeling for crabs in Peggys Cove the red caps of white lighthouses, the little swells of little blue, translucent jellyfish at the beach in Caribou, Nova Scotia. She told me about dark bars that smelled of cigarette smoke and whisky in St John's, grizzled fishermen who came on very strong but were absolute gentlemen in the face of Carmen's consistent rejection, about fiddle players and bartenders with Newfie accents so thick you could hardly get a word in edgewise but they brought you cold pints anyway, about people laughing and hotel rooms with impossibly white fluffy towels. By the time dinner arrived we'd polished off the first litre of wine. We ordered another. Carmen was aghast that I had never had lobster—rich, white-fleshed, buttery lobster with its taste like the sea and sunshine—but showed me patiently how to crack the claws and scrape out the green tomalley, which she said some people ate but that was, in her opinion, quite gross. The lobster came with a big pile of green beans and a steaming hot baked PEI potato with sour cream, and it wasn't until I started eating that I realized how hungry I was, for food and for company. I hadn't had a hot meal or anyone to talk to in over a week.

Carmen told me about her work at an ad firm in Toronto, a city I had only ever visited as a child, about city nights with towering skyscrapers and people as numerous as stars. I told her about riding a motorcycle down an open, twisting highway and drinking warm beers on the side of the road. She told me about the sea moving beneath her feet on the ferry and long days in meetings and the happiness of finally being out in the sun. I told her about the old painter I'd met along the Gulf of Saint Lawrence who, seeing the dark clouds coming in over the ocean, had called ahead to the hostel owner here in Pleasant Bay and made me a reservation so I wouldn't be left sleeping out in the rain again. I told her about the whales and the white sea birds with yellow throats bobbing listlessly in the water. I told her about Lonesome Thelma, and her strange, golden eyes.

We finished dinner and the wine. The plates were whisked away. We ordered apple pie and coffee. She was smart and sweet and funny. She had read not only *The Idiot*, but *Grapes of Wrath, Anna Karenina*, and *For Whom the Bell Tolls,* and was a great fan of historical fiction. Whenever she said anything my heart fluttered about in my chest like a fledgling bird, uncertain of its wings but determined to use them. Over the course of the meal we had closed the space between each other imperceptibly, so that now when we spoke we were almost leaning in to whisper to each other.

She was twenty-nine with an apartment in Toronto, a professional in a career she liked. I was twenty-one, living in a dive with duct tape over the holes in the walls, a wannabe writer working as a waitress at a tourist-trap in Ottawa called *Yesterday's* where all the booths were upholstered in some dingy floral fabric that looked as if it had been torn out of your grandmother's retirement home. A customer had once remarked in an online review that our burgers had *run through him like a rat through a drain pipe.*

"You must think I'm very silly," I said.

Our pie had just come. It turned out that we both took our coffee black. I found that instantly charming, couldn't help but compare her to Emily, who had always dumped two heaping teaspoons of sugar and a generous glug of cream into hers. Carmen had a slice of cooked apple halfway to her mouth. She had a lovely mouth, plump-lipped, well-shaped, lush. Her fork paused in mid-motion.

"Why would you think that?" she asked earnestly.

"Being out here by myself. Sleeping in ditches. Eating cold beans. Getting lost."

Carmen put down her fork, the metal clicking lightly against the porcelain of her plate. She regarded me carefully. She was wearing the blouse that bared her collarbones and the way her hair fell perfectly over her shoulders made me run my hands through my own short, shaggy, dirty blond hair self-consciously. After a moment she seemed to intuit what I was really saying, what I really meant, what I was too embarrassed to say out loud, which was:

You're too good for me. You're way out of my league. What the hell are you doing having dinner with me?

She smiled imperiously, one corner of her mouth slightly higher than the other, and reached out across the table to lay her perfect, white hand over top of my cut-up, sun-freckled one. At some point I had forgotten how awful they looked and put them on the table again.

"Jane, I'm on vacation. You're on an adventure. We're just different people doing different things. I don't think you're silly at all."

I looked down at our crossed hands. Carmen turned my palm over and threaded our fingers together.

"Thank you," I said, softly, although I wasn't quite certain what I was thanking her for. We paid the check.

Carmen had rented the only private room in the hostel.

———

The next morning she was gone.

We had coffee together in the common room, the portrait windows wide open, the green shadow of a maple tree crawling across the table. A few other guests were up and about, making breakfast, having showers, talking softly, but for the most part it was early and people were still asleep. It gave the illusion that we were alone. We sat in silence for a long time, knees touching, watching the sea.

Then she got into her rented car, a red Corolla with lightly tinted windows, and I watched her drive away. She had to be in Charlottetown in a couple days. That's where she was flying out of. Her car kicked up dust that didn't settle for a long time.

After she was gone I went back inside and lay down on my bed and stared up at the ceiling. There was suddenly a big aching hole in my chest, an unexpected wound. I cried, and I felt silly for crying, because I had just met Carmen, there was no way I could be in love with Carmen, I'd known her less than twenty-four hours and what I was doing was stupid and childish and ruining a perfectly good thing.

I cried anyway. Then I got up, ate a slice of toast and went for a hike.

I did the Skyline Trail this time. It's well used and very popular, running along a narrow path through a bog in the mountains. They say Cape Breton Highlands National Park is as close to being in the Scottish Highlands as a person can be without being in Scotland. I've never been to Scotland, but it seems likely; rolling heather marshes, peat giving softly under your feet, little birds flitting about in the willows, the sea gleaming like the blade of a wet knife far beneath you.

A few years later, on this trail, the young Canadian folk singer Taylor Mitchell would die in a tragic and freak coyote attack. I remember thinking at the time that, if there was ever a beautiful place to die, it was there.

I saw it all, and each time I looked at this great beauty, I knew I was alone—without Emily, without Carmen, without *anyone*—and a deep, bone-cutting pain filled me.

I reached the peak of the trail. From my vantage point I could see the cove where I had taken the whaling trip the day before. I squinted. There was a bird down there, flying above the water but still beneath me. I have no way of knowing for certain that it was Lonesome Thelma, but I like to think it was, and at the time I believed it to be so.

Thelma was turning in slow, geometric circles. Riding the thermals.

I watched her for a long moment. Something in the smooth, easy motion of her solo flight was so soothing and calm I felt hypnotized.

Thelma was alone but Thelma was alright. Thelma was better than alright. Thelma was free.

My mind cleared. I felt full and empty at the same time, as I had after seeing the whales.

I finished the hike. I thought of nothing.

I ate at the restaurant again that night, a simple meal this time of fish and chips and a beer. I went to bed. I read for a while.

I slept early. In the morning I rose at dawn. I showered and dressed. I had coffee again in the shadow of the same tree. I put my boots on, then my leathers. I mounted my bike and put the key in the ignition. I turned the engine over and flew away.

———

A couple hours later I had come down the mountain. The racing, buzzing hum of the engine had broken the calm of Thelma's spell and while I was no longer sad and aching, I was myself again. I stopped into a restaurant in Cheticamp, a little French-speaking town at the base of the mountains. The restaurant made wonderful bread and the loaves, sitting to cool on racks at the front of the house, filled the air with their welcoming, yeasty aroma. I sat at a little table by the window and ordered bacon and eggs and rye toast and black coffee. When the young waitress went away with my order I reached into my bag and took out *The Idiot.*

I had been using a dried sumac leaf as a bookmark, and it was gone. In its place was a business card printed on fine, firm white paper, stiff and professional. It read *Carmen Greyson,* her job title and her phone number and email. I plucked it up from between the pages, running my fingers over her name. The letters were embossed. I turned it over. On the back, in crisp, flowing script she had written *Good luck on your adventure, Lonesome Jane. Call me when you get home.* And then her private number.

I held it disbelievingly for a moment. Then I laughed and took another drink of my coffee. The second sip seemed better than the first.

PROTECTION TO GO

KAREN J LEE

When I heard my name I moved from a soft chair in the waiting area to a harder one at the counter and placed my immunization record on the bare surface in front of me. I had received all the major vaccinations at this travel clinic before my first trip to Africa a year ago and only needed boosters for hepatitis A and B. The counter was divided by partitions to create a semblance of privacy, and a map from the World Health Organization was tacked to the inside of the particleboard on my right. It was an infogram, describing why I shouldn't leave home. According to the WHO, Canada didn't have uncivilized diseases, whereas Kenya, my destination, had eight of the ten most unwanted.

Sensations from my last trip swirled: thick mango juice sliding down the back of my throat, the heave of water when two rhinos mated, the accumulation of sweat between my breasts and behind my knees, delicate mosquito netting pooled like spilled milk on a rough plank floor, and a man's hand loosely clamped around a steering wheel, its thumb curled back to reveal the pink underneath.

There were as many shades of brown in Kenya as there were tribes, but this particular hand was black—black on top, pink underneath. He was Luhya, born in Kenya and educated in Uganda. As he guided our group from one game lodge to the next, he laced bits of himself into his tales about local culture and African wildlife. I learned his family fled Uganda when Idi Amin came to power and, in addition to raising three children alone, he was head of his extended family. As "the big man," he was responsible for everyone's welfare, including the care of his elderly mother and the family farm near

Lake Victoria. His earnings supported many; guiding was a coveted position in Kenya, where the average annual income wouldn't buy a one-way ticket to Canada.

From my seat behind him in the van, I memorized the creases in his neck, the slope of his shoulders and the way the curls on his head crawled under the collar of his shirt. Whenever he offered a hand to help his passengers through the sliding door, or climbed back to lift the roof for a game drive, or pulled his machete out of its sheath bolted to the floor, the women in the van exchanged looks; we were all drifting in the same fantasy.

A young fellow whose name had been called ahead of me was sitting to my right, on the other side of the partition. He was college-aged with blond hair, arms that looked too long for his body, and a rear end worth watching. Events in Kenya had left me hyper-aware and curious about men; a salacious voice that had been muzzled my whole life was now live streaming on the left side of my brain.

I made a mental note to raise the question of men's butts the next time I talked to my sister and then scrounged in my purse for pen and paper. Lately my "mental notes" had been evaporating like gasoline on a hot dock; one minute a whiff in the air, the next—zilch. I had started using Post-it notes months ago, sticking them to mirrors, the bottom edge of the big-screen television, the inside of the front door and the side of the bottle of Crown Royal whisky sitting on the counter in my kitchen. I'd learned not to scrimp on the notes after the glue on the bargain batch let go and my reminders began drifting into crevices and behind furniture. I found "bank" under my yoga mat, "call Krista" behind the dieffenbachia, "library books" under the fridge. Now I carried sticky notes that cost more but adhered tenaciously to any surface.

An article in my weekly news magazine suggested ways for the fifty-plus crowd to cope with day-to-day forgetfulness. (I joked that when the big one hit the West Coast, I would already be hovering in a protective doorframe, wondering why.) The author of the article advised Boomers to speak the task out loud as soon as the intent formed, which gave seventy-seven million North Americans a reason to talk to themselves.

I wasn't old. Not old-old. I was still downwind of retirement. But every day something reminded me I wasn't young either: forgetfulness, a morning ache in my finger joints, a drop of pee when I sneezed. I was still what my grandfather used to call a fine figure of a woman—narrow shoulders, deep bosom, defined waist, broad hips—but I had never embraced the cornucopia. Instead I wore loose sweaters that could be pulled closed or pushed open, depending on the circumstances.

I shrugged out of today's cover-up and allowed my shoulders to roll back and relax. The simple motion, so foreign, thrilled me. Since Kenya, the paths I'd avoided in life occupied my thoughts more than the paths taken. I hadn't learned to downhill ski. I'd missed my chance to hitchhike. There were no tattoos hidden near my private spots or pictures of myself skydiving. I'd never tested my body's capacity for pleasure or proudly celebrated its lines. A different kind of clock was ticking in my head now, and it ran fast.

I jotted "men's butts" and "article on forgetfulness" on sticky notes and pressed them against the back of my cell phone. The consultation on my right was winding down and the doctor's voice drifted over the partition.

"Be sure to take North American condoms. Local ones aren't always reliable."

I froze, blinking rapidly, but had no time to consider the ramifications of what I'd overheard because at that moment my physician arrived, offered a perfunctory greeting, sat down, and reached for the yellow travel immunization record lying on the counter between us. She confirmed the country I planned to visit, made a note on her file, gestured back toward the soft seats in the waiting area, and said it would be ten minutes before I was called for my booster shots. I continued to stare into her face, but she stood and pivoted away without offering advice on condoms. I felt as if I'd pinched information without paying for it.

While I waited for the nurse to call my name, I crossed travel clinic off the top of my list and added condoms to the bottom.

———

The next day I met with my family physician. Dr. Hepner had been at my side through a couple of suspicious lumps, menopause, clinical depression and late-life divorce. So far, nothing had fazed her.

"I'm going on a trip and plan to have lots of sex." The words tripped over one another in their rush to escape. "I'm worried about bladder infection."

Her lips twitched as she sat down on the little stool with wheels. She pulled a prescription pad out of the pocket of her lab coat. "Let's not take any chances then. Do you have vaginal dryness?"

A sensible question. I considered for a moment, mentally located the terrain, tried to remember its climate on my last visit, and frowned.

Dr. Hepner weighed my uncertainty. "Let's not take any chances," she said again and leaned into her task. Antibiotics for unexpected upper respiratory problems and little blue pills to fight jet lag fell into the same category. With a smile that bordered on giddy, I pocketed four prescriptions, crossed Dr. Hepner off my list, and headed for the drugstore.

———

Metaphorically, I considered myself a born-again virgin; I hadn't had sex with a stranger since the Beatles appeared on *The Ed Sullivan Show*. My last encounter with a condom was years ago, when two square, waterproof packages went through the wash/rinse/spin cycle and fell, static-free, into the bottom of my laundry basket along with the kids' jeans. The end of my thirty-seven-year marriage had been a shock; rediscovering single life had been a revelation; so far, protection had not been necessary.

Condoms occupied a significant piece of real estate directly in front of the prescription-dispensing counter. The scope of decision making was mind-boggling: ribbed or studded, clear lubricated or colour lubricated, baggy head, cool tingle, or ultra-thin. There were strength ratings and expiry dates and promises of ecstasy. I was searching for a get-the-job-done house brand, something like President's Choice at the Real Canadian Superstore, when I realized the little discs came in sizes. My mind flashed to the last time I'd seen him, standing in the shadow of his van at the Nairobi airport.

"Will you come back?" he'd asked in that fabulous, melodic accent. It accompanied a gorgeous smile, impossibly white teeth, close-cropped hair, strong arms, a thick neck, and hands that made my stomach clench. I couldn't remember the size of his feet.

He had touched my foot once. I was sitting in the safari van with my left sandal resting on the running board and instead of telling me it was time to go, he pressed one finger against the frosted varnish on my big toe and then allowed his hand to drift up until it wrapped around my ankle. For a millisecond, we both stared at the dark hand on the pale leg. Then he gently lifted my foot and tucked it inside the door. When he straightened, his eyes were hooded; mine were wide and staring.

A young woman with three piercings in her ear and a tattoo on her neck was standing to one side, watching me dither. No doubt the girl had a working knowledge of condoms. She probably preferred a certain brand. Maybe she thought her generation had dibs on sex. I drew my brows together, executed a full-body turn to the right, zapped the young woman with a mother stare, and blew her ten paces east—to the section housing eye drops and nasal spray.

Stay, my look said.

I continued to ponder. I didn't want to offend, but I didn't want the damned things falling off either. I pulled a box of Trojan Thin Intensity™ with Warm Sensations™ Lubricant, size medium, off the rack hanger and tossed it into my basket. Then hesitated.

On the final evening of the safari, vans transported us to a spot far from our lodge where tables had been set and a bonfire burned and cooks in tall white hats tended sizzling chunks of meat on barbeques. He had waited until the other passengers were out of sight before he pulled me into the shadows. The move was fast, like two dancers coming together in a jive; I landed with a thud against his chest. His arms circled, his hands memorized my shape, his lips brushed the crook of my neck. I wanted him to throw me to the ground and take me, hard.

"Next time," his eyes promised as he backed away.

"Next time," he whispered every time he called.

The thought of next time set me on fire.

My friends warned of Somali pirates and white slavers and the possibility of being held for ransom. One of them recommended *The White Masai,* a book about a white woman and a black man that doesn't end well. I wanted to throttle them all. I was infatuated, not dense; I'd worried the bad bits a hundred times.

The Nairobi airport was chaos: dirty, noisy, a free-for-all. People surged toward conveyor belts where bags rolled endlessly. Large women in customs uniforms pawed through side pockets, shooting questions. Hawkers sold Kenyan shillings and cheap necklaces. Hundreds of taxi drivers and tour operators waited outside, waving signs and jostling for position. The group I had travelled with last time had moved through the Nairobi airport in a pack, like soldiers in a war zone, eyes darting, alert to danger, clutching branded bags, searching for a pale-skinned host carrying a Vintage Africa sign. I'd be alone this time. How would I find him? What if he wasn't there? What if he was there, but wasn't the man I remembered?

The young woman was edging back toward the rack of prophylactics. I multiplied mentally and grabbed two more boxes. This was my chance—he wanted me, I wanted him. Screw the rest. At the girl's look of incredulity, I popped a fourth box into my basket, lifted my chin, and pivoted toward the cashier, crossing condoms off my list.

The pager in my pocket vibrated; my prescriptions were ready.

CONCRETE JUNGLE

MIRIAM MATEJOVA

The jungle has awakened," I murmur, standing on a chilly yet relatively dry side of an entrance door to a high-rise apartment building. The rain had come heavily and abruptly, at the precise moment the iron door closed behind me with a click of a lock to which I don't have a key anymore.

I sigh and lean backward, letting nothing but my shoulder blades touch the cold metal behind me. My small bag on wheels sways as I let go of it. The wooden handle of my umbrella is not sticking out of the bag's front pocket, its usual spot. Instead, it is lying uselessly on the floor several storeys above.

I could return upstairs and get that umbrella. I could see my mother again and then reenact the goodbyes, the hugs and the repressed tears. I could let another wave of guilt wash over me—the guilt of leaving for Canada, the home of my estranged father, all that time ago. And then returning ten years later to merely visit, not to stay.

I draw the zipper of my jacket higher and frown at the broken intercom. Someone would have to let me in. The surrounding walls are preventing the rain from reaching me, but they are no good at halting the damp chill that is clawing at my flesh. "And it's not going to get any better," I mutter as I watch the rainwater pooling in the cracks of the path ahead of me. It is stretching for some hundred metres, linking my hideout with a covered bus stop that I need to reach in order to catch a bus to the airport. Years ago, the path was nothing but a thin layer of dust in the summer and a shallow bed of mud throughout the rest of the year. Now it is made of pink symmetrical cobblestone that complements its concrete surroundings.

"Petržalka is an infamous part of Bratislava," I used to say to introduce my home borough to foreigners. When Linda, my life-long friend and Petržalka's enduring resident, was around, she disagreed. "It is infamous only because you grew up here. Otherwise, no one gives a damn." She would snort and dramatically roll her eyes, and I would ignore her.

Petržalka is one of the five municipalities of Slovakia's capital, Bratislava. The borough is located south of the Danube River and connected with the rest of the city by several rather unremarkable bridges. Built by the communists in the 1970s, Petržalka's primary purpose was residential. Accordingly, the borough is marked by a sombre appearance, relatively identical building design, scattered artificial patches of green spaces, and a lack of any obvious centre.

Petržalka is not a tourist destination; yet, foreigners who wander over from the north banks of the Danube have been discovering the borough with the curiosity of uninformed explorers and the passion of pleased adventurers. These are the streets of a jungle, a sea of grey that long ago suffocated the intended white. Patches of colours—red, yellow, purple and green—have seeped through here and there, determined to beat the grey overgrowth. The shadows of the jungle conceal treacherous nooks. There, the smell of urine, pieces of shattered glass and darkness, the shade of which seems deeper than anywhere else, tingle the hair on your arms and prompt your pace.

Yet, enclosed by a patchwork of painted concrete, there are oases too. Some are full of rough-grained sand, sturdy plastic and coloured metal that leaves a sour smell on the palms of your hands. Some are fields of short-cut grass surrounded by poplars and chestnut trees. And a few are natural bodies of standing water, inhabited by toads, tree frogs, spotted salamanders and some inevitable municipal waste.

A decade ago, I roamed the concrete jungle with a pack of my fellow animals. Now, upon my return, I cross the streets alone, feeling a sting of unease. I am haunted by Petržalka's criminal past, the past I grew up in unaware of its existence.

I hunch under the unfriendly stares of the passersby. I listen to the people surrounding me at the bus stops, in grocery stores, public parks and shopping centres. I hold my purse close to my side. I wait an extra few seconds at the traffic lights after the pedestrian light turns green. At night I walk under the street lamps, avoiding the shadows in a grotesque caricature of my once favourite children's game, the one where the goal is to dodge all the cracks on the sidewalks.

"The pampering kindness of Canada has made me soft," I whisper bitterly, still in my damp hideout. In a pursuit of foreign opportunities, I have traded my home for a vision of future that was mine to choose. My guilt is a recurrent reminder of that trade-off. By moving to Canada I drew an emigration line that can never be wiped. Like a line in sandstone, it is being smoothed and deepened as the time passes. I have become a visitor in my old home, trapped on the wrong side of the door to which I don't have a key anymore.

A high-pitched monotonal sound escaping a human throat in about three-second intervals interrupts my musings. I turn my head toward the small glassed-up area to the left of the door I am still leaning against. The high-pitched "iii" ceases; it is now replaced with an old Slovak folk song.

"*Slovenské mamičky, pekných synov máte* (Slovak mothers, you have handsome sons)," sounds slightly off-tune in the depths of the building. I grin. Even after a decade Palko still lives at home. He must be in his late thirties now.

"*Vychovali ste ich, na vojnu ich dáte* … (You've raised them and now you send them off to war)." His voice is growing louder, closer.

"*Vychovali ste ich* …" Palko's face appears behind the glassy patch, just above the building's intercom. He is staring straight at me, his song cut at the last line of the first verse.

For a moment I watch him silently. His hair is curly and of the colour of dust. His face is round, almost as round as his blue, squinting eyes. He used to wear glasses that emphasized his misaligned pupils. He wears no spectacles now. His face is pushed against the glass, the proximity slightly flattening his nose. In a childlike way, he has placed his palms alongside his cheeks.

"Hey, Palko," I address him, my voice squeaking with phony friendliness. It is the type of fake kindness I used to force into my voice when, as a child, I couldn't avoid facing this mentally handicapped man. Palko says nothing but flattens the tip of his nose a little more.

"Palko," I say, turning my body toward the door to face him fully. "Can you open the door, please?"

He pulls away and starts nodding his head. But those nods are slightly too short and considerably too numerous to signify a "yes." It is the kind of nodding that Bobblehead figures engage in when placed on dashboards of cars that encounter nothing but mild city traffic.

I sigh and glance at the closed door before leaning my back against it again.

"*Na vojnu ich dáte*," Palko says, finishing the last line of the first verse of his song. Then he begins the verse anew, his voice being hushed by the concrete within which he is disappearing.

The rain seems heavier, meaner, snider. I walk away from the door and lean against a stucco wall, my palms flat against the rough surface. The building is humming underneath my fingertips. I feel the echoes of footsteps on the dim, malodorous staircase; young voices resonating throughout the hallways; barking dogs, likely locked in tiny bathrooms; someone's fingers running over piano keys and failing to get an A note right in Schubert's Moment Musical; and underlying all, the soft humming of many television sets. "The evening news must be on now," I mutter. Growing impatient, I stick my face out into the rain, stretching my neck to look around the corner. There is a dent in the wall, at the level of my eyes. Below, crumbling concrete and white dust have been pooling on the ground.

The wind is snatching tiny white dust specks and carrying them across the road toward a lone group of poplars. The trees mark a re-emergence point of one of Danube's dead tributaries—the Croatian Arm, or Kanál as it has been known. It is a body of standing water, snaking throughout the concrete jungle. Its banks are lined with willows, poplars and common reed. They are remainders of Petržalka's once luscious riparian forest cover. The jungle appears to devour Kanál at times, barricade it with its stony fingers, but the tributary always resurfaces somewhere full of mud, bulrush, abandoned pet tortoises and lost hockey pucks. I can't see its murky waters, now likely covered with a thin sheet of translucent ice. What I am able to see, however, is a long red bus passing the group of poplars I am eyeing. I breathe out and peel away from the wall. I grab my bag and start running.

I run across the pink cobblestone. The wind is whipping my face, hurling thousands of raindrops in my direction. They are stinging my eyes and prickling my exposed skin. At the end of the path I don't cross the road to catch the airport-bound bus. Instead, I make a sharp right turn and traverse a patch of yellowed grass, burnt by the excrements of the jungle animals, both four-legged and bipedal ones.

The jungle is pulling me, and I wish to blend in once again. I want to hear my footsteps echoing against the colourful concrete, sending a message to my old borough, making my presence felt. I want to hear the buildings speak to me as they magnify the sound of my footsteps and bounce it against the concrete structures, the plastic slides and the rusting metal of the climbing frames that used to leave that sour smell on the palms of my hands.

I run toward a stretch of urban forest that used to be the territory of a streaker. Wearing nothing but a long brown coat, he roamed the bushes after dark, crossing the sidewalks in the dim light of the street lamps. The same light is now illuminating my way as I pass a low-rise building surrounded by a rusting fence. Although it is a music school now, I have always remembered it as my pre-school. The building's yard is now almost entirely lost under a creeping vegetation overgrowth that is striving to reclaim its previous territory.

Kanál's bulrush is moving in the wind, out of rhythm with my pace, as I leave my former pre-school behind. I run in soft mud that squishes underneath my shoes and composes an abstract painting of muddy dots on the back of my legs. I am too fast for the disgust from my soiled attire to catch up with me.

I run alongside the paved sidewalk, invisible, engulfed in the shadows of the concrete jungle. A decade ago, I left my home and now returned a stranger. I recognize nothing but the imprints of the times long gone. An old Slovak folk song, sounding in my ears slightly off-tune. The humming of television sets with the evening news on. The barking of small dogs, the sea of greying concrete, the yellowed grass, the sandy playgrounds concealed by the towering structures.

To those reflections, those shadows of the past, I am invisible. Like Bram Stoker's Dracula, I am unable to see myself in any reflecting surface—in the raindrops glistering in the pale light of the street lamps, in the darkened windows flickering in my peripheral vision, in the waters of the dead Kanál. I am a lone tourist in the hometown I have willingly abandoned.

I should have left something behind. The thought bounces off the surrounding structures as the sound of my footsteps fills the cracks of the painted concrete.

I should have left a trace.

WELCOME TO CANADA/
SPEAKING MY OWN LANGUAGE

DESIRÉE JUNG

My hand shakes a bit as I hold onto the varnished handrail. It is my first morning here. I'm nervous and too close to my dream. My father had said I should behave quietly in a foreign country, so I step carefully, trying not to make noise. But the house is old. Everything seems to creak and crack, as if the floors and the walls are alive. I don't know if anyone is up yet.

I think about the emptiness of words, and I like the silence. The best thing about being here so far has been waking up alone without having to listen to my parents argue. If they are fighting so much at that age maybe couples should rethink their lives. Travelling abroad is a way for me to get distant from them as much as I can.

My parents are always going through a crisis and I feel stuck in the middle, having to take sides. As a child, I searched for solace in my room, but it wasn't enough. When the opportunity to travel came along in high school, I didn't think twice. I spoke to the counsellor and filled out the forms to start the procedures. I convinced my parents that English was essential for my future, and that I had to go to another country to learn it. "It is mind-opening going overseas," I told them.

My grades weren't the best, but it didn't matter as I wasn't being evaluated or applying to university. I was attending a language school. All I had to do was pay the tuition, send the application, apply for a visa and hope for the best. When everything was ready, I couldn't wait for the day of my trip to arrive. After crossing the customs and security area in the Brazilian airport, I felt a surge of panic and fear to be travelling on my own and wanted to go back to the safety of my home.

But slowly I got used to the idea of the unknown, of tracing my own destiny alone. I made friends with an older lady, not exactly old, but around forty, sitting beside me. She was going to Vancouver to visit her sister who lived there. She did this every year. "Aren't you afraid of travelling on your own?" I asked. I was not embarrassed about my high school English. The woman replied, "You get used to the silence. It is very soothing."

And I know this is true now. I walk down the stairs as drops of rain fall heavy on the window. It feels welcoming after such a long journey. I watched movies in the plane for nine hours and changed aircrafts in Toronto, headed to Vancouver. On the train from the airport to downtown, the city seemed grey and industrial at first, with greenery and residential areas as I approached the city centre.

I took a cab to the house after getting off at the Skytrain station. All I could think of was falling asleep in the bedroom of the homestay where I would spend the next few months. I found the key under the mat, just as the email had informed me. I was staying in the basement suite and there was a private entrance to my room, furnished with a small kitchen.

Upstairs I could hear people moving about, but thought I'd better not disrupt their routine. I didn't know if they were like my parents, who didn't like to be interrupted after dinner. I changed my clothes and had a shower. Tired, I ate a bowl of cereal with milk just like I had seen people do on television.

The fridge had bread, milk, cheese and jam. There were also other items I had never eaten before at home, like peanut butter and maple syrup. I read the welcoming greetings my homestay parents had left me at the entrance and watched the news, trying to understand what the announcer said, but he spoke very fast. I was falling asleep on the couch when I decided to go to bed. I put my shoes near the heater, as they were wet from the storm.

Because it was raining, my hair became flat and formless, despite the blow dry I had received before leaving Brazil. I wanted to look beautiful when traversing the Pacific Ocean for the first time.

There was no real winter in South America, not as far as I was concerned.

There were many small details I had to learn about my new routine. There was a set of instructions telling me what time to get up, which bus to take, what to recycle. My homestay parents would be establishing the rules. I was supposed to have dinners at the homestay and lunch in the school.

Because of the time difference, I ended up waking up in the middle of the night. With nothing else to do, I started to unpack my bag and fill the drawers with my pullovers. I had to write down on a sheet of paper what kind of meat I wanted to eat. I chose chicken most of the days, because my mother had said that in Canada it was free range and that was very expensive and hard to find in Brazil. The other days I chose salmon, because it was supposed to be good and was from the Pacific Ocean. I liked sweets, but I watched my weight.

At home we had a maid, Rosita, and my mother used to tell her what to do for dinner and lunch every day. The week before I left for Canada my mother accused my father of being too flirtatious with Rosita, and they had another fight.

This homestay was a house well looked after, though I suspected they didn't have a helper. I was advised in the list about when to clean my bathroom and change my sheets.

Now that it is finally morning I am free to explore. I discover that the main floor is dark, sober and penetrating. Great windows cover the wall descending from the attic, but rose curtains wrapped with a red lace block the light. From the kitchen, I can see a park and a covered green area for children.

"I wish I was your age," my father told me before I left. "I would make other choices." That comment made me think about my own decision to leave the country and my fear of being too close to boys, wondering if they would be like him, demanding, unfaithful but also unsatisfied. My father liked to complain, and his middle-class apartment with two bedrooms, a small living room and a view to other buildings was just one of his problems.

I found it difficult to understand what he wanted from life after his retirement and I think he didn't know either. I truly didn't know if there was any other kind of love apart from the one I learned at home. My mother explained that this was what frustrated people liked to do, regret, and that's why my trip to Canada was so necessary. It would introduce me into a new world without so much anger.

"It is important to speak your own language," she said.

"What do you mean?" I asked, wondering if my English wasn't good enough to live in a foreign country.

"I'm not talking about your English. Your English is fine, you will improve it if you need to. What I mean is your own way of being in life, your desire, your decisions," she said, as if just mentioning it made her anxious. "I didn't have this opportunity."

Now, after travelling for almost twenty-four hours, I already sensed that my mother was right. A foreign place can change your way of being in the world just by offering its unknown space and new possibilities.

In the living room, the fireplace is lit and two blue couches are protected by a plastic cover. When I enter, Mr. Robert is there, the hems of his pyjama pants dragging on the blue and white rug. He is a man of small stature, wearing flip-flops. My father would *never* wear his sleeping clothes outside of his own bedroom. He can't ever really relax, and is always dressed as if he is going to work. This other man, on the contrary, seems at ease in his house garments. I follow him as he walks to the kitchen with a sleepy face. He appears very calm as he starts to slice round pieces of bread.

The radio is turned on. Not bothered by my presence, he goes to the living room and grabs two different cups from a special cupboard. "I like to serve my guests the best," he says. The American kitchen style is identical to the ones I've seen on TV. On the speakers, the classical music is a tranquil piano intermixed with English sentences. I sneeze. The blow calls his attention. "*Bom dia*," he says in Portuguese, pulling out a chair for me to sit. "How was your trip?"

I tell him everything in my rough English, tired of being inside of my own head for so long. He is patient and moves his eyebrows as if used to this ritual of listening. Once again I think about my dad, and how every single morning he used to complain about the weather and the political conditions of the country. He never really asked how my day was.

"Do all Canadians listen to CBC?" I ask, trying to sound casual, not knowing how to make conversation with a man I've just met.

He raises his shoulders. "I really don't know." He has almost imperceptible grey, round glasses that fall from his thin and delicate nose. It makes him appear younger.

Maybe he is just different, more attentive, because he is not my father. I wonder how it must feel to be married to a man like that and I am immediately ashamed of having such thoughts. I am still deciphering my mother's wisdom.

His nose doesn't have hairs coming out of his nostrils and he doesn't have hairy hands. His kindness is foreign, strange. I only know men with tanned skin and brown eyes. His are penetrating like an angora cat. He smiles and gives me an empty cup. The music continues to play. Imprinted on the porcelain of the cup is the saying *Unified Health System*. "Are you a doctor?" I ask.

"Music teacher," he replies.

Perhaps if my father had more opportunities, he would have been a different man, less bitter, my mother suggested. I feel guilty for being critical in my judgment. But it is hard to know what kind of woman I am. I don't have a boyfriend yet, despite being eighteen. Most girls in my school have already dated but I am shy and confused. The pressure of getting married is a concern of many girls in Brazil.

Two slices of bread jump from the toaster, interrupting my thoughts. Mr. Robert grabs the electric kettle and pours water into his cup. "Do you want coffee?" he asks. I don't know. Nobody has ever asked me this question before. At home, I only drink chocolate powder and milk. He opens a jar of instant coffee and gives me a spoon. I add the same quantity to my cup as he does to his. The wooden table occupies half of the kitchen. There is a newspaper wrapped in a plastic bag.

The rubber soles of my shoes make noise against the tiles. Once in a while I touch my backpack on the floor, trying to emanate naturalness. "Is your class at nine?" he asks. I nod yes, sipping the bitter coffee with difficulty. He eats his bread with jam. A red stream runs down his fingers.

Without understanding why, I want to touch him, making our inadequacies concrete. I don't remember hugging my dad before I left. I unwrap the newspaper's plastic cover instead.

"Have a good class," he says. "Later you will meet my wife and children." This takes me away from my strange inner fantasies. Suddenly exposed, I rush out of the room, realizing I will be late for class. In that moment, I project my life into the future: I want to have a home like this one, an assurance of who I am outside of the world of my family. I don't even know if that is possible.

I pass an aroma of lavender and mint coming from a cupboard with spices. Near the entrance there are many different sizes of shoes piled in a dresser. Outside, the cold air invades my skin, despite the long coat and merino wool pullover. I identify the bus stop on the other side of the street. The seats are soft and the place has maps, not like the public transportation in Brazil where everything is precarious and there are rectangular signs attached to tree trunks in the avenues.

Still, I already miss it. Here, the grey light of November leaves everything monochrome. At this time of the year in Brazil there is lots of sun, mangoes and persimmon.

Alone again, I feel relieved. In the bus, people talk hurriedly and words are pronounced without pauses, different from how I learned at school. When I enter the classroom with its small chairs I place my backpack against the wall. The students are the same age as me. The teacher wears a yellow dress with blue flowers and doesn't seem cold, taking off her jacket and exposing her white skin. On the break, adults drink tea and coffee. The bell rings.

Carelessly, I brush against a boy ahead of me going up the stairs. Distracted, I apologize in Portuguese, *desculpe*. His smile is open and receptive.

"Are you Brazilian?" he asks with a thick accent. "I'm ..." I say, my heart beating fast. I don't answer, suddenly nervous, and I hurry toward the classroom.

He follows me. "My father is Brazilian but I'm from Spain," he says. "I came here to learn English. It's nice to meet you. I'm Juan."

He extends his hand and I grab it sideways while we walk.

Feeling afflicted, I sit at the back of the room and flip through the phrasal verb book compulsively, hoping I can find words to help me say something else about myself. Once in awhile I see Juan looking at me. The teacher distributes a list to be memorized.

My own world, veiled inside, begins to speak, surprising me. I move my chair close to Juan's and we practise the exercises together, breathing deeper whenever we are lost or without words.

DANCE THE CURVES

WAASEYAA'SIN CHRISTINE SY

I'm looking for an Anishinaabemowin word for travelling, as in "we travel," "we are preparing to travel," or "we will be travelling." I'm looking for a word and a meaning—the cultural, spiritual, or sound meaning. I need it. I need it because our words, our language brings cohesion into my world, simultaneously illuminating it, making it bigger than it was before. A word and a meaning would act as a cloth, bundling these stories lovingly. This endeavor is important because travelling is one of many significant elements of Anishinaabewiziwin, which, when loosely translated in English, refers to all the elements that make up the Anishinaabe way.[1] Travelling is so Anishinaabe.

Travelling is also, and always has been, an important element of being Anishinaabe'ikawe. That is, Anishinaabe woman.[2] Historically, travelling kept us alive as we moved through Turtle Island from the east, making our new territory within the Great Lake region. Here, we travelled about seasonally for sustenance and flourishing life: winter camps, rice beds, sugar bushes, summer fishing. Embedded within all this travelling and making camp was exchange—political, material, social, ideological, etc. Travelling, for woman, is also significant in a

---

1   This definition comes from Helen Agger, *Following Nimishomis: The Trout Lake History of Dedibaayaanimanook Sarah Keesick Olsen*, (Pentiction: Theytus Books, 2008): 286. Agger also reveals, through oral history shared from her mother, so much of the old travelling lifestyle and the nuances of this life.

2   The word ikawe actually refers to the changing nature of this being. Woman, as a translation, is an English translation, and does not reflect the Anishinaabe worldview as understood through its sounds. For more on this or on the sound-based method of Anishinaabemowin, see Caroline Helen (Roy) Fuhst, *Introduction to the Sound Based Method of Understanding Anishinaabemowin* (Canton: Niish Ishkidoen Productions, 2012).

contemporary world shaped by colonizing nation-states and settler colonization. Both are invested in keeping indigenous women immobilized or controlled. Settled and domesticated. Silent. Dependent. Dead.[3] Invested in keeping us contained and regulated within man-made borders of rural to urban, off rez to on rez, and US to Canada. Anishinaabe women on both sides of all these borders share this history and these experiences.

Knowing this word-meaning bundle would allow me to ground myself deeper into the spirit of who I am as Anishinaabe, who we are as Anishinaabeg; ground myself deeper into the spirit of who I am within who We are as a Nation as well as within/outside the colonizing, dominating Canadian society.

Deep grounds allow sure flight.

This word-meaning bundle would shelter yet another sophisticated element of all those elements that make up the lives of Anishinaabe ikawewag (women) in Anishinaabegogamig.

But, I have neither.

What I have, in the absence of a word and a meaning, are stories, reflections, and some knowledge. What I have, for the time being, is the spirit of Anishinaabe (physical) travel that moves without an Anishinaabe name. One part of this travelling-Anishinaabe-woman story is inspired by my most recent experience.

———

A week ago yesterday I found myself driving my longest distance in one period of time ever. This long haul took n'ikawewizehns (my little girl) and me from Naminitigoong to Nogojowanong—a point on the eastern shore of Lake Michigan to the lands north of Lake Ontario. We departed at 11:00 a.m. and arrived home the next morning at 3:30 a.m. That's about thirteen hundred kilometres in about sixteen hours.

Naminitigoong is what the Ottawa (Odawa) Anishinaabeg call

3   Epidemic rates of missing, murdered, and traded indigenous women is a significant social and political concern for Indigenous peoples in what is popularly known as Canada. It is also a concern for the United Nations and various Canadian political parties. At the present time, Prime Minister Stephen Harper refuses to address this matter as one of national importance.

one of their homes—Land Beneath the Trees.[4] English Americans call
the city they built there Manistee, Michigan. Nogojiwanong is what
the Mississauga Anishinaabeg call one of their homes—Mouth of the
River.[5] English Canadians call the city they built there Peterborough,
Ontario.

I let my thoughts wander to what I imagine were the ways of
our old-time Anishinaabeg, envisioning that a trip like this one would
have been epic. It would have been navigated with jiimaan (canoe)
and portaging through waterways and bmose (walking) on trails. It
would have been travelled in the same ways we travelled for thousands of years. And then I re-think this because I know I'm heavily
influenced by lenses shaped by the occupying society I live in. Re-
think and reconsider: our people may not have described aspects of
their travelling life with such grandeur.

Not epic, just necessary.

I consider the possibility that a trip like this would have been
carried out pragmatically and without excessive pomp. In my case,
however, this one was significant because it was the longest bit of
driving I'd done in one stretch of time, most of it without adults to
provide companionship, support and safety.

I recall another trip—an eight-hundred-kilometre trek that re-
quired me to drive a moving van with a trailer attached carrying
my vehicle. A friend who was helping with the packing said to me,
"I'd be scared shitless to drive this thing. How are you not scared?"
My response was, "I can't be. I have no one else to drive it!" Again,
necessity compels us to do things we typically might not. Pragmatism
reigns in the life of a solo woman, sole head of household. We do
what we must.

Getting my child home in time for summer daycamp and saving
cash that would otherwise be spent on a motel room were important
factors in deciding to make the trip in one run. Subsidized funding
and low-income shape many of our decisions.

We were all filled up, returning from a three-day Anishinaabe
language and culture camp hosted by the Little River Band of Ottawa

4   Cecelia LaPointe, personal communication, Facebook, July 31, 2012.
5   Doug Williams, personal communication, Waawshkigemonki, n.d.

Indians. This tribal community is located midway along the eastern shore of Lake Michigan. After five hours of driving with my niece and one-year-old grandniece, there was a brief stop in Bawating to drop them off. My girl and I picked up our cat and made a pit stop for some beads so she could have something to do for the remaining trip home. She had learned to bead at the camp and was excited to keep at it.

Bawating is the Ojibway name for our traditional gathering place where Gichi Gaming (Lake Superior) and Odawa Zaagi'gan (Lake Huron) meet. It's also the fifth stopping place on the Anishinaabeg great migration from Gichi Ziibing, the mouth of the St. Lawrence.[6] Settler colonialism has seen our place become re-named, re-landscaped, and re-intentioned. Today it is popularly known as Sault Ste. Marie on both sides of the Canada–US border in Ontario and Michigan. This border is technically arbitrary to the Anishinaabeg Nation because we were not involved in its creation.[7] Despite its arbitrariness due to our non-involvement, it generates problems for us because it imposes a geo-political division within our Nation. It interferes in our movement, lifestyles and livelihoods and prohibits the movement of our goods.[8]

Onward and onward into the day we went, and being safe into the night was priority. Making sure the car is okay (tires inflated, oil okay, wipers working, etc.), phone charger for the car accessible, having emergency roadside assistance and enough money in case of emergency is always key. It was on that trip as well. Late into the night, however, these matters seemed less important as fatigue became a factor. Staying alert to drive and to watch out for waawaashkeshiwag miinawaa moozo (deer and moose)—two big animals whose territories I was driving through—became a primary concern. I laid asemaa

---

6   For more on this migration, see Edward Benton-Benai, *Mishomis Book: The Voice of the Ojibway* (Hayward: Indian Country Communications, Inc., 1988): 99–101.

7   Phil Belfy, *Three Fires Unity: The Anishinaabeg of the Lake Huron Borderlands* (Nebraska: University of Nebraska Press, 2011).

8   The Jay Treaty was created between Great Britain and the United States in 1794 and provided that American Indians could travel freely across the international boundary. However, to my knowledge, Canada does not recognize this treaty. For more, http://canada.usembassy.gov/visas/information-for-canadians/first-nations-and-native-americans.html.

(tobacco) and whispered a pray to the wiingaashk (sweetgrass) that sits on my dash and to the wesiinh manidooyaag (animal spirits); and, I petitioned migizi miigwan (golden eagle feather), who was flying around from my rear-view window on the currents of a/c and the open window.

I knew my ancestors would have done something similar and drew comfort from this. I realized that maybe, travelling a lot by water, they would have asked for kindness from pinesiwaag (thunder beings), miizhu biizhu (water lynx), or nebaunaubaewuk (merpeople). They may have asked for kindness, like I did, not because these beings would be out to harm them but because we know we are impinging on their surroundings by virtue of moving through their landscapes. We know the animals and water beings have their moving lives that do not stop simply because we are travelling through their territory. Essentially, after all the things that can be controlled for are considered, I asked gizhewe manidoo (the great, kind mystery) and my pawaaman (spirit protectors) to look out for us, to bring us safely to our destination.

This carries a lot of power.

But the mind—the colonized mind—has a funny way of letting doubt, fear and worry interfere with humility, faith and pragmatics. I immediately go back to words James Dumont, an Anishinaabe professor and Midewewinini (member of a particular kind of medicine lodge), shared in an undergraduate class at Laurentian University in Northern Ontario: doubt is a tool of colonization.[9] I reminded myself of this. I did something else too. When she was sleeping in the back, the new music suggestions solicited from social media friends were played out and it was just me, the high-beams, occasional transport and Nokomis (grandmother moon), I got to thinking about the women I know who travel. While the theory of colonization explained the doubt and removed it, it was the women—the real lived experiences of women, who filled up the space where doubt once dwelled.

My mom. Ngaashi. Mary. She was a traveler. She travelled by foot three times with her sisters up that trap-line to where her step-dad,

---

9 Personal communication, Laurentian University, Sudbury, Ontario, 1995.

Paddy, was. Three times my mom and my aunts left Pelican Falls Residential School and made it to him successfully. Two times, the Royal Canadian Mounted Police came and got those ikawewizenhsag and brought them back to the residential school. The third time, those RCMP, and the school, finally left those girls alone.

I think of this, this story my aunt told me; and, those little girls, my relatives, navigating the dominating colonizing world as well as the bush that loved them. I think of my mom some more: She was a hitchhiker. Something her second daughter, my unknown younger sister Celine, has in her bones too. Ngaashi hitched to New Orleans once. Wanted to go, went. Likely didn't think of it as 'epic'—and she was alone. She travelled to Winnipeg, too. She didn't like it their either; left. Went to Sault Ste. Marie, liked it, stayed. She had her babies there, lived her life there, and died there. I don't know if she ever knew Sault Ste. Marie as Bawating.

So I think of my mom, aunts and a sister (all whom I hardly know) and it makes me proud in a humble way. It makes me want to hunker down and just do the thing that's got to be done. It reminds me I have this ability in my body, my bones and my cells. It's in my DNA. It also reminds me of my huge privilege: I don't have to hitchhike or walk, like some of these women had/have to. I have a vehicle.

I wonder if my mom or my sister were ever hurt while hitchhiking, and for self-preservation purposes I don't live in that thought too long. I think of all the indigenous women on the Highway of Tears who didn't make their destination.[10] I put my window down and offer asemaa (tobacco) out and away for all these women. I think of all the times I walked or biked Hwy 17 North or Hwy 556 alone and always made it to my destination; how I always made it safely. I think of the time it was minus-thirty degrees Celsius and I had to walk to work at 5:00 a.m. to open up the restaurant. The extreme cold compelled me to hitchhike. It was the one and only time I ever hitched alone. I remember a carload of men stopping, asking me where I was going. I was nervous, checked out the scene beyond the rolled-down

---

10   A website illuminating the deaths of women in this particular area can be found here: http://www.highwayoftears.ca/.

window. The heat and cigarette smoke enveloped me. Glorious. The passenger, who said he knew my boss, Kathy, said, "Hop in. We'll give you a lift and we'll get some coffee before we head out."

I got in.

The drive was only about two and a half kilometres away, meaning only a matter of minutes, but getting in that vehicle was long enough for them to be the kind of men who sexually assault, torture, kidnap, beat up, murder young Indigenous women. They weren't, however, at least not in that case. I think about those minutes of my sixteen-year-old life. So naïve. So stupid. So lucky. I didn't have a clue what was happening to Indigenous women in Canada back then in the late '80s and '90s ... throughout history. What were the adults in my life thinking, letting me walk the highway like that alone?

I put my window back down and put more asemaa out. Thankful they were just a bunch of men heading to work themselves and giving me a lift, being helpful. Protective? It's memories like this that re-ignites a profound realization and acceptance: life is very much ultimately shaped by gizhewe manidoo.

I return to thinking about my mother, Mary Chisel, and the women in her line—Mary Gray (my grandmother), Martha Gray (my great-grandmother), Sarah Chisel (great-great grandmother) and so on[11]—whose travelling stories I don't know and will likely never know. I think of those women travelling with people, travelling alone or travelling with their young children.

I know I can do this.

On the road alone at night, with Nokomis rising up, I also think of the other Anishinaabe women I'm aware of today who travel about here and there. Whose trusty jiiman is a daaban. Who travel, travel, travel. Going here and there keeping life going for people. I think of one strong, vital woman, Mary Jane:

Mushkego esqauo. Northern Cree woman. Grandmother. Mother. Poet. Musician. Philosopher. Language speaker. Warrior. My last visit with her was a few weeks ago. It started abruptly at 5:00 a.m. with her

---

11   I'm eternally grateful to Elsie Chisel, younger sister to my mother, for sharing my maternal family tree in October 2009. Her work on reclaiming our family history and sharing stories about our family has been life-giving.

banging on my door. She was returning from an all-day and -night round trip in her trusty vehicle. Alone. The purpose: a family member was in need. After driving all night, she needed a place to sleep and knew I was close by and had a couch.

The first time I met MJ, I was returning from Fort Albany to Bawating with a colleague. She caught a lift with us. It was a five-hour drive and that was just the right amount of time for the story she had to tell. I was tired and although I weaved in and out of consciousness I learned a few things that stick with me while on the road. One, the Mushkego word her dad taught her that means "not to be arrogant; do not think that you know what is going to happen up there ahead of you in the future." I've since forgot what that word is and have asked, but we both forget. Two, I learned that the curves along the Chapleau River are beautiful and they make for a treacherous highway. I learned that MJ's method for negotiating them in her daabaan was to just "dance the curves" and go. That's it. Just go. "Don't be arrogant to think that you know what will happen up ahead the road there, just dance the curves, child."

Thinking of my family and Mary Jane genereates swirls of thoughts of other women.

Shirley. Odawa Anishinaabekwe. Gichi Piitzijid (Elder). Anishinaabemowin Chi Ekinomaaget (Language Professor). Water walker and ceremonialist. Academic. Traveller.

Edna. Odawa Anishinaabeg. Gichi Piitzijid. Artist. Singer. Storyteller. Plant teacher. Ceremonialist. Language Speaker. Traveller.

Josephine. Anishinaabeg. Gichi Piitzijid. Ceremonialist. Water walker. Her daabaan has a name. She is a traveller.

I think of our ancestors and imagine all the women who travelled. I shake my head, a bit embarrassed, and chuckle at my immaturity.

I think of all these women and conclude this: to travel alone is Anishinaabe'ikawe. How can I not have this?

Still, the fear, worry. There are possible dangers out here on the road other than animals or fatigue. Weird travellers. Power-hungry police officers. If my skepticism about police officers is disturbing to anyone, please note that as an Anishinaabe woman in colonial Canada, not all police officers—man or woman—serve and protect.

Some intimidate, threaten, patronize and make a person feel unsafe. Some hurt indigenous women.[12]

And as if to test my resolve on the last leg of this journey where I am driving on a desolate rural highway, I see lights travelling perpendicular to me across the dark landscape. I don't know if I should be comforted that someone else is up this late at night or if I should be worried. The car comes to a stop sign and I, on the main highway, drive past. *A police car. A police car? What the heck are the police doing way back here this late at night? The landscape is dark. There's nothing here but farms. It's 2:30 a.m.* My heart quickens and more so when the car turns and quickly catches up to me, following me. I'm tired and strive to be very vigilant in my driving. *Oh shit. Am I swerving? What if s/he pulls me over for fatigue? Shit. What if s/he pulls me over and gives me a hard time out here in the middle of nowhere? What am I going to do?* I keep driving, keep glancing in the rear-view mirror. The car slows down, turns off at the next major intersection.

Nothing happened beyond my rundown of imaginary possible scenarios. I think it says something, though, that I felt safer when the police car stopped following me and turned onto another road. I think it says something that I was contemplating not stopping if they were going to pull me over and instead driving to a more well-lit public area. I was contemplating calling 911 if they did pull me over, as I knew I wasn't doing anything illegal. I think this all says something.

In the deep of the dark highway and bright moon, the glowing yellow and white lines, I think of all the little kids. All of our young people here and elsewhere who have had to walk long distances to get away from harm adults have imposed on them historically and still do today. I think of all the little kids who ran away from residential school, like my relatives who ran away and didn't make it home or were never found: death by freezing or summer hardships. Maybe lost to the bush. I think of their travels in this realm, in this country and other countries. I think of their spirits travelling beyond.

I think about my daughter and my nieces and the people who have come and gone from my life. All the ones coming up after us

---

12   Human Rights Watch, "Those Who Take Us Away," February 13, 2013, http://www.hrw. org/reports/2013/02/13/those-who-take-us-away

who are stuck and are trying to get out; who, for whatever reason can't get unstuck, who can't afford the train, bus or plane ticket or tank of gas to their destination. All those immobilized by/in some neo-colonial institution. The women finding the courage to travel, whatever that means to them.

I think about how I want all of them to know travel and movement across our homelands the way our ancestors did. I want their worlds to go beyond the parameters of settler/Canadian good life. I want them to have the means and confidence to move their bodies, their lives and their spirits across our landscapes—both physical and spiritual—visiting, learning, teaching and living.

Moving under a sky that was turning dark and then turning bright. That's what I was doing with my little girl sleeping. Thinking all the things over the long haul, thinking *I can do this I can do this I can do this* until there I was, turning the corner to home and then into our parking lot. Until it became *I did this*. Niminitigoong to Nogo-jowanong in one day. Me, my girl, our kitty, trusty daaban, and a lot of different kinds of relatives.

Like Sky Woman.

Moving through the world with her children and all her supports. zaasaa'ikawe[13]

---

13   This is a shout-out to the spirits.

No More Named Johnny and Other Panics

SHANNON WEBB-CAMPBELL

I cracked open in Malta. Without Internet, telephone or television I drank too much, read Anne Carson exclusively and entertained myself by writing letters to my ancestors and inner children at various stages.

On the other side of the world, everything amplified. As if breaking up with my first girlfriend, having an affair while we still lived together and abandoning my degree one credit shy of graduation wasn't enough. Amongst a myriad of culture shock, loneliness and displacement, I found myself on the outside looking out.

It was late fall in 2009, and I was twenty-six years old, bound for Malta International Airport after ten days listless in Paris and another week Gaudi-struck, tapas-stuffed and beach-bummed in Barcelona. Even though I am a heavy-set queer woman, I had already kissed half a dozen strangers on my first overseas trip, an attempt to explore and broaden my horizons. Own my desire.

I was trying to shed skins of sexual shame, though had encountered half of Europe's creeps—a taxi driver who felt me up and propositioned me for a threesome in the Latin Quarter, a bookstore stalker and countless come-ons from Spanish men. I was exhausted and depleted, yet according to my therapist, selectively promiscuous.

With its sun-bleached crumbling houses, 365 Catholic churches and bluer than blue Mediterranean Sea, I landed in Malta, a place more foreign than my night terrors. I rented a vacation home in Senglea on Portu Salvu. I had no idea where this tiny far-flung archipelago at the boot of Italy was. Never even heard of it. All I knew was I needed to go somewhere exotic, a place far away from myself.

I pulled up in a taxi to the old house and scrambled to find the key in my purse. The house had been vacant for seasons—musty, dark and rather eerie. Made entirely of stone, which crumbled at the touch. Nothing felt welcoming. A rotting couch in a dark living room and a little kitchen set a bleak scene.

As I dragged my oversized suitcase up the stairs to the bedroom, I wondered what the hell I had got into. The romantic balloon of renting a house in a foreign country popped. It was a small bedroom, two single beds pushed together, spring-lined old mattresses unaligned. The bathroom was a recent addition, though a big bathtub and stand-alone shower lack luxury when the hot water heater is broken.

I opened the window to let the house breathe and unpacked my belongings. Dresses, leggings, sandals, a sunhat, a notebook and a tattered copy of Carson's *Decreation* were my sum. I hung what I could in the armoire and tossed my undergarments in a basket.

My days in Malta moved slowly, and cold showers were a brutal start, even in October. For the first week, I mostly ate *pastizzi*, a traditional Maltese pastry with ricotta or mushy peas, and drank cheap Italian wine. I frantically scribbled letters to my inner children and ancestors, a therapeutic attempt to come to terms with family trauma passed down generation by generation.

Even though I wear the weight of genealogical abuse, I drew family trees and traced the branches and fault lines between us all. There were always forms of love. Night after night the demons and I mingled, but the heartfelt saints kept watch. Thundershowers stirred, and I often cried myself to sleep.

By the second week, the boys on the bread truck gave me an extra loaf, an older fella perched outside the fruit and veggie stand inquired about my daily travels to and from Senglea and both restaurants in the area knew my order by heart.

Most days I'd make my way down to the Grand Harbour for a swim and I found temporary relief in the Mediterranean Sea. Swimming always brought me back to my body. I floated on my back to watch the birds fly overhead, their beating wings filled with perseverance. Such freedom. I didn't bother with a towel. My footprints led to the house where a neighbour practised classical piano. I'd stand there long enough to hear a few movements and dry off in the Mediterranean heat.

By the third week, a familiar loneliness washed ashore. There were only so many hours I could entertain myself. I made my way down the marina for pizza, or a pasta and rabbit dish. Under the stars, half-broken conversations with a Maltese waitress waltzed around tourist speak. She mentioned Notte Bianca, an all-night arts festival in Valletta. I took the bus into the capital city the following night.

It was relentlessly clear. The full moon hovered over the bus shelter. Thousands of people gathered, beautiful royal red and gold drapery hung in the streets, bare light bulbs dangled like dancing night bugs. A flash mob in the streets danced to hits from the 1950s, onlookers gawked in awe while men sold half-price *pastizzi*. One joked they looked like women's sex organs, and they sold like hot cakes given their vulva-like shape.

Built in the seventeenth century, baroque in nature with its unspoiled buildings and grid streets, Valletta was stunning with its cathedrals, shops and art. Malta has an old-world charm. It's a country of resilience, as it suffered 154 continuous days and nights of bombing during World War II. While the Grand Harbour protects, Notte Bianca transformed the ancient city.

I paid a visit to the National Museum of Archeology to soak in traces of our beginnings, stone phalluses and headless breasted bodies. In 4000 BC the women looked like real women—wide hips, round bellies, big breasts and strong arms. The most enchanting figure: Mal'ta Venus, or better known as "The Sleeping Lady," with her brownish red ochre body, a creation that embodied Maltese prehistoric art. Her beauty was discovered in the depths of a dark pit. To me she looked like a lover, a sleeping goddess, a soft animal of a woman at rest, bound by the bliss of an eternal sleep. No longer aware of carnal concerns.

Back in the streets, paper cups of wine and hard liquor spilled. For ten euros you could get a Maltese platter: bread with tomato sauce, refried beans, corn, olives, feta and a Cisk beer. On one corner there was an opera, on another a marching band led a parade. The city was a baroque carnival draped in costume and performance. Folks smoked in bars; even The Gut had a one-woman show about the rise and fall of Rita Hayworth's fame. Dress shops stayed open after midnight, and a choir sang outside St. Paul's Anglican Church.

One cup of wine after another and I felt like I was moving through a fever dream surrounded by thousands of bodies, but deeply detached. Eventually spent, I headed back to Valletta's bus terminal to make my way home to Senglea.

Men with white teeth and skin like night sky circled me like vultures. One after another they taunted: *where was my boyfriend, why was a girl like me out at night all alone.* Despite several attempts to ignore them, they were relentless. If one simmered, the other sizzled: *you need another boyfriend, a second boyfriend. Baby, I'll be your real boyfriend.* Catcalls became lion's roars. Two men with British accents stood nearby chatting about their flight, almost on guard.

Finally Route 3 arrived, a retro orange and mustard painted bus, twenty minutes late. Passengers filed onto the bus one by one. The two British blokes boarded behind me with small suitcases and took seats in the back. One looked grandfatherly, with his snow-white hair, the other could be my father. I sat close by.

"We were watchin' out for ya. We had your back if he did anything stupid." The British accent a stark contrast to the Maltese I'd been hearing for weeks. "What's a girl like you doing in Senglea, anyway?"

I explained I had rented a house from a Canadian friend not far from the church. I was a writer, though not sure what I was writing. Next week I was headed to London for a week or so, and then to visit friends in Norwich. Apparently many Brits visit Malta, despite their complicated history. Malta is only a wee three-hour flight, far away from England's damp fog. The men introduced themselves as John and John, or as I differed them, Young John and Old John.

"The refugees really fancy you," said Young John, more fatherly than grandfatherly.

"It's like that every time I wait for the bus."

"A girl like you shouldn't have to put up with such bullshit."

When the bus finally came to a stop at Senglea's Jesus statue, I had agreed to go for a nightcap to shake off the hour-long commute.

The Johns took me to a secret little bar in Senglea with arched doorways. Young John knew everyone and introduced the locals who had once eyed me suspiciously on the streets. The bartender gave us a round on the house. A beautiful Maltese woman came by, kissed Young John's cheek. Hardly looked over.

Baffled to hear I hadn't made it to Gozo, or travelled all around Malta given its less than three hundred square miles, the Johns were most shocked I'd been living for a month without hot water. I shared stories of bathing at St. Paul's Beach, visiting Mdina, the silent city where no cars were allowed, and Birgu by Candlelight, a night when Vittoriosa was only aglow by millions of candles. Every shop, home and street solely lit by tiny dancing flames.

By the second round, Young John had introduced me to the entire bar, offered unlimited use of his hot water and made a promise to take me around my last week in Malta, certain the tail end of my journey would be filled with sightseeing, proper showers and company. No more bus stop swarms. No idiot taxi drivers. No men but them.

Young John had a strange charisma, told me he was a landlord in Ipswich, owned a few properties in England, Sweden, another in Bangkok, and loved Malta's carefree spirit. Old John had met him at the pub in Ipswich, and they had travelled to Malta several times together. It was hard to tell what they had in common aside from their name and a taste for drink.

Old John offered up his wallet, but Young John brushed him off. As he paid our tab, the gruff bartender extended his hand. Young John leaned over to the shapely Maltese woman now seated at the bar and whispered something in her ear. We all sang out goodnight.

Together we stumbled on into the night. Young John's house was halfway between the bar and my spot. The Johns offered to walk me home, but I assured them I could make my way back one street over. Young John told me to come over and shower whenever I woke up.

Now late morning, with alcohol-clogged pores, I pulled on last night's black sundress and floppy hat and sauntered back up to Young John's. I tapped the lion's head knocker on the old wooden door and waited. Young John opened it with a devilish grin, sporting the same red T-shirt he had been wearing the night before. With two showers to choose from, one downstairs in the garage and another upstairs by the master bedroom, I opted for the closest shower, no frills. He pulled a spare off his key chain, told me I was welcome anytime.

Warm water pierced through my skin, and I stayed in the shower until I cooked my body lobster red. After drying off and getting dressed for the day, I went upstairs to say thanks and found Old John sipping tea in the kitchen. Young John barrelled in, mentioned I cleaned up well, and offered to give me the grand tour.

The house felt like a movie set—three renovated floors, a large living room, a fair-sized kitchen and even laundry. Young John's guest bedroom, a spacious room with a North American double bed, was twice the size of the house I rented. The master bedroom overlooked the main drag. Though it was the rooftop terrace with its panoramic vista of the Three Cities that stole the show. Young John mentioned he bought the house a couple of years before, a fixer-upper with his son who had since lost interest.

Old John finished his tea, and we all went for a long drive to the sand dunes. Like a trio of misfits, we toured the area where they were filming *Moby Dick* and shot some of *Gladiator*, explored old caves, and eventually the Johns and I went for a swim by the dunes. Old John stayed ashore, while Young John and I swam in the caverns of the sea. I noticed snake chain tattoos laced around his ankles.

For the next three days we ventured around Malta. Our unlikely friendship extended beyond the generation gaps. In moments it felt like a Woody Allen film, or an obscure remake of *Lost in Translation*. We laughed, told stories, explored markets, swam some more, went for drinks and shared dinners on the marina. After weeks alone, it felt so good to be amongst other people, strangers who became familiar.

On my last day in Malta I dragged over my suitcase to do a round of laundry. Young John showed me how to set the rinse cycle and cracked a joke—if only I was a few years older he'd push me up against the machine and do very bad things to me. I laughed him off, reminded him he was too old … and I was queer, anyway.

The Johns took me out to dinner and we shared two bottles of Italian red. In the bathroom, I checked my cell phone thanks to free Wi-Fi, and got a Facebook message from a man who had sexually assaulted me as a teenager at a party, an apology note a lifetime too late. He was sorry, and since married with two daughters. Couldn't forgive himself. I deleted it and was thrown into a tailspin. I returned to the table only to guzzle my drink and then another.

Old John suggested we head back to the house, have a nightcap on the rooftop. We sipped a bottle of wine until Old John retired. Together, Young John and I looked out at the night enveloping the Three Cities. It felt like a picture-postcard. Fuelled by confession juice, I told Young John my story, how the hands of that man shaped and stole many relationships, how I struggled with my family and the seasons of shame.

The bald eagle tattoo and snake chains around both ankles merely hinted at his sordid past, while my aches were more internal ink stains. Young John shared a story that he'd done time for nearly beating a man to death who raped his daughter. That's when he got the tattoos. As the hour grew colder, he wrapped himself around me and wiped my tears with his callused hands. I stayed in his embrace too long, desperate to feel anything but the waves of trauma wash over me. He tilted my chin and kissed my very drunk mouth. He tasted like beer and garlic. I told him I had to go to bed. I hiccupped, said my flight left early. Young John took the couch.

In the sober light of morning, cradled in the arms of a hungover dreamless sleep, Young John softly parted my thighs. I half-woke up as he pressed the weight of the world into my darkest pit. Whispered: if you were really a dyke, you'd never get so wet.

Time slowed, and my entire being was taken over by a temporary paralysis. I didn't fight, or even try to push him off. My brain couldn't connect to what was happening. I drifted far, far away. I lay there limp, half-dead like Mal'ta Venus.

Young John left the room to shower, and I opened my eyes just enough to take in the ceiling fan. Light poured in through the curtains. I closed my eyes again, unable to feel my legs. In between states of consciousness, Young John returned, told me if I didn't get out of bed I would miss my flight.

Dizzy and disoriented, I made it to the bathroom and stood under the shower. My body felt no temperature.

The Johns and I drove in silence to Malta International Airport, Tracy Chapman's "Fast Car" played on the radio. Young John turned it down. I sat in the passenger seat and stared out at the sun-bleached, desolate landscape. Hardly even a tree.

When we pulled up at the airport, Old John took my suitcase out of the trunk and passed me a post-it note with his address. Mentioned if I eventually found myself in Ipswich to look him up. Gave me a side hug.

Young John wandered off to the gift shop. We never said a word. I checked in and came back with my suitcase. When we met, he handed me a bottle of water and a granola bar, a peace offering. Stunned, I searched his face, tried to unscramble his features. He looked at me in a way I'd never seen before—primal, yet human.

An announcer called my name over the PA: last boarding call for Flight 364 on Ryanair from Malta to London, England. In one jerk reaction, Young John pulled me close, kissed my forehead, and mumbled the words *I'm sorry*. I didn't dare exhale.

I reached for my things as the two Johns waved me off. My suitcase doubled in weight. All I wanted to do was curl up in the fetal position and become another Maltese relic. But I kept walking, one flip-flop after the other, down the terminal.

I was the last passenger to board the flight, my purse filled with illegible letters, a bottle of water and two different Maltese keys. I was seated at the very back next to the bathrooms, a window seat.

As the plane took off and climbed higher, I held the barf bag and looked out to the plush clouds. No landscape, memory or person could touch me in the sky.

REFLECTIONS ON THE WATER

KIM MELTON

The prow of my kayak juts out in centre frame, just above the eighteen-inch circular crack in my windshield. It strains at the ropes that tether it to the car, drawing me onward like a dowsing rod, veering to one side and then the other as we climb and dip along the base of the mountain. This is a taste of what is to come for me: a week with only that narrow blue nose for companion. I swing a sharp left onto a potholed, sandy track that leads down to a campground.

The boat launch consists of a simple twenty-foot-wide gap in the shoreline brush where the sand slopes gently into a little bay, and it is currently occupied by a green SUV carrying a canoe. I slide in beside it. Three trucks with trailers are parked further up the sandy bank, one nosed into a campsite that amazingly still has shade. It's only 9:00 a.m., but the sun is already high this close to solstice.

The aluminum boats tied up to the stumpy willow to the right of the SUV belong to men, middle-aged and older, who come here from Whitehorse for a day's respite from whatever it is that weighs on their minds. They come on their own, ostensibly to fish, but I suspect any catch is incidental to the pleasure of silence—once they've shut off their outboards. I come here too for the quiet, and wonder that other women seldom seem to do so. I am curious to see another paddler, also a relative rarity on this lake. He sports a red bandana and the kind of sunglasses you wear for extra speed, and looks to be around my age, which is thirty. We exchange pleasantries as we unload gear, and though I try to appear interested, I'm already imagining the peaceful solitude that now lies so close. He's up from BC for the summer, and I don't catch what he's doing. I say that I'm a local working on a biology contract and immediately regret it because of the curiosity it engenders.

"So what exactly are you doing out there?" he asks as we help each other lift boats from their racks. I pause as I clip my paddle float to the deck, wondering which answer to give—the big picture, the ecological questions, the conservation issues or just what, physically, I'm doing. The latter wins out for ease. "I'm looking for otter scat," I reply. At his blank look I add helpfully, "You know, shit." He wrinkles his nose and I barrel onward. "I collect it to find out what they eat. And count what's fresh each month." A pause. "And I'll be taking habitat measurements," I add, in a bid to sound more professional.

We salute each other as we shove off, he no doubt chalking up another Yukon experience and I shaking my head at my persistent childlike angst over being taken seriously. My passion for biology has been with me my whole life, though I took a detour from the career path a few years ago. I found that high-tech equipment, politics and bureaucracy were interfering with what made me fall in love with the discipline in the first place—just being out in nature. I hadn't even been looking for work when this contract showed up, right in time to re-instill my faith: someone did value on-the-ground, boots-in-the-mud, no-helicopters-required kind of work. (I learned later that part of the reason for the bare-bones approach was budget constraints, but hey, I'll take it.) The interview included questions like: *Do you have your own canoe or kayak? Backcountry gear? Are you comfortable being out in the bush alone?* Yes, yes and yes. The hardest question was *Do you have someone to check in with on a regular basis via satellite phone?* I live alone now, and I cherish my solitude to a fault when I'm out in the bush. But it was a small concession, and a reasonable one.

I round the headland that puts the little campground out of sight and earshot, relaxing into the rhythm of paddling. Looking down at the lake, I see high clouds reflected in the surface, vying with the lake bottom for backdrop—in the foreground a large grin between sunglasses and a slightly too-large lifejacket, topped with a dark, wide-brimmed Tilley hat. I watch the twin blue prows cutting through the water, then movement below leads my eye through the looking glass and I become an inter-elemental voyeur. Rays of sunshine are visible reaching down to the lake floor, a gently rippling yellow-green. It looks inviting, like it would be suede beneath my feet, but I know this muck. I know how it lies further below the surface than it appears. I've stepped into it and sunk down, down, frighteningly far down as clouds of silt rose around my disappearing legs.

This and other lessons I learned a thousand kilometres to the east, where waters run clear and cold above two-billion-year-old rock, pooling and running in the wrinkles of the land's wizened skin. The beginnings of soil have been slowly filling in the creases since ice last scraped the surface clean, to make peat bogs where scraggly black spruce lean drunkenly on one another and sandy benches where jack pine stand tall and erect. There lies my first lake, prelude to all the others, near Yellowknife, NWT. Perched high on a cliff above one of its many bays is the ramshackle A-frame cabin of my childhood. I left when I was twelve and imagine the lake unchanged, though the cliff may be smaller now. From that lake I learned not only that things are not always as they seem, but that a lake spells freedom. In winter she was unobstructed travel, waves frozen to a standstill for eight months of the year. Summer days were spent crawling about the rocky shore enthralled by insects that stride and row, or skimming the surface in a small aluminum boat with my dad. I once snuck down to the dock—I couldn't have been more than nine—and took the canoe out alone. I remember vividly the headiness of the freedom of my first solo command and also something that approached awe at the magnificent stillness.

That freedom of being self-propelled and self-sufficient returns to me now even as the wind picks up and is funnelled toward me. I make slow progress, my paddle dipping alternately to one side, then the other. *Straighten up. Shoulders back. Lead with your heart.* Funny how so often a similar message comes from different directions: paddling and yoga instructors, my neighbour, my mother. I guess they are messages I need to hear. I do as they suggest, feeling my centre of gravity sink into the seat of the kayak, how my lower body sits below the waterline. There is a satisfying resistance in each pull of the paddle, contrasting with the smoothness with which the hull slips through the water. I try to focus on this, to find a balance of effort and ease as in a yoga practice. In the boat as on the mat it comes and goes, slippery as a fish.

And then, like a savasana, a final relaxation. I can finally let it all go. I've arrived at a place where a round mound of a hill emerges from the water, bristling with an open forest of mature pine trees that have carpeted the earth with decades of red needles. The hill creates an eddy of calm in the choppy channel and invites rest.

As I slide across the drop-off toward the undercut bank, the underwater world comes into sharp focus. Criss-crossed logs, stumps, branches and all of their shadows dance below with the school of small fish that move through and around them. Sometimes the fish move as one body; sometimes one veers off for a solo performance, then returns to the main troupe and their choreographed steps. Always with the shadows moving below. Even swimming solo, the image is that of a pair. I feel a darkness suddenly balloon out from a small, hard pit in my heart. Where is my partner in this watery dance?

There is a part I left out, but that is still part of the story, as Margaret Atwood would say: I wasn't anticipating being alone this time. I was intending on sharing canoe and camp, days and nights and all of this glorious world with the woman I love. I had it all planned. She was a year in the north, a year in my life, and I was taking every opportunity to show her my world. The one where I really feel at home. It was perfect. Except that as the field season began a few short weeks ago, she had a change of heart. She chose a path that I couldn't follow. Instead, I now find myself trying to comprehend the incomprehensible reality of being unchosen.

In a moment I have moved from that sweet freedom to a different alone: the keen absence of an anticipated presence. I see but do not take note of the beauty of the moment, overshadowed as it is by a woman-shaped void by my side. As the late-afternoon sun brings out the richest reds and umbers in the trees, grief rises and takes me over. I surrender to it with the abandon I have only ever known in the arms of nature. Sounds I don't know how to make escape my throat and leave it raw. A loon sends a haunting call in reply. I slam my paddle on the water, hard, and the trees answer me just as they do the slap of the beaver's tail. Drops of lake water join the tears that run down my face. Eventually, I'm empty. The peace of the sheltered cove remains, untroubled by my outpouring. I had somehow forgotten this power of a lake. Without knowing it, I have been in need of one.

I used to think the ability of a lake to moderate emotions, like the sea moderates the climate of the land, was rooted in immensity, because this was the most obvious quality of the lake where I rediscovered the gifts of water as an adult. She lies only an hour to the southeast of here, long and deep, filling in a yawning furrow that marks where tectonic plates collided 150 million years ago. A lake so large she seems a great sessile beast, breathing with the seasons, but never really moving from her anchor. She is a *thing* with inertia and mass. I would share in her moods, channelling rage or frustration or joy or grief into her violent whitecaps or wide rolling waves, and when they subsided to glass reflecting the midnight sun, I would know stillness within as well. Always she was able to take in whatever I needed to let out, remaining incredibly unchanged while I felt a new being.

This lake is different altogether, a shallow, sinuous creature made up of channels, bays and backwaters. She is less a massive thing than a space that is filled, a place where water slows but never comes to a standstill. And yet, she seems equally able to take in what I need to let out; constant motion gives *her* a capacity for listening, for calming. Perhaps motion in fact is what is at the heart of this quality in even the vast lakes of the world—without movement, any sink will eventually be overwhelmed.

I sigh, exhausted with the catharsis of tears and sound, and lean back on my lifejacket, resting my paddle on the cockpit. I see the colour now, the play of light. As I gaze at the shore, a beaver climbs dripping out of the water a short distance away, and I feel the kinship of just having surfaced. Her fur gleams golden brown in the sun. As if recognizing her responsibility to this display, she seats herself upon her tail and commences a fastidious toilet. She grooms meticulously, cleaning and waterproofing her fur by running it through claws smeared with an oil from a gland near the base of her tail. She spends half an hour at this task, while I pull out some crackers and salmon jerky and recharge. She begins with her face, then her forelegs, her hind legs and finally her belly, above which I can make out the twin halos of bare skin that surround her nipples. I feel calmed, as if it is I being stroked in that gentle act so common in social creatures.

———

It is an hour or so since I left Mother Beaver, and I have recovered my equilibrium. I have just—maybe—seen my first otter. Or heard it, in the form of a sudden *ploop* to starboard as I entered a tiny channel near the northern tip of the lake. It sounded too large for a muskrat and was accompanied by no beavertail slap. I scan the shoreline in vain for my quarry. Though research is such that a successful field season could be accomplished without ever setting eyes on one, I long to be invited into their private world.

I push and pole the boat over a mud bank and see the local beaver has been busy here. I haul the boat out onto the shore of a small pond. After unloading the heavier items, I heave and slide and slip and strain, eventually making it over the small rise that separates me from another little lake. I don't have enough breath left to curse when I lose my footing on the steep slope. I pause a moment to stretch; then, goaded by early mosquitoes, I am back on the water to visit my first set of field sites. At one seemingly random spot on the shoreline after another, I pull my legs out of the kayak and tie up to a bush or a log. I walk carefully, scanning the ground for little piles of scat peppered with fish scales and the exoskeletons of dragonfly larvae, until I reach a camera—this one fastened securely to the trunk of a pine, about a foot off the ground. They are triggered by movement, and I plan to try and relate the number of otters who have visited the site to the amount of fresh scat I find each month. I don't always tell people about this part of the project, worried that some might go looking for the sites. As I unlock the case that holds the camera, I sigh, still getting used to the idea that there is no second set of eyes scanning the forest floor while I work, no set of hands ready to take mine when we finish.

The round takes only two hours, and all too soon I find myself staring at the bottom of the portage trail. Suddenly I realize I am ravenous. On no one's schedule but my own, I sometimes forget to break. I turn back to the middle of the bay away from the bugs and pull out some food, knowing I'm only putting off the inevitable. Once my hunger is sated and I have rested a little, I reluctantly return to shore and do the whole thing in reverse. There is a certain satisfaction in brute strength, but for the sake of my back perhaps next time I'll bring a pulley and some rope. Or someone else.

———

I retrace my route of the morning and take a left over a beaver dam after another hour or so, a few kilometres before the campground. It is more sheltered here, in these linked lagoons patrolled by rusty blackbirds who alert the next sentry with a sharp *chat*. The uniform lines of forest that separate the ridges from the sky are punctuated occasionally by single, taller pines. They bear witness to time that existed before the rise of the current cohort. They remind that what is normal now is not how it always was, nor how it always will be. I imagine the fire that crackled and roared its way across this landscape a half century ago, destroying and creating in one instant. I try, without much success, to take the lesson to heart, to remember that I, too, will change.

Three hours upstream over five more dams and I'm on another lake, this one a larger, straighter incarnation that lets the cries of loons play back and forth along its length. It is the loon, I think, from whom I learned that loneliness does not come only to the lone—their duets can be hauntingly lonely—and also that beauty and sadness can share the same note.

It is late, the sun's last rays slanting from rather far to the north, and as I make my way down the lake I can see signs that I am in human company, past and present. There are a number of well-used camps visible as patches of bank conspicuously clear of shrubs underneath the high pines. Some have stumps for seats; all have firepits surrounded by blackened stones. I drift by, imagining the ghosts of all those who have passed through and committed that primal act of making camp, perhaps for centuries. Then I see two bright blue tarps on the far shore, a motorboat moored below. Current denizens. I give them a wide berth and aim for a tiny island to the south.

By this time I am feeling the day's movements, both physical and emotional, weighing on my body. I circle to the far side of the island, wanting my entry to go unobserved. Not that any of the other campers are within sight. I remember the same desire for privacy when entering the little haunts I discovered along that long-ago lakeshore of my girlhood ramblings. I pull up to shore with only a single loon for witness and am greeted by a cluster of large white orchids, their pendulous flowers nodding their assent to my landing from too-delicate stalks. A brief reconnaissance of the island reveals a bald hump fringed by a thick monk's tonsure of mid-sized spruce and pine, thick too beneath with soapberry and Labrador tea. I choose a small clearing north of the hump and lay out the raw materials of home: an eight-by-ten-foot compact tarp, a bivy sack, a cold-weather down sleeping bag and a Therm-a-Rest. It all goes up in no time, the fabrics expanding exponentially when I release them from their stuff sacks, like a magician's endless scarf unfurling from a hat.

At times I have been accused of being a minimalist and I accept the charge when I survey my spartan camp for one. The bivy sack is a tube of a tent that just fits my sleeping bag, a single pole arching over the head in a concession to avoiding claustrophobia. Once inside, I have one position: prone with legs outstretched. To some, it may feel a nylon coffin; to me, it is the closest I can get to being fully in the world of earth and wind and sky without the bug bites. Everything safely stowed for the night, I slide into my sleeping bag. The square digits on my alarm clock stand out clearly in the twilight: midnight. I'm asleep almost before my head hits the ground.

———

I wake roughly after what feels like only a few minutes. The dim light gives no clue as to the time. The sounds that lulled me to sleep, the creaking pines and lapping waves, have given way to silence. I listen for a moment, my ears held taught, and then remember. There is no one to make the sleep noises I expect to hear. I feel a darkness descend over me again, and the tidy, self-sufficient camp is transformed to a broken half. The hours in the week ahead stretch long before me, an endless, desolate road filled with absence. How do I imagine again a future that inspires an eagerness to explore? I roll over and cover my eyes, falling into a fitful sleep.

———

The next time I wake it is proper morning, and a squirrel is cheerfully contesting my claim to this little patch of turf. The glade is bathed in warm yellow light filtering through the tarp. I open my eyes, squint at this bushy-tailed challenger and grin. I feel rested. I feel, dare I say it, hopeful. The ghosts of the night are forgotten. I watch a pair of pine needles—our only pine, the lodgepole, always twins her needles—twist lazily in the air a foot or so below the squirrel. He lets out another rattle, the audio equivalent of my tarp and bedroll, marking a boundary across which others are not welcome except by invitation. The message is clear within species; it takes a pathology or urgent need for a person to cross such a line. But what does this thin nylon shell say to the other animals who call this place home? I feel safe snugged in my flimsy sarcophagus, as if bears and moose will respect this backcountry equivalent of a picket fence. Though clearly I am not respecting the squirrel's line. I hope they at least notice me; I am more worried about being tripped over than sought out.

My feet dangle in the cool water as I eat my breakfast next to the kayak before heading out for the morning's work. Homemade oatcakes and a granola bar, zucchini chips, a peanut butter cookie. So much preparation to lead this simple life—cooking and dehydrating, packing and repacking and wondering what I've forgotten. Yet as soon as I get out here, whatever I didn't bring is not missed. Everything I do have is a luxury. The trappings of life at home, material and relational, feel increasingly irrelevant the longer I am away.

———

I return to the island in the early afternoon after the same routine as the previous day: check camera, look for sign, bag scat and repeat. Out on the water I was pleasantly cool with my lower half ensconced in the cockpit of the kayak, but now the ever-present June sun threatens to burn a hole through my dark shirt. I hasten to strip off my wetsuit before I overheat. Knee-high Labrador tea sends up great puffs of sun-warmed fragrance as I push my way through to the eastern point of the island. There, a thin yellow-white spit extends far out into the bay below a foot or two of water, edged by a narrow band of teal descending quickly to deep blue. And it is deep. I have sent down a weight on the end of a twelve-metre rope without touching bottom. The effect of the colours is striking, a coral atoll in the midst of the boreal. Stepping in, I grimace a little. The algae-covered rocks do not quite feel like white sand, and they give a little in the muck, but I don't sink too far and it is blessedly cool. I wade out in the shallows to circumnavigate my temporary home, walking slowly to avoid stirring up the sediment and so preserve what I can of the tropical illusion.

I start suddenly, stopping stock-still, my heart in my throat. A loon has erupted in a flurry of feathers from a shoreside nest, calling wildly. She flaps her wings, raising herself high out of the water to impressive effect. I back away slowly as the pounding of my heart recedes in my ears. She is huge, seen up close. I see now the other half of the pair making wide circles between the island and the shore. So the witness to my arrival was not, in fact, alone. I feel like yelling in frustration, "Is *everyone* paired up but me?" A rattle above me reminds me that my resident squirrel at least isn't shacked up with anyone. His romantic trysts are perhaps many but short-lived, limited to a single day for each female he can smell on the wind. I escape my own mind by diving into the bracing cold water.

As I head out of the bay for my second round of the day, I pass a pair of canoeists. I nod mutely, wrapping my solitude around me like a cloak, wishing I could fade into the landscape that surrounds me. I catch sight of my brooding reflection and the corners of my mouth twitch a little. It is a little funny, how much I resent these other explorers. I resent them for being couples to be sure, but even the singletons remind me that I too am part of this thing we call the human race, in all of its arrogance and frailty and ugliness and beauty. In being rejected by one single human I would reject all of humanity. I give a half laugh that threatens to become a sob so I conjure anger, drowning in a mess of emotions topped off with the frustration that they rule me so. I thrust my paddle violently into the water, which responds as usual, by doing nothing but waiting for me to calm down.

I turn to my work and try to lose myself in left-brain activity. I break only when my stomach begins to growl in earnest. I extricate myself from the kayak, with only another squirrel to marvel at this one becoming two, and build a small fire in a well-used pit. While it burns down to coals, I wade out into the water and cast over the drop-off. On the second cast a pike follows the lure in. I wonder about the relative roles in fishing of luck, karma, intention and skill. I cast again, and this time it bites. We fight, and I win. I wonder about the roles in love of luck, karma, intention and skill. I knock the pike between the eyes and say my thanks.

I return to the fire and add a little more wood, settling down to stare into the hypnotic flames in a ritual as old as our species. Once it is reduced to a pile of white-hot embers, I strip a green willow stick and slide it through the mouth of the gutted fish and out a hole cut just in front of the tail. It hovers just above the coals. While it cooks, I make my daily check-in call. I feel torn between wanting my neighbour to pick up, to ask how I am so I can fib a little, and fearing that she'll see right through me to the brokenness inside. Or that she won't. It's a moot point because the answering machine clicks on and I let out the breath I was holding. I leave an inane message.

I pick bits of flesh off the skeleton of the pike—it is delicious. I love catching my own food, cooking on an open fire, feeling the wind and the water. In the same moment I hurt, am frustrated, am angry. I feel no need out here to reconcile the conflicting emotions that tumble through me, to present any sort of coherent self to the world, another gift of the lake. I toss a piece of fish skin into the coals and listen to it pop and sizzle.

A splash wrests my gaze away and I look up to see the sleek heads of two otters heading out into the bay. Their antics bring a smile to my face and I settle back against a pine to watch them until they disappear from sight.

THE HILLS ARE ALIVE

SARAH PAYNTER

Walking alone for four weeks had a profoundly calming effect on me. Without even trying to have a significant meditative escape or "find myself," I somehow managed to shed any heavy thoughts. With each step, I took individual anxieties about work, family, regret and so on, mentally examined them and discarded them one by one as if into thin air. I read of a similar experience in *Being Caribou*, where Karsten Heuer and Leanne Allison follow the porcupine caribou on their annual migration in Northern Canada. Karsten recounts singing every song he'd ever known before finding silence. He needed to encounter each song before his mind was clear.

On the Adlerweg, or "Eagle's Way," trekking route, my brain was a washing machine. It was too easy: All I had to do was put one foot in front of the other for 320 kilometres. Stop to rest when tired.

I rarely worried about my safety, despite walking solo on some precarious paths and scrambling along some "ropes-optional" routes. The Austrian huts and villages were safe. I never felt threatened. I was not concerned that a fellow hiker would harm me and didn't see any evidence of thieves hiking along remote trails to catch unwary travellers.

I did, however, meet a man who was walking the same stretch of the Adlerweg as me. He wasn't dangerous, but he quickly became a royal pain in the ass.

He was an Austrian father hiking the Eagle's Way alone. He was the only other person I met who was trying to complete this obscure long-distance route through Tirol in Western Austria. He had walked the rest of the track over two years and was trying to finish the final section that week in his third and final year. He was loud, racist, stinky, mostly drunk and apparently trying to break some sort of record for burps per minute.

Worst of all, he was a "mansplainer." He was going to tell me what I needed to know about Austria, the European Union, tourism, the alpine hut system, the cost of food, parenting, Germans, Americans, and so on and so forth.

I'd spied him while rehydrating at a pasture farm called Hintere Tarrentenalpe, a rest point that was miraculously open in late September. The Alps are spotted with farms and shacks that sell drinks, and sometimes food, to travellers throughout the summer walking season. As I continued on alone, each time I stopped to catch my breath I could see him downslope working hard to catch up with me.

Eventually he did. "Hello, so you are from Canada?" he asked. Apparently he'd overheard me speaking with the farm owners earlier. "You are hiking alone?" He was smoking.

We were standing on a ridge about six hours' walk from any road or village and I almost said, "No, my husband's joining me soon," a common lie I've told on trips before ("My husband is at a conference, I'm meeting him for dinner later.")

"Yes, I'm walking alone," I replied, stepping back and waving my hand at the smoke now surrounding me.

"Are you going to Anahalter Hutte, the next hut?"

"Yes," I said.

"Good, we'll walk together, then." He seemed to have decided that we would now be hiking together. Oh goody. He reeked of beer and cigarettes, which was exactly what I'd hoped the Alps would smell like.

His name was Julian and he proceeded to tell me that he was happy I wasn't German because they were all jerks. "They think they are better than us, but really we are more happy and our Alps are bigger than their Alps."

"Ohhhh, aaaare they?" I replied. He couldn't see me grinning from ear to ear, because he'd taken the lead. Of course. Man first, woman second!

I was also informed about his family, Euro monetary policy, and why it was better to divide long distance walks into shorter stages instead of tackling them all at once like I was. Silly me.

I don't consider myself an anti-social person. I actually love talking with people. One of the joys of solo travel is that you meet more people than you do travelling as a couple or group. I'd expected to encounter many more people hiking in Austria but the few I'd bumped into while walking were invariably going the opposite direction. So I had walked more than three hundred kilometres across the Tirolean Alps almost entirely alone. I did, however, spend a lot of nights in mountain huts and village pubs socializing with whoever was there. I found Austrians very willing to chat over drinks, especially if you ordered a local craft weissbier or wheat beer, and then took your turn buying a round of schnapps.

When Julian insisted we take a shortcut along a scree slope, a very stupid idea from my perspective, somehow I just fell in line and followed him. I clearly was not thinking straight. As I stared down at my impending death I thought, What the hell am I doing? Why am I allowing this guy to hijack my holiday?

"Don't worry, it's safe." According to Julian I was "overreacting." I could see the headline: *Kanadische frau stürzt in den Tod.* Canadian woman falls to her death. The obituary would comment on how courageous and thoughtful I was when really my solo vacations were entirely selfish escapades.

After covering the dangerous terrain and arriving at the mountain hut, I came firmly to the conclusion that I would do everything in my power to avoid hiking with this man again. Anhalter Hutte, or Anhalter hut, with its red and white window shutters, sits at 2030 metres above sea level, perched beneath the imposing Tschachaun peak. It's surrounded by rocky crags just above a blanket of alpine pasture. Like all good hikers, I removed my boots before checking in with the hut warden to arrange a bed and food.

"You are travelling alone?" she asked. "Yes," I replied. I still don't know whether her smirk was a "You go, girl!" or "Stupid foreigner!" Some people are more transparent about their disdain for women travelling alone. I've been told time and again that it's too dangerous.

"I travel alone a lot," I said. "I'm fine, really."

Kind folks all over the world do not seem to understand why I enjoy some time to myself, by myself, with myself, on vacation; that for me, the vacation is in the solitude. Some offer spurious "facts" to help me on my way. They tell me that I'll likely get robbed, lost, lonely and/or hurt.

"You might get attacked," said a concerned local in Austria. I'd heard the same thing from "helpful" people in Belize, India, Australia, Slovenia, and all the other places I've travelled by myself. The only narrative dispensed is that the world is too big and scary for those of us with boobs and vaginas. But I don't want to let fear stop me from travelling, and so I carry on.

"Yes, I'm married. No, he's at home working," I would explain again and again.

"That's strange," said one woman I'd met at a Maurach bed and breakfast. "So he gave you his permission?" We were sitting outside sipping rowanberry schnapps surrounded by Austrian hills and the very glacial Achensee or Achen Lake. How do I even respond to this?

"Um, I didn't ask him for it," I replied.

At Anhalter Hutte, I discovered the lodge was nearly full. The only beds left were in the lager, the communal sleeping rooms where mattresses barely wide enough for one are stacked side by side, usually in an attic or outbuilding. My Alpine Club of Austria card guaranteed me a space; however, I was going to have to share quarters with my new pal Julian and several Germans who seemed disinterested in talking to us.

"See, they are all snobs," said Julian later, downing yet another beer. I won't even relay what he had to say about other nationalities. Thankfully, I escaped his verbal diarrhea with the help of Marieke, another solo hiker, who whisked me away while Julian was outside smoking.

At bedtime, however, there was nowhere to hide. Happily for me, my mattress neighbour Julian got himself thoroughly hammered and turned up at some ungodly hour to trip over people's bags before tumbling into bed in his underwear. To be exact, he fell onto the mattress next to me while trying to remove his pants. Great. He woke everyone in the room and then kept us up most of the night.

Besides exhaling pure alcohol and smelling like an ashtray, he snored and tossed and turned continuously. My earplugs were useless. My attempt to create a wall of blankets between his sprawling, naked limbs and myself was futile. On a midnight bathroom expedition I even searched in vain for anywhere else to sleep. About a week previously I'd escaped a lager with about thirty people snoring and farting to sleep a few restful hours in a walk-in linen closet without anyone noticing. To this day, I derive a great source of pride from that particular misadventure! My lager-mates then were a group of mountaineers taking advantage of Oktoberfest to get royally pissed in the Alps.

With Julian, however, there was no escape. After a sleepless night, I was groggy and oh so cranky. I felt like I'd been the one smoking my guts out. This is not what I want to deal with on my holiday.

I'd packed the night before, and I was able to sneak out of the room quietly. I cleaned up and rushed downstairs for a quick break-fast. Despite my best efforts to disappear unseen, Julian caught me as I was walking out the front door of the hut. He was outside smoking, naturally.

"So you are on your way?" he stated.

"Yes. You snored all night."

"My wife says I don't snore," he said.

"Um. Okay. Have a great day."

"That's what Americans say," he stated matter-of-factly.

"Okay. Bye?" And I turned and left as fast as I could.

I felt so liberated! I was happy to be on my own again. The sun was rising over the mountains and suddenly I could see that the pastures below the hut were flanked with horses. After seeing cows, cows, cows, cows, goats, goats, goats, sheep and sheep for days on end, horses were a great alternative, and I like them. Walking through the Alps is like pulling up to an amazing viewpoint every five minutes. The sights are breathtaking. I wanted to take lots of pictures but I also wanted to put distance between Julian and myself. The air smelled like the mountains now with the distinct lack of cigarette smoke and alcohol fumes. It was lovely. The hills are alive with the sound of music!

After two weeks of consistent hiking, I was feeling fit and fast.

The track was downhill, so I could practically jog. As I got further and further from the hut, I settled back into my happy daydreaming.

Two hours later I stopped to get some water and take one last look at the horses when I glimpsed Julian out of the corner of my eye. I was shocked. There he was, tearing down the open meadows, leaping and bounding in a straight line, ignoring every switchback turn. He was gaining on me. Soon he was only a hundred metres away. He looked like he was moving as fast as he could and much faster than he needed considering his long speech the previous day about how Austrian hikers took their time to smell the roses while the Germans all competed for speed, missing out on the experience itself...

Twenty kilometres lay between me and the village of Haselgehr, and I could imagine it filled entirely with his "let me tell you about the world, little girl" banter.

That's when I turned and bolted.

I was pretty sure he hadn't seen me catch sight of him. My back was still turned and the tree line was close. I put my water back in my bag and started walking. I moved as fast as I could without running and hit the tree line in a matter of minutes. After the first turn, I started sprinting as fast as I could with a forty-litre rucksack on my back. The path was a series of twists and turns through dense trees along a river gorge. After a quarter kilometre I glanced back to make sure the coast was clear and scurried upslope and behind some bushes to a hidden vantage point over the trail. It was exhilarating and liberating, just like every other time I decide to say, "no, that's not what I want to do today, thank you very much!" and instead make my own journey.

I sat on my perch and waited nervously. I felt like a kid again. I was playing tag, catch the flag, or hide and seek with my friends and I was doing well (but I might get caught). I held my breath and waited. Sure enough, Julian eventually came rushing by. He was covered in sweat, straining to catch up to me. He had a confused and beaten-down look on his face. I almost felt sorry for him. I'm sure he meant no harm, but I was insanely happy to see him go. I wasn't sure whether he just wanted a walking companion—that he was lonely—or whether he was trying to prove his masculinity by out-walking a woman. Maybe both.

I sat for a long time in that spot. I snacked. I reflected on my favourite moments of my trip. I flipped through my photos in my camera. I enjoyed the sun on my face. And I agreed that I would not feel guilty for ditching Julian. He would be much farther ahead of me by now. I decided that if I ran into him—if he'd stopped to eat or had thought that I purposefully dropped him and then he stayed put to wait—I'd tell him that I'd had to pee and had gone in the woods. "You must have passed me on the trail," I would say. "You're very fast."

I wanted to avoid him entirely. We were both headed along the same route so I consulted my map and found an alternate path. I hiked along the main Adlerweg for another hour. There was no sign of Julian. Then I turned west. The new path took me to the other side of a massive gorge. The main path was on the north side of a ravine, and the shortcut I was now walking took me through trees along the south side, leap-frogging me a day ahead of my Austrian companion. I was officially free of Julian.

While I've sometimes lamented the fact that I had to change my plans, shortening my long-distance trek in order to avoid an un-savoury character, the shortcut ended up being a highpoint of the trip because it was a largely unmarked, wild route away from the villages and roads on the north side of that gorge.

And I treasure that moment when I scrambled up into the bush-es to hide. I was not hiding in fear. I was not threatened. I was enor-mously happy. I felt exhilarated and mischievous. I did actually have to pee. And I got to spend another day hiking alone, breathing in the wilderness and absorbing the extraordinary sights in my very own adventure.

I channelled my inner Julie Andrews and began to sing to the mountains, to the solitude and to my well-worn hiking boots and sore feet.

These are a few of my favourite things ...

LITTLE COFFINS

NANCY PINCOMBE

Full of Pilsner and desperate for a pee, I am about to drop my pants and squat on the street, which might be the stupidest thing a woman can do alone at night in a strange city. It is dark and very late and I cannot work the key to my apartment. I am useless with keys. And this is one of those large, cartoonish keys on a wide ring that fit into a massive, splintery, wooden door. The narrow, cobbled street and the echo of distant footsteps make the city seem medieval and menacing. The footsteps come closer. No, actually, this is the stupidest thing a woman alone at night can do: I approach the strange man, the large strange man, whose face, in the dark, I cannot read at all, and give him my key. I gesture to the door and mime using a key, and shrug helplessly. The man understands, shakes his head at me disapprovingly, inserts the key into the lock, just so, and gives it a twist. The door swings open and he goes on his way. "*Dekuju!*"—thank you in Czech—I call softly. The trick, I learn after much practising the next morning, is to push the key in only halfway, to where it will engage with the clumsy ancient workings of the lock inside the door. Push too far and the long key goes right through to the other side.

Inside the building, the stone steps have that distinctive, cool, old-building tang. Close to wetting myself, I am anxious about my actual apartment door, but this smaller key I am able to work after a couple of tries. I flip on the lights, throw down my bag and jacket and run for the toilet. I don't bother closing the bathroom door and hear a kind of scuffling across the room where a door—with another of those large keyholes—leads to an adjoining apartment. I am certain someone is watching. Annoyed rather than alarmed, I finish up and deliberately hang my jacket on that doorknob, covering the keyhole.

Starving and jetlagged—it must be mealtime at home—I devour the breakfast that the landlady (she lives in the adjoining apartment and is most likely the peeper) has left for me: slices of tasteless white cheese, some thin disks of salami, a small white roll and some processed cheese spread wrapped in little foil wedges that is quite nice. I drink the orange-coloured beverage that passes for juice, but save the cup with a spoonful of Nescafe in the bottom for the morning. It takes me a long time to fall asleep. And the next morning it is difficult to get up, knowing there are only those little grounds at the bottom of the cup waiting for me.

———

Prague is everything I'd heard. It is weird and beautiful, a city of classical music, a textbook full of European architecture, spires, stonework, stucco, a mecca for cuckoo clocks and similar oddities. A friend who'd recommended the place to me added a few observations that the guidebooks missed:

"And Jesus, it's Kafka-strange. To the back of the main square, there's a church where, dangling from the roof, is the arm—flesh still intact—of some saint, accused four hundred years ago of using her limbs in a presumably sacrilegious way. At Christmastime, Czechs keep live carp in their bathtubs until the poor buggers think they're going to be made a pet—then on Christmas Eve they kill them and eat them with boiled potatoes. Outside of town, there's a place that's decorated entirely with human bones. And, chillingly, there are no cats. Not one. You don't notice it until you do; then it becomes creepy. You won't know what to think."

Perfect. It is my thirtieth birthday and this trip is my present. A counsellor has recommended it, that Ian and I do more things on our own. I enjoy travelling alone and I have a lot to not think about. Our relationship is floundering, but in interesting ways, so that the last ten years have gone by in a blink. Together we've filled our days with going-nowhere jobs, and in our off time we climb mountains and sail boats and paddle kayaks and win races of various sorts. We've achieved an impressive degree of fitness and failed utterly at making a home together, and could I really be THIRTY? I soon realize that these exact things—my age, travelling solo, my Gore-Tex and fleece garments—make me stand out here. I encounter many groups of young backpackers, and of course a lot of retired couples touring in style, but I don't belong in either group. Here, a thirty-year-old woman should be married, busy with children. By thirty, I might have actually said it out loud, once or twice, that I felt like I was using up all my mothering energy in the wrong place, on a man who spent more and more time behaving like a sullen teenager. One of those "not think about" things I hoped to avoid, at least for the span of this holiday. And maybe my choice of Europe, rather than Patagonia or some such place, cushy culture rather than windswept mountains and low-fat granola, is the antidote to the way I've been living this past decade. Still, I vow to go running as often as I can.

My neighbours back home are Czech and miss their old country a great deal. They encouraged me and insisted that I visit Moravia and stay with family they have there. Also my good friend, quoted above, spent some months in Prague recently on a work-study program for her graduate degree. She raved about it. I have been quietly jealous of her travels, her studies, her focus in life. I have the telephone number of a friend of hers. I ring up Lucie and get a young-sounding voice in perfect, Canadian-accented English. Lucie works at the Canadian embassy in Prague. We get along well. She is petite and dark haired, with warm brown eyes, and looks strangely like my friend who recommended her, right down to a small scar on an eyebrow. I have the ideal guide for my stay in the city.

Lucie takes me to embassy parties as her date. We drink strange blue cocktails late into the night with some British friends of hers. I have a photo of us all tangoing, falling-down drunk, on a dark cobbled street, and a hazier memory still of a young man from the British embassy lying with his head in my lap, touching in fascination a small hole in the knee of my black stocking, recalling that scene in the movie *The Piano*. These expats drink in a way that makes my sailing friends back home seem like amateurs.

Lucie is excellent fun. I treat her to a fancy meal at a small restaurant in the Malá Strana, down a series of narrow, curving stone steps, where we eat an enormous meal of venison with juniper sauce. My dining experiences in the city until now have been hit-and-miss. A meal in a restaurant is inexpensive here, but the proprietors and waiters find ways to make you pay. Your entree, as listed on the menu, will be very cheap, as will your beer or wine, but if you are careless enough to allow the waiter to set a basket of bread on your table, you will pay as much again for the often stale sliced white bread. Experienced diners quickly wave away the bread. Our restaurant this evening is upscale and its staff need not stoop to such tactics. Yet even at a posh place, with all we can eat and drink, I am unable to spend forty dollars. I cannot fit in another morsel, but petite Lucie insists that we must not leave anything, certainly not meat; Western-European-style abundance is recent, here. She lifts more of the tender meat with the tangy sauce onto my plate.

Stuffed, we continue our evening at a nearby beer hall. Carrying beer in steins so big I have trouble lifting mine, we take the stairs down into the basement where there is a large room with a wooden floor. People assemble; most are young British expats. We are here for Scottish country dancing. I want to lie down in a corner; my digestive resources have never had such a test. The music begins and a slim, dark woman explains the steps briefly. Everyone is game, particularly a perspiring, graceless but grinning young man who whirls me with such gusto that I turn my ankle. There goes my running resolution. Luckily we take frequent *pivo* (beer) breaks and I forget to be depressed.

Lucie and I take the train to visit a man she knows, a Canadian man named Matthew, who runs a large farm west of Prague. He is my age, from Ontario, but came over to claim the farm of his grandparents that had been taken over by the government so many years ago. And whereas at home he might be selling cars or aspiring to middle management somewhere, saving up to buy a condo, here he is master of a big stone house, two beautiful German short-haired pointers, horses, acres of farmland and forest and some thin, elderly aunts who keep house for him. He's wearing breeches. I feel like I am in a Jane Austen novel. He looks like Ian, medium height, strongly built, thick dark hair. A version of Ian that Ian would love: wealth and status, family money.

It's a guy's fairy tale. He takes me riding. Lucie stays with the dogs while I mount a big-boned mare named Marguerite, quietly admiring the expensive, well-oiled tack, and we gallop up a hill into a block of beautiful deciduous forest full of fall colour.

When we return, the aunts have laid out a modest lunch for us: bread and grilled sausages, salads; we are offered beer or wine. The dogs lounge on solid leather furniture. Everything is solid. I feel insubstantial, mousy and old. Our conversation is friendly. He and Lucie have many friends in common, but he is just a bit remote. I have the impression that he is spoiled for choice, here, with women, in a way that he would not be back in Ontario. And Czech women are so notoriously beautiful. I am reminded of the equation the guys at work use, to calculate the ideal age for a female partner. It is half the man's age, plus seven. So, a man of thirty should date a woman of no more than twenty-two. And of course that woman won't be the right age for long. Lucie is only twenty-six—close enough—and has the advantage of her perfect Canadian English. We talk of little else but this visit for the next few days. She wants him. Of course she does. So do I. But she has a chance, so we strategize on her behalf.

———

After more than a week, I leave the city to travel east. I ask Lucie to telephone the parents of my neighbour back home. They live in Brno, in Moravia. Yes, they are expecting me and will meet the train.

I love trains. The landscape is tame and flat and open, comfortable. The autumn burning has started and the air is peaty and hazy. I relax and enjoy a rare feeling of timelessness. Brno has the feel of a town rather than a city. On the platform, a sturdily built man with a large, drooping, grey moustache holds a sign with my name on it. Valer, the father of my neighbour back home, is a glass artist who has exhibited internationally. The twinkle in his eye and that astounding 'stache give the impression of charisma and a naughtiness that surprises me. He guides me to his car using a firmly placed hand on my elbow.

Their home is a spacious townhouse in an upscale part of town. Liba, his wife, seems a kind and pretty, well-made-up woman who has lunch on the table for us. I know enough now to recognize that this is a special meal for a guest. It's not soup or stew, or the much more usual white bread, ham and cheese; this is a chicken dinner. They solemnly serve me the choicest pieces. We eat and do our best at conversation. I am brought to understand that they have arranged, in fact hired, a man to take me around their city. This man used to be a school chum of their son, and he speaks a little English. He is an artist, too. I learn that in the Czech Republic, artists are entitled to a small salary from the government, just for being artists. It is not enough to live in any sort of style—for that the artist must be well connected and successful—but it is enough to keep him from starving.

Orlik arrives at the appointed time to take me out. I have changed into a sundress—the weather has been almost hot—and do my best not to look rumpled. My guide is about my age, but his untidiness makes him look like a teenager. He has a careless, frizzled ponytail, bad teeth and the look of someone who stays indoors too much. But he is sweet and earnest and is obviously uncomfortable in his role; he seems unsure about shaking my hand. Our first stop is a museum of "dried, dead bodies." Orlick speaks the words carefully—he doesn't know the word "mummies." This is to be followed by an exhibition of implements of torture. He does see the humour in this, but doesn't quite have the language to make the joke.

After dutifully admiring the gruesome displays, I feel an even stronger desire for fresh air and suggest that we just stroll around the city. And so we walk in the breezy, warm, late afternoon. Even in the centre of town the air smells like burning leaves, and although it is only late September, I am aware of winter approaching in the swirls of leaves and the whiffs of mulled wine near street-vendor carts. Liba handed Orlik a fistful of money as we left the house, and I understand that he is to buy me dinner.

We order goulash with dumplings and pivo. My host eats ravenously, pointing out with pride the texture and size of the dumplings at this restaurant. I clean my plate and wrestle him for the bill, explaining that it is my pleasure, and that he should pocket the cash. I am really grateful for his time and give him a Canadian-style hug when he drops me off. He is more than a little startled.

The next day, Liba drives me out to the country. We both do ourselves credit by managing the communication: we are going to pick rosehips for tea. It is exactly what I feel like doing. My Gore-Tex jacket is appropriate, for once. The weather is cooler and we enjoy ourselves on the outskirts of some town, the name of which starts with O, picking fat, orange-red rosehips the size of plums. Afterwards, she drives me to Valer's studio—I have noticed that he does not seem to live at their house—and leaves me there with a wan smile. His studio is, well, bohemian. It sprawls over several levels and has many blankets and cushions. He is pleased to show me around. There are, of course, some nude sketches. He offers wine, and for a moment I imagine dropping my guard, dropping my clothes, becoming a variously flesh-toned figure in a frame. Would it change anything really? Or would acquiescence startle him into shyness? I suspect his attentions are *de rigueur*, and not personal, and decide that this is a good thing. I decline the drink and show interest in some glass work in the corner. It feels very Canadian somehow, nice, but not quite getting it. And there's a thread of this that reminds me of who I am at home, in a relationship where I pretend not to see what's really going on.

"I've got it all worked out." Six months ago Ian walked over to the couch with a bit of paper scrawled with figures in his small, neat writing. We sat, blinking at it, in the strong spring sunlight. My heart sank, because I knew that a) he'd spent the entire morning on this, rather than on anything that might get us somewhere, and b) that it would involve me giving him more money. I was already paying the mortgage, and for all our food, making regular handouts of cash for cigarettes (even though I hated that he smoked) and gas. We had all the utilities in my name, but he had agreed to pay them as his contribution to our living expenses. Except he didn't. I finally intercepted a hydro bill that said final notice and checked the others ... all in arrears. It was a mad scramble to pay them all and preserve my credit. This time his idea was for me to buy some life insurance from him, and with the commission he got, he would pay me back a full year of premiums. I knew I had to be positive, convincing, but a little vague. When he came up with these plans he was really vulnerable and would fly into a rage if I showed any signs of what he considered betrayal. Other schemes have involved using my line of credit so he could buy materials to fix up the house, but he'd only ever complete the demolition part, or ideas for taking elaborate holidays which I would then excitedly plan and research, only to have him cancel at the last minute. On my birthday, in the summer, he'd proudly handed me a cheque to cover the airfare for this trip to Europe. It was something the counsellor had suggested, that Ian contribute a little to my taking a trip. That cheque bounced, so he'd written me another for half the sum but cautioned me not to cash it until he gave the go-ahead. Which of course never came.

Valer takes me to lunch in another small town nearby and orders for me. What arrives seems to be the highlight of the menu: three kinds of meat, or perhaps three treatments of the same meat (pork), and cabbage cooked with salt, lard and sugar. Oh, and dumplings. And pivo. I feel I may die, but remembering Lucie's reaction to leftover protein, I plough through the plateful. As if making conversation, Valer asks if I like ice cream. I say sure, I like ice cream. But what he means of course is *would I like* ice cream. And I, stupidly, have said yes. A mountain of the stuff arrives, piled with whipped topping and flecked and drizzled with bits of canned pineapple. I barely touch it and endure disappointed looks from my host—the tips of his moustache come near to colliding—and the server looks like she wants to slap me.

Our outing for the afternoon is the Moravian Karst: caves, quite spectacular ones. Indeed, there are stalactites and stalagmites thrusting in all directions as we walk through the extensive, barely lit paths and past the smooth, wet walls. My host becomes concerned that I might lose my footing and grasps my upper arm, bringing his body close. Until we finally emerge, all communication is accomplished with the aid of his moustache nuzzling my hair. Yes, at thirty, I have finally perfected a useful obliviousness that serves me well. When I return that evening to Liba—who seems to be a cosmetics representative—she looks at me intently and makes me a present of just the right combination of lip glosses for my colouring.

I need a day on my own, so I declare an interest in Moravian wine and plan to visit some wineries. My hosts seem to feel that this means they have been remiss, and so on the eve of my departure for the wine region they arrange their own wine tasting. Orlik is invited. Liba has a surprise for me. It is frozen pizza, which she understands to be a North American delicacy, and I fear she has paid dearly for it. We sit under the hanging lamp in their small, contemporary kitchen and share the tiny, tasteless pizza, a thin wedge each. Then, to properly prepare our palates for wine, Valer pours us each a tumbler of whiskey. I am not as aghast as I should be and gamely down mine. After the whisky, we drink a few bottles of white wine, and then a few bottles of red. I swirl and exclaim like a good guest. The wine is pretty good. At some point I visit the washroom off the kitchen, where I fall asleep on the toilet. They wake me, unfazed, and the evening continues. At a later point, Valer suggests that I call home. I do. I am too drunk to be apprehensive. It is a cheerful, slurred conversation in which I praise my hosts and ask about pets.

I am up early the next morning to catch my bus to the vineyards, and I find Liba tending a pot of boiling water in which floats a large, pink kielbasa, my breakfast. "Liba, no!" I grab her arm and give her a haggard look. She understands and spoons some Nescafe into a cup for me.

In the next room I hear my own drunken voice. It takes me a moment to recognize myself. Higher-pitched than I imagine myself to sound. Could it be nervousness? Even after all the wine? And yes, wholly cheerful, determinedly oblivious to the tension at home, light and positive about my travels and my hosts. Just as well, for Valer, who has stayed the night, is playing and replaying this tape he has secretly made of my phone conversation the night before.

I pretend not to hear and quickly prepare for my outing. Valer drives me to the bus depot. I sleep the entire way on the bus. The driver wakes me at the end of his route. I am surrounded by large, flat stubble fields. After a short walk to the centre of the small town, which is shuttered and still, I make a few inquiries and find that all the wineries and tasting rooms are closed on Mondays. Relieved though depressed, and actually hungry, I wander for a while, not quite able to enjoy the long views, finding the wind chilly, missing home and the familiar, forgetting how hard it was. A good hot lunch is available at the bus depot cafeteria. Goulash. My hangover has subsided to the ravenous point. I clean my plate and catch the afternoon bus back to Brno, where Valer is waiting to take me out for goulash. And pivo. Starobrno is the ancient local brand of beer, of which he is justifiably proud.

Afterwards he is pleased to tell me that we are to visit some special friends. Georgian Mafia, I think he says. Though at another point in the conversation it comes out as Georgian minister. Either way I have trouble raising any enthusiasm. I am again stuffed and longing for bed. We arrive at what might be an office building but seems to be a block of private apartments. I am wearing a scruffy, loose grey sweatshirt, sneakers and jeans. Valer's special friends are in business attire. A woman in a smart suit and heels is freshly made up. I try to shake hands tidily, and before I am allowed to sit, Valer's arm on my elbow guides me to an enormous table of pastries that has obviously been laid out just for me. Thick cream atop chocolate and hazelnut, pastries filled with cream and topped with more cream. When I am back home recounting this scene to my Czech neighbour, I describe a particular rectangular pastry covered with cocoa-coloured cream. "Ahh!" His eyes widen and gaze heavenward, his hands clasp in reverie. "Little coffins! How I loved them as a child!"

The woman opens a bottle of vodka and hands me a dinner-sized plate. They all watch as I make my selections. Valer offers me orange drink with fizzy water, or vodka. Or both: "Mishmash?" he suggests. I opt for the fizzy orange. I have nothing to say to Valer's special Mafia/minister friends, nor they to me, even if we did share a language, which we don't. I am miserable in more ways than I can tally. But I try: Thirty. Hungover. Directionless. Rumpled. Unilingual. Unmanicured, seriously unmanicured (I find I am staring at the smartly attired woman's hands), and jewellery-less. Alone. Alone even when I am not alone. Stuffed. And, judging by the way my loose jeans aren't anymore, at least five pounds fatter. I haven't gone for even one run since I've been here. Well-laundered strangers are smiling at me, gesturing at a table full of calories. I reach for another pastry, this one topped with a sweet curd cheese that, even feeling as I am, is worth it. I catch Valer's eye and nod in the direction of the vodka. This not thinking—maybe it just takes practice.

Na zdravi! Your health!

THE PHARAONIC VIBE

JULIA SELINGER

APRIL 2013

I wake up alone, in pain, in a strange hotel bed. A faint glow from the first fingers of dawn is creeping in the edges of the window. I think the call to prayer must have been what roused me, but I am accustomed to sleeping through it by now. Every morning the muezzin calls, *Prayer is better than Sleep*. I don't agree.

I lie quietly, taking stock of my body, assessing my abilities to function, to rise. I gently adjust, carefully easing onto a flat back to avoid any contact with the angry incisions on my chest and the bruised and tender area where the frankenstein knob of portacath rises, surgically implanted in my other side. Eventually I stir, reaching for the pain medication, ineffectual as it is. Pain relief in an Islamic country is abysmal. They lop off a body part and the nurse offers you Panadol, as if you only have a headache. "Don't worry, Madam," the same nurse exhorts. "You will get through this. You white people can be very courageous." She looks bewildered when I laugh so hard I can hardly breathe. I may have peed myself a little.

Full consciousness arrives in increments, and I remember that I have awoken in Luxor. Today I will walk in the Valley of the Kings. Earlier this week I was inside a pyramid in Cairo. A freaking pyramid! I stood before the Sphinx with its ruined nose and shivered. This journey is my gift to myself before I leave this side of the planet. It is my reward for completing the year of cutting, puncturing, poisoning and burning meant to save my life.

Everyone thinks I am crazy. It is not just the matter of my sickly and debilitated female self stubbornly insisting on this solo excursion. This is, after all, the Arab Spring. Cairo is in and out of a state of emergency. Sadly, I didn't get to see the museum at Tahrir Square; the driver wouldn't go there. Demonstrations, he explained. No one is going to Egypt. There is not a single cruise ship on the Nile. Fleets of feluccas sit moored and empty along shore. There were more men offering camel and pony rides at Giza than there were tourists to accept them. I felt sorry for them, but I have ridden enough camels. Besides, everyone knows it is one price to get on the camel and take your ride into the desert, but a much steeper price to be permitted to return and get off that camel.

The staff at the hotel are largely idle. There are few guests to care for. They seem genuinely pleased to see me, grateful that I apparently don't read or heed the ominous travel advisories. Their faces split into wide grins as they spy me across the hotel gardens. They wave and call out in booming voices, "Welcome back!" It makes no difference that I have never been here before. "Welcome back!" A uniformed employee rushes over to me, his face glowing. "Welcome back! Are you happy?" he asks me. Yes, I decide. I am happy.

I spend a couple of days in Cairo at the home of friends before heading to Luxor on my own. My hosts are firmly in agreement with my Egyptian friends back home that I should not venture out alone, considering the current political climate. I can tell they are also somewhat alarmed at my diminished appearance: a sliver of the woman they knew in Dubai. They generously arrange a guide while they are at work, a slender Egyptian woman in a long swirling skirt. A knowledgeable and passionate historian, she has a comforting air of serenity about her I am drawn to, and I immediately like her. She tells me that the story of the Sphinx's nose getting shot off by French legionnaires is false. She leads me through the Citadel of Salah Al-Din, its shrubbery manicured into the names of Allah, as if the Arab brother of Edward Scissorhands had run amok. We visit the Hanging Church, an astonishingly suspended splendour, the air inside redolent with frankincense. Later, wandering through the vast Khan el-Khalili souk, she cautions me not to speak to any vendors. They are relentless, she warns, and will not leave me alone even if all I say is no. She thinks I might even pass for Egyptian, if only I would hide my camera, as apparently I tie my head scarf in an Egyptian manner. I had no idea. It's just fastened with a simple bow, the only scarf technique I have mastered, aside from Pirate and Aunt Jemima, neither a successful look for me. This is not hijab. This is what bald looks like. My clothes are uber modest today, after yesterday's unpleasant encounter with a scary old man at the Giza pyramids. He had unsavoury things stuck in his beard. It was the head scarf that did it. My arms and legs were covered but a fair swath of skin was visible below my neck—more than adequate coverage for a tourist but not acceptable for a Muslim woman. He spoke loudly and angrily at me in Arabic. I got the gist of it. I kept glancing over at a nearby blond tourist sporting cleavage in a tight pink T-shirt, hoping he might redirect his efforts towards her. Perhaps she is beyond saving.

For my daughters, I buy silver earrings with lapis inlay in the shapes of ankhs and scarabs. I keep forgetting not to speak to the souk vendors. I am Canadian. I say no thank you and sorry in my sleep, and in the market I smile and say it automatically, although I say it in Arabic. I chat briefly, ask questions at a few stalls. No one plagues me, despite my guide's predictions. More than one compliments the apologetic smile I flash with abandon. But not when the camera is out. The camera breeds hostility. I confess to my guide that I am not doing well on the no speaking thing and she wryly comments that she noticed. I can't help voicing my belief that it is wrong to perpetuate this ignorant tourist behaviour of hysterical blindness, with in turn the locals harassing the shit out of travellers until they flee. She smiles politely, but I get the feeling I might be an idiot having a lucky day.

My children are natural masters of foreign interaction. Expat kids, third-culture kids, they feel quite comfortable in unfamiliar cultures and surroundings. I have rarely travelled alone since I became a mother, toting my eager offspring along through more than a score of different countries. It feels strange to be in Egypt without them. Right about now, I figure the oldest one would be pleading with an artisan to let her have a try at whatever it is they are making, and the youngest one would be busting out her schoolgirl Arabic skills in the secret hopes of a reward. The now-familiar pangs of longing and despair clutch at my chest as I forcefully push away the pervasive Bad Thoughts, thoughts of the distinct possibility I will not survive to witness the unfolding of their remarkable lives. Unthinkable, unthinkable, unthinkable …

Cairo is littered with an endless array of unfinished buildings, most of them occupied. Curious conical dovecotes adorn their roofs. These brick structures are exempt from the tax levied on completed buildings and will never have facades built. They are inhabited in various states of construction, many alarmingly ramshackle, yet immensely superior to the sprawling city slums lacking in any kind of infrastructure or basic facilities. We drive past the City of the Dead, where squatters fill miles of densely packed mausoleums, residing amongst the remains of deceased strangers. I am informed that these tomb dwellers are considered fortunate in this deteriorating landscape, teeming with millions of unrecognized poor scrabbling to secure any type of rudimentary shelter. The wealthy make their homes in suburbs, separated from the squalor where revolution foments and now violently erupts with increasing regularity.

Later in the evening, my hosts throw a small dinner party in their home. The guests are all expats, mainly Brits. One woman is fairly frothing about Bloody Canadians when I walk into the room. I listen politely in silent amusement until our hostess breaks in and reveals, "J is Canadian." Ranting Woman has the good grace to blush and apologizes profusely, explaining she is married to a Canadian and it is he who has drawn her wrath. Later in the evening, she goes off on a tangent about how much she hates Fucking Egyptians and doesn't appear to be slowing down until once again our hostess cuts in, this time to inform her that "J is married to an Egyptian." Just for the record, I'm not actually, but it was quite a lot of fun to see Ranting Woman blanch and sputter. "Oh God, are you really?!!" she asks. I nod and look disgusted. The rest of the night goes by in a blur and I drink too much wine, cackle too loudly, blowing away my Polite Canadian Guest status. Early the next morning I hop a plane to Luxor.

I have heard that the beach resort of Sharm el-Sheikh is the only place left in Egypt with tourists. Luxor certainly has few. The visitors are sparse at Karnak, where the long rows of sphinxes flanking the entrance stand sentry. I meander through the immense colonnade in quiet contemplation and awe. Luxor Temple is even quieter, almost completely empty. I spend some time wandering and drinking in my ancient surroundings until a vague feeling of unease washes over me. I become uncomfortably aware that the temple is deserted as far as I can see. A shadowy *galabeya*-clad figure detaches himself from a nearby pillar. I recognize him as one of the temple "caretakers" who wants to make a few coins by leading me to the best temple photo ops. I decline and hurry back to the gate where my guide waits, the beckoning caretaker trailing in my wake.

I'm not liking my Luxor guide a whole lot. As in Cairo, having one seems to be mandatory for a lone woman, in stark contrast to my home in Abu Dhabi where I go as I choose, in relative freedom and safety. I arranged him through the hotel, and he is a brusque young man, a recent university graduate with not enough employment. He gives his rote speech at each destination in a flat voice. He points to a statue of a pharaoh with his giant foot over the necks of three warriors. "It was important for Pharaoh to show power over his enemas," he says. I snort. "His what?" I snicker a bit inside like a schoolchild when he repeats himself. "His enemas. Pharaoh had many enemas."

I have requested that longer history lessons be given in the shade while I sit, and that he walk more slowly, have explained I am not feeling well, but still he motors ahead, looking vaguely annoyed at my slow pace.

Back at the hotel, I am too exhausted to eat supper. I feel shattered. My body is not up to this trip. I eat my battalion of meds with a granola bar and go to sleep.

Brusque Young Man is waiting to take me to the Valley of the Kings. He seems to move even faster today and I allow irritation to seep into my voice. "Excuse me, but I did mention yesterday that I am unwell. I just spent a year in bed, and there is no way I can keep up with you. You must slow down, please." He comes to a halt, stares at me for a moment and blinks, possibly noticing that my scarf isn't covering any hair. Remarkable how few people notice that my scarf lies smooth and tight to my scalp. "Do you have breast cancer?" he blurts out. "My mother has breast cancer and she also has been in bed for a year. Are you Christian?" he inquires in a rare moment of animation, eagerly displaying the dark blue cross tattooed into the webbing between his thumb and forefinger, marking him as a Coptic.

Well holy cow, that was a weird exchange.

Brusque Young Man becomes less so after that, but he doesn't suddenly become solicitous and is only somewhat friendlier. He never loses a certain stiffness that is possibly inherent but I suspect is largely due to my presence.

Hatshepsut's Temple has many, many stairs. I regard them resolutely. It is worth it, no question. Hatshepsut was badass. She ruled during a time when a word for a queen regent did not yet exist in the Egyptian language, only that for consort. She was a warrior and is widely regarded by historians as one of the most successful pharaohs, bringing prosperity and innovation during her reign. Her exquisite mortuary temple, in Deir el-Bahari, is carved into a cliff face that rises sharply above it. I convince myself that I can feel a strong female energy in this place and open myself to it, wanting to be infused by some type of ancient strength, some uniquely feminine power to restore my depleted wells. Much later I discovered Hatshepsut died of cancer and wished I could unknow it. Giggling schoolchildren come running up the stairs, breaking the spell with their shining little heads. A couple of them speak to me, ask me where I come from. In my broken Arabic, I offer that I am Canadian and I have daughters their ages. They titter, and although I am reasonably certain of what I have told them, I wonder briefly if I may have had an "enema" moment myself.

The Valley of the Kings looms ahead. Monotone, sere, it stretches out into the desert, cloaking its secret treasures. A long arcade separates the car park and the entrance to the valley. Almost immediately upon our arrival, a bookseller approaches, reminding me that photography is strictly prohibited inside the tombs and offering his slim souvenir volumes. Tall and lean, he has smooth caramel skin and smells like amber. I promise to remember him and consider his wares on my way out.

We reach the entrance and my guide inspects the list of tombs open for the day, available for viewing on a rotating basis. He selects three to recommend to me. Tutankhamen is not among them. Not only does the boy king's tomb require a separate fee to enter, he explains, but it is among the least impressive in the valley, with little ornament and having been emptied of all the riches that have garnered it so much fame. Older, more powerful pharaohs with the advantage of years and resources boast the most elaborate tunnels and chambers. I take his word for it and go with his suggestions.

I sit and listen to Brusque Young Man give his monotone delivery about the sites he has chosen. He then joins the small yet boisterous gathering of waiting guides as I steadily make my way toward the tomb of Ramses III. I enter, my head swivelling, slowly taking in the visual feast surrounding me. The Valley of the Kings normally sees upwards of seven thousand visitors a day and there are cordons inside many of the tombs to direct the procession of tourists. Typically, one follows in a queue to the end of the site and then back, proceeding at a constant pace with the flow of bodies. Like a ride at an amusement park, the amount of time it takes is never long enough to satisfy, leaving one with a wistful mix of disappointment and exhilaration when it is over. This is not the case today. The valley is lucky to attract three hundred visitors per day lately. This means I can spend as long as I choose in each tomb. I can lean back, my face tilted upward, and gaze uninterrupted at the Pharaoh god's travel across the night sky of the ceiling fresco, until my neck muscles protest. I can inspect at leisure any detail my eye falls upon and wish I was fluent in hieroglyphics. It sounds cliché because it is, but I get goosebumps. My skin tingles in the cool atmosphere of this regal and mysterious place, filled with its sacred ghosts of millennia past. The disjointed feeling I couldn't shake earlier in the morning, as I stood engulfed by the towering shadows of the broken Colossi of Memnon, is now replaced by one of unaccountable fulfillment. I think I must be experiencing the Pharaonic Vibe.

Passing back through the souvenir arcade to reach the car park, I tell one stall keeper after another that I have promised my sale to another already. Before long, my bookseller approaches and I discreetly remove some cash from my purse and pay him for the books I have chosen. Mistake. I really should have thought to have him escort me to the end of the arcade before completing my purchase, but it didn't occur to me. The instant they see me buy something, I am rushed by every vendor in the place. I walk briskly toward my car, and the small throng surrounding me, moving with me, is admittedly uncomfortable, but I figure it's their job to sell me stuff and I am not really rattled by it. Their aggressive nature parallels the desperation they must feel to be paying the high licensing fee for this coveted area, which currently draws no custom. I keep moving ahead until one man puts his arm across my chest and physically restrains me. He could have grabbed my arm, touched me practically anywhere else and I would have kept my cool, but when he makes contact with my chest, I freak out, and I freak out loudly, somewhat inappropriately. I scream a long blue streak at him ending with the accusation that he is a Big Sinner. Everyone stares and he releases me. I re-evaluate the advice of my guide at the souk in Cairo.

Later, back at the hotel, I chafe at the travel restrictions and long to walk along the verdant banks of the Nile by myself, despite the fact that by this point I can barely put one foot in front of the other and pause frequently, my gait swaying with exhaustion. At the concierge's suggestion, I opt instead for high tea on the hotel terrace, with its magnificent Nile view at sunset. I grew up looking at the Nile River, on the wall of our living room in Canada. My mother often painted scenes from the pages of *National Geographic*, and my favourite work of hers depicts children bathing in the Nile, a boulder inscribed with hieroglyphics hovering in the foreground. This river has inhabited my dreams as long as I can remember. It carries a magical presence for me, imbued by a lifetime of childhood longing. I am the sole patron on the veranda this evening, and a waiter approaches quickly, the bright red fez perched atop his head bobbing in his haste. Another single woman appears and the waiter turns back to inquire if he should seat her at my table. He looks deflated when I demur and seats her at the table directly beside mine on the large and otherwise empty terrace. We exchange brief pleasantries and then sit in companionable silence, gazing at the blazing neon orb slowly sinking into the river before us. Our tea eventually arrives, accompanied by tiered silver trays arranged with tiny cakes in lurid colours one generally doesn't associate with food, and we fall into conversation. The waiter reappears to refresh our teapots, and I somewhat sheepishly request he move her things to my table after all. He looks quite pleased by this. The other woman tells me she is in Egypt as a volunteer, teaching business skills to local women. I am impressed and wish that I were here on such a selfless mission, that my purpose were more noble and profound than "Hey, I am still alive and I got out of bed and went to see the pyramids!" Survivor—I love/mostly hate that word. Awesome Volunteer Woman's trip is also coming to a close, and she is spending her last days here sightseeing before returning to her home in Bali. It so happens that I am wearing a handmade shirt I purchased in Ubud, and we smile at the small-world connection when she reveals that is the same village she lives in. No other diners arrive, and once the sun has set, the terrace closes for the evening with our departure. I am loath to leave, as I must fly back to Cairo in the morning, and then home to the Gulf.

My measure of Egypt has run out too quickly and so has my life in the Middle East. I return home to Abu Dhabi and begin the painful process of packing up my daughters and our belongings in preparation for our move to Canada. I sell my car and my stove for less than I would like, but I lack the energy to hold out for a better price. I end up giving away my washer and dryer. I have been an expat for most of the past twenty years and I am not ready to repatriate. My children, however, are ecstatic. They think they miss snow. They are delusional. Still, I am twelfth-generation Canadian, and I will always be home when I go there. It is comforting and familiar, but I'm not quite ready to be comforted yet.

THINGS THAT DIDN'T HAPPEN

JANE EATON HAMILTON

Why not February?

1)
That day I landed in Paris, alone, no French to pout my lips, anti-gay protests spilled into the streets, shooting rapids of hatred. Queers had to navigate them, no oars. When I walked down Avenue Henri-Martin to find an open store, I looked like what I was: a MEC-bedecked North American dyke, shapeless as a continent. Two men radared in. Their words hatcheted toward me on streams of spittle; vitriol tones language. The guy closest shoulder-checked me and I stumbled into a wall, scraping limestone.

Then they were gone, and I still needed oranges.

2)
A week later, Rue de la Pompe, arrondissement 16, outside Casino supermarket. Serrated needles of rain raking sideways. No umbrella, just a thin wire pull-cart I needed to pile with groceries if I wanted to eat, launder, shampoo.

A Roma girl hunched on the street, no coat, one-shoed, hair divided into oleaginous shanks functioning as eavestroughs. Shoulders heaving. One foot maimed, red, shaped like a soup bone, the raw socket of a cow's tibia. A paper begging cup exhausted by rain crumpled under her left knee.

Trafficked, I thought, tears and misery the tools of her job. Maybe later, when she was plucked off the sidewalk, the gratitude of Stockholm Syndrome or familial bonds or simple lack of options would keep her in her place, but for now, thrown to the Paris pavement by her pimp or aunt or older brother, she was the picture of all that was wrong and nothing that was right.

My anger in Paris was a simmering thing, small at first, then growing. It was at first the size of the palm of a hand laid against a hot burner, but it flared. It was that worst thing, that touristic thing, impotence with a strangling desire to "help."

"Madame, ça va?" I said as I pressed soggy pastries, fruit, hidden money into her hands. Nothing that would make it better. Nothing that would buy her options.

What do I want with pastries*?* her eyes said. *Are you* kidding *me?*

She was right; I was an asshole in any language.

3)

Colours of paint for women's skin. Words to describe love between women. Sweet love. Soured love. Dancing women. Women laughing. Women being exploited. Corrective rape. Women being murdered. Women of all races. Women honoured. Exiled women. Women rising at night to mother. Dependent women. Trafficked women. Women in poverty. Battered women. Women in marriages. Affluent women. Women in lesbianism. Women leaving womanhood. Women arriving at womanhood. Women who made scientific discoveries. Women who saved chimpanzees/pigs/dogs/elephants. Women in literature, in art. Women and feminism.

Hamilton, get a goddamned life, I told myself.

4)

And always my pressing question: *Am I just one wife away from welfare?*

5)

Paris, five intentional weeks alone.

I'd been married for eighteen years to an able-bodied woman, and she had been my legs. I wanted to see if, alone, I had legs of any kind at all. Legs that could transport me toward a future.

Was my cerebellum, at least, capable of squats?

6)

At the mouths of metros, mothers slept next to children all in a row, biggest to smallest, as if their mattresses were magic carpets flown out of bedrooms on purpose because the pavement was memory foam, because it was the *best place to be.*

(They dreamed of roast beef and dripping sauces. They dreamed nightmares of their social workers. They dreamed of men who pushed them, pulled them, threw them down. They dreamed of labours where the children arrived as cotton candy, able to turn the world on with a smile. They dreamed of Elysian Fields where poppies blew them toward extinction.)

Watching the babies, I thought: The adults of tomorrow.

Tell me what happened, I wanted to say to the mothers. *Wake up. What the hell happened to you? Wake up. Wake up. Wake up. Tell us how to fix this.*

One social security net with gaping holes, mothers teetering on the lips of buildings, babes in arms, almost falling, falling, falling—

7)

Why do you notice these things, Hamilton? Walking down the street with you is not like walking down the street with anyone else I know. Stop meeting people's eyes. You almost got knifed last time you were here. Didn't it teach you a goddamned thing?

I almost got knifed because a man had a knife and planned to use it.

Because you looked at him.

Oh, well, then. I looked at him.

Don't look at people. Ne pas regarder les gens.

8)

Years ago, I stood in food bank lines with my little girls, begging scraps. I couldn't have purchased a cup of coffee, a barrette, a Care Bear.

9)

Eventually, I married a doctor.

10)

Who left me after eighteen years. Who wanted to send me back onto the streets to beg, only now not at thirty and healthy, but at sixty and disabled. I was sliding toward asphalt but just hadn't landed.

11)

In Paris, a few boring things happened and a few boring things didn't happen.

12)

I stood by dog crap in vaporous light, unable to move forward. I was seconds away from a slump, to knees, to my side. Short of breath, angina, hips screaming, ankles puffed and pit-able, long muscles shrieking. *Measure your pain out of ten*, I heard my doctors say. "Eight," I whispered on Rue de Franqueville.

After that, I sat wrapped tight in ice packs and could not go out again for many days until the pain wore away, and so, marooned, while on a bridge not far away lovers' locks, ridiculous things, pulled down cement, I painted and wrote. I slept. I wasted Paris.

What I wrote was perhaps identical to what I might have written in Vancouver. What I painted was perhaps identical to what I might have painted in Vancouver.

13)

In my borrowed flat, indoors, it was not Paris. Nor London, nor Luxembourg, nor Athens, but stateless and devoid of personality. I couldn't go out until my larder was stripped bare and choice was minimal. And even then, to go out was only to invite more pain. I hung my paintings on the walls as I produced them. There were a lot of them, minimal things, all done on paper for ease of carrying home, a painting a day.

When I ventured out, rolling across acute bursitis, rolling through heart failure and torn rotator cuffs, rolling through tendonitis and arthritis and ulnar pain, I gazed at the pale limestone walls, the architectural details, the sky pushed impossibly far overhead and I said: *It's still Paris.* A trick of the light. A trick of a plane ticket.

A trick of being unmoored from the life where I thought I would live until death.

Constant pain is only sometimes synonymous with unhappy.

It was Paris. And since it was Paris, I reasoned, something was bound to happen.

14)

Small things happened:

My friend A, from China, arrived for a quick overnight and brought me thick tubes of paints and reams of delicious paper. We went to look at an art deco exhibit at Palais de Tokyo and took weird photographs of the Eiffel Tower through its rain-slicked windows. Pansies opened in my flat's courtyard. I met D, a psychoanalyst/artist. A friend from Medicins Sans Frontiéres blurred through town and we attended an exhibit of young European photographers, and over bread, cheese and wine we discussed what evasive actions she needed to take given that a nearby Syrian medical team had been kidnapped—an IUD to minimize her periods/pregnancy, get her eyes fixed. Ways to be less vulnerable. See. Don't get pregnant. Don't bleed. I met with a poet, and this poet decided to translate a piece of mine for a lit mag in France. I met with a non-fiction author who was writing about the lesbian artist Rosa Bonheur, and a novelist finishing a book on assisted suicide in Switzerland. I went with the psychoanalyst to the Poo-poo, to dinner, to the Lesbian Archives. In a burst of physical stupidity, I trekked to Auvers-sur-Oise with a friend from London to visit Vincent van Gogh's gravesite.

15)

Things that didn't happen: I didn't grow a set of balls to start helping out the tormented women left to rot on Paris streets.

16)

I wept in front of only two paintings: *Woman with Blue Eyes*, Modigliani, 1918, at Musée d'Art Moderne de la Ville de Paris, and *Fille rousse*, Modigliani, 1915, at L'Orangerie.

Colours and brushwork jumped. Like the models themselves,

I became, myself, canvas. Modigliani painted me. I was touched with sable fibres, a cloth, turpentine, fingers.

17)

Define an ekphrastic experience?

18)

There really was so little women's art.

19)

Something female happened to me, though—here and there. On my other major hike, into Montmartre, I stood in Suzanne Valadon's house scrutinizing the paucity of her sketches. In the Pompidou, from a wheelchair D pushed, I saw Louise Bourgeois's last works on paper. At the women's centre, I opened the tome of the book Anna Klumpke wrote about her lover. I held buttons from feminist protest marches in 1970s Paris.

I laughed and talked with women long into many nights, so something definitely happened to me.

Although nothing changed me.

20)

Maybe this inchoate thing I craved was not satisfiable. Maybe what was to happen to me was not satisfaction, but, eventually, sooner than later, only death.

But I had stood with the hooded man and his scythe and had been revived and been set down like a milk bottle into these Parisian streets. Please, please, couldn't I skim a little milk from under the cap?

21)

One week a friend told me that Mavis Gallant had died and invited me to her funeral. It poured all night the night before, and I woke and fell asleep and woke and fell asleep again dreaming of umbrellas. I was too shy to go even there alone, but I forced myself out the door, down the elevator, across the courtyard. I had a hat and gloves. I had bought reasonable pants in a second-hand store. I short-stepped to the Rue de la Pompe metro, down into its filthy noisy depths, and stood wide-legged on the platform. Four minutes, three minutes, two minutes, one minute and then I was pressed up against a man in a Canadian winter hat. I changed trains from the M9 to the M4 at Trocadéro, and then we rose to the light on line M4, and on our left pressed the Eiffel Tower, close enough to be stripped of its romance, to be just rusted metal pick-up sticks.

I scoured faces on the metro looking for some sign of shared humanity, whether, for instance, our aspirations collided (the longing for warmth and affection, a new carpet or pair of shoes, money), the point at which we acknowledged we were more the same than we were different. I thought, *If there were an emergency in the tube, these are the people with whom I would share it, who would variously help me or step over me, whom I would crawl to.* Which one of us would become a hero, which one would lie broken, which one would sneak away like a cur? *What are your stories?* I wondered. *Which of you is on the way to a birthday party, an English class, a violin lesson, or is going home from an assignation? Which of you has just fallen in love, or lost love? Which of you has danced this week? Which of you is stunted with boredom and complacency?* People moved through the underground muted, their human-ness turned to low.

Used to a car, public disaffection shocked me. In every train there was a woman whose portrait I longed to paint. In every train there was one man I wanted to sketch. In every train, some situation worthy of Mavis's short fiction played out—secretively, between seats, a woman slid her hand toward another woman; a little kid hopped along on crutches, then kicked someone in the ankle; a young woman in a purple hat touched the hair of an old woman sitting next to her so tenderly I ached; a man scratched his groin; a girl picked her nose; a baby chortled and her mother laughed back, delighted.

But most eyes were glazed over, dazed, unamazed: *I do not notice; I am not vulnerable. You can't see me, you can't hear me, you can't smell me.*

The week before, Mavis Gallant was able to do very human things. What was she now? I wanted to shake strangers on the metro. *Tell me, what is death? Goddamn it, tell me. Stop keeping this big secret. What is death?*

Montparnasse Cemetery. Man Ray, Jean-Paul Sartre, Simone de Beauvoir, Susan Sontag, Samuel Beckett. Once Sartre said to de Beauvoir that he wanted to love her with an open door.

A grave is not an open door. On the contrary. But it was through a grave that we had now to love Mavis.

22)

Given we were all going to die, all we mourners, and very soon (relatively), were we making every moment matter? Could we rise toward the valiant, the foolhardy, toward forgiveness?

23)

My wife had taken me to Paris just before we broke, when she already despised me and was with someone new, and I felt her estrangement but hoped whatever it was would sort itself out because we were an item, a long luxury of love. I was baffled over the purpose of the trip—could it have been that she just wanted to impress the new woman with tales of her largesse?

Was her estrangement, there, the softer version of what shortly became her hard workboot to the door?

(Whoever leaves the marital home loses. Whoever has less income loses. Who knew this going out?)

That week with my wife in Paris, I walked a thousand times as much as I could, so that, in memory, pain is what I recall. *Paris is a city for walkers,* my wife kept saying. I hobbled up the hills of Montmartre and along the Seine under the water jets of Paris Plage, pain in my feet, my diseased hips, pain radiating from my heart, anginally, trying hard to keep up with her, begging her for cabs, and still she kept saying, *Too bad, too bad. This would be a lot of fun if you weren't handicapped.*

She said, *Paris is really not a city for people like you.*

24)

Once a new friend invited me out, and I, without a phone and too myopic to follow a map, and too language-challenged to understand instructions from people I stopped, got lost, and walked and walked, and then I could not walk any longer, or ask again, and saw a metro with its sleeping mother and children, and I went past them in silent shrieks of pain down the stairs and home, standing my friend completely up.

25)

There were only about fifty people at Mavis's funeral, most of whom knew Mavis well. Mavis had been my tutor at the Writing Studios at Banff in the early nineties and gave me her address in Paris, but I did not write her, since I had no function to offer her beyond that of sycophant.

We were a small procession at the Montparnasse Cemetery for a small Catholic roadside service. It had been pouring; the sun came vividly through the quince blooms. Marilyn Hacker read a John Donne poem, and Mary K. MacLeod, Mavis's executor, read biblical verses. Some others of her friends spoke. The gathered sprinkled holy water on her coffin. The minister read the 23rd Psalm and the Lord's Prayer and exhorted us to kindness. Pallbearers carried Mavis's coffin to the Péron family *caveau* and lowered it on ropes. Each of us then dropped in a long-stemmed white rose. I was surprised to see that the casket was perhaps fifteen feet down; the deep, dark hole knocked the wind out of me, the blond casket with its subterranean river of white roses, and I started crying. I watched the cemetery workers struggle to put the stone on the grave, sliding it incrementally over a thick metal rod and with crowbars and shims made of fragments of wood, finally settling it into place. I could not bear this; it was hard not to anthropomorphize the dead Mavis. I'm sure I was not alone in my urge to rescue her, to lift her in my arms and run on swift feet down Boulevard Edgar-Quinet. *Do something, do something*, I thought and looked wildly at the mourners. I longed to shout, but then it was too late, the lid was firm in its place. A man with a caulking gun sealed Mavis Gallant into the Earth. Bouquets of flowers were set into place, and Mary K. gave us each a yellow rose to take away with us. Later I would fasten this yellow rose, dried, into my scrapbook, and I would hold my hand against it, thinking about Mavis, for some reason about her short story "Scarves, Beads, Sandals," about Montparnasse.

26)

I sank into the catacombs below Paris. It was foolhardy of me to go alone. There was a long walk (*les carrières de Paris*), many stairs, and I could easily become trapped by either claustrophobia or heart failure.

In the late 1700s, Paris cemeteries began to overflow and grow in height, and in inclement weather skeletons began to crumble into citizens' basements. Decisions were made to exhume the bodies from nine graveyards and re-inter them into quarry tunnels below the city. For years, at night, horse-drawn carts pulled black-shrouded wagons across the restless city until fully six million skeletons had been moved.

Workers stacked the bones, fibula on fibula, skull and skull.

For more than a hundred years now, people had paid to walk among them. To contemplate whatever we contemplated there.

Ghost-din. Deaths from plague, from fever, from childbirth, from accident, from abuse. Someone had written, *Pour moi, mort est un gain. Pour moi, pour moi, pour moi,* I whispered.

27)

I stood at 27 rue de Fleurus imagining Picasso, Bracques, Barnes, Beach, Hemingway, Cézanne, the Cones, Matisse. Stein, Toklas. All dead. I stood under 5 rue Guy de Maupassant imagining Tamara de Lempicka. Dead. I stood in Montmartre imagining Suzanne Valadon falling from the circus tightrope, a fall that led her toward modelling and then painting. Dead. Her son dead.

Death rose up from the streets of Paris. Death: Paris's exhalation.

28)

A man on the subway played "Evening in Paris" on the accordion. It was the three-year anniversary of the date I left my marriage, and I was very grateful it had been that long. She wanted to endlessly fight but the battling only hurt my heart, sapped my strength, stole my money.

We'd renewed our vows under the Eiffel Tower even as she was involved with someone new. We had renewed our vows in other places, too: in a hot-air balloon over the Namib-Naukluft Park; in a tuk-tuk in northern Thailand, at the top of the Empire State Building, on elephant back in Ubud, Bali, under our rose arbour cascading with 'Ilse Krohn' and 'Ballerina.'

29)
I wondered if I would ever marry again.

30)
In the metro, my friend from London and I were stalked by two men. We retraced our steps. *What do you think they wanted to do to us?* J asked, and I answered, *Rob us, probably.* But of course the bigger story was that no woman ever exactly knew what they wanted to do, and robbery was our optimistic hope—the wallet lost, the iPhone scooped. I was aware of my vulnerability, my inability to run. We waited a few minutes, then tried again. They were still there, hiding while we hid, still intending an ambush. We got on the first train backtracking anywhere.

31)
A boy on the tube looked like young John Lennon—black fedora, mimic wire-rimmed glasses. Man of magic fingers, a deck of cards in his hands that flew alive, climbed in the air and jumped without parachutes.

32)
M9 train toward Pont de Sèvres:
I love Paris, said a bristle-haired man holding a pole.
Dude, fuck Paris, said a young woman holding on just below his hands. She switched her hair that reminded me of horses' tails into which I'd braided ribbons. *Do you love a girl? A vagina? Do you love a vagina? Ya gotta fuck the city and love a vagina. Dude, Paris! Who gives a shit? Vagina. That's where it's at.*
I don't do that kind of thing. He looked down at her, frowning.
Why the fuck not? Are you asexual? Homo? What the hell. Why the fuck not? What the fuck is wrong with you, dude? She cracked gum, blew a turquoise bubble.

I'm married.

She kicked the pole. *Married! That is so fucked up. How the fuck long have you been married? Whoa, married! Married is like some kinda thing. You're fucking married?*

I could see he didn't want to answer. He swiped at his hair. *Five years.*

Five years? Are you nuts? Dude. How the fuck long have you been together?

A pause. *Ten years.*

Like, is she here?

Now he sighed. If he could have pulled his wife through the night-wet air, right then, he would have. *No, in Canada.*

The woman laughed, pulled her chin back to say how screwed up she thought his wife was. *Well, fuck, dude, is she, like, joining you? Does she have a job?*

Yeah. Sure.

She rolled her eyes. *I mean, like, fuck, a career? Does she have a career? 'Cause a job is nothing, man. Nothing. You can fucking quit a job. A job is like McDonald's. You can quit McDonald's. Don't fucking look back. Why isn't she here?*

She has a career, he said, lips thinning.

Is she in the FBI? The RCMP? Surrey? Where the fuck is Surrey? That's in Ontario, isn't it? There's a Surrey, Ontario, isn't there?

Vancouver, he said, his voice now sullen, thick.

There's a Surrey, Vancouver? That's fucked up, dude. Ten fucking years. Dude, you totally gotta get moving. Ten years is way too long to spend with someone. How the fuck old are you? Like, you must be a hundred. I'm twenty-eight.

I'm thirty-five, he told her reluctantly.

I tried to imagine how the two of them might know each other.

She leaned forward and licked the pole. Slowly. Then she looked up at him. *Thirty-five! Dude, that means you've been together since you were twenty-five. That is so majorly fucked up. You gotta get a divorce. Do you love her?*

I love her, he said, his voice firm.

And she loves you?

She loves me. I could hear something in his voice, something about love faltering, but he didn't say more.

You gotta get a divorce, said the woman. *That's fucking pathetic. You need some vagina, dude. You seriously need vagina.*

33)
I gave myself Paris because that's where I found out my wife loved another, and didn't love me, and hadn't loved me (so she said) for thirteen years, even though during that time she asked me to marry her, joined in the court case to fight for the right to marry me and married me.

34)
I slept with the psychoanalyst.

Come here, my smoky treasure, I said, and held out my arms.

She moved to the bed, stripping her clothing.

You are too young, I said and kissed her nicotine lips, pulled long hair from my tongue.

She was an atheist, but she believed that her small grandmother had received a special dispensation to go to heaven.

35)
Things I did that were wrong just to do them. Things I would do again. Women like bowling pins I was knocking into my bed.

36)
I had raised two children. I had loved long and well and honourably, forsaking all others. I had kept the secrets she wanted me to keep about anger and violence. And still I had been catapulted into a blue beyond.

37)
In Paris, I was the spikes I'd shoved into my own heart. I was the burrs I had rubbed against my grey matter. I was the warfarin of my own rat trap.

I didn't need Paris to teach me that. I already knew that spikes, burrs and rat poison were half of all I'd managed to understand in sixty years and that understanding didn't mean cessation.

The other half was beauty. Babies. Silk. A blossom. A sunset. Eyes. A forest. An artwork. A baby goat. A woman. Grass. Poppies. Skin. Scent. Breasts. Lilacs. Ocean. Palm trees. Warm wind. Butches.

A cabin with a lake.

My youngsters.

Friends.

Work.

Hope.

38)

Why Paris in February and what was I waiting for?

Just for anything.

39)

Nothing happened in Paris except that spring arrived, daffodils like miniature sunshines across the courtyard, hopped up on renewal and promise.

THE ALCHEMIST

ELIZABETH HAYNES

WARNING: Women tourists should not in any circumstances take tours on their own or in pairs with independent guides but should stick to larger group tours run by reputable agencies.
—*Lonelyplanet.com on Bolivian jungle tours.*

We drift toward the camp spot just as dusk is settling on the brown Ibare River. Fish splash the still water. Papacho noses the boat into the bank then jumps out to haul it in. I scan for the crocodiles I've seen all afternoon slipping down the mud and into the drink. Papacho motions me out and we hike up to a clearing on the edge of the jungle where we will spend the night.

It's dark when Papacho begins setting up a tiny pup tent. Where is mine? I ask, having insisted on two tents when I hired him in the jungle town of Trinidad in Bolivia to take me up this tributary of the Mamoré River. One tent is better, he says. One tent is not better, I say. You will be frightened, he says. I will not be frightened, I say. There are caiman, jaguar, bear, he says. My country is full of bears, I say. We haven't passed a single boat all day. We are miles from anywhere.

I know nothing about this man except that his sister ran the hostel where I stayed. That exactly one waiter and one travel agent said he was a good guide. I wandered the dusty streets of Trinidad looking for other backpackers who might want to ply a river. For days, I sat in the ice cream parlour at the edge of the plaza, watching cars and motorcycles roar by and listening to sound systems trying to out "*La Vida Loca*" each other. Listening to church bells, which rang for ten minutes, took a break for five and resumed on the quarter hour.

I searched for tourists among tidy families who strolled the plaza, knots of teenagers at the *heladería*, but found no one.

Well, there was one other woman. A Frenchwoman I'd see striding around town or out to the Laguna Suárez in a pair of long hiking shorts, a button-down shirt, wool knee socks and a safari hat. She was heading to Guayamerín but told me she'd met a New Zealand couple who wanted to do a river trip. They, however, eluded me.

I debated with myself: *You've come all this way to go on a river, just hire him. It's stupid to go on your own. Papacho seems like a nice guy—but what about the German girl who was raped by her guide in Rurrenabaque? Papacho doesn't speak English—but it could be a great opportunity to practise your Spanish. You've been travelling for six months and nothing bad has happened to you—but what about the bus hijacking in Mexico? That was years ago and it was because you took a night bus.*

Shut up, I told the voices and over yet another dish of chocolate ice cream, I wrote down the pros and cons. The pros won, so I hired Papacho to take me down the river.

The first day of our trip came—as did Papacho, two hours late, on a borrowed motorcycle with no gear.

"Desafortunadamente," his friend had borrowed the motor from his boat to go fishing. He would take me to the town of Loreto to see the old Jesuit mission instead, and we would be on the river early the next day. We bumped down dusty roads, stopping to look at Jabiru storks, egrets and herons on the Pampas. An anteater ran across our path, forcing him to slam on the brakes and me to crash into his back.

Maybe it was me hanging on to his waist for dear life as other motorcycles and trucks roared by pelting us with stones and dust that gave him the "one tent" idea. Or maybe it was because I bought him a beer in Loreto while we ate *gallina picante*, hen with hot sauce, as their sisters pecked the scrubby yard. Or maybe it was just because I was a gringa alone.

The next day, the motor restored, we set off. Just me, Papacho and Gabriel García Márquez—in the form of a tattered copy of *One Hundred Years of Solitude* I'd found in Santa Cruz de la Sierra. I swung in the hammock he'd rigged for me, alternately watching the river and reading, smugly thinking it was fitting to read a book set in a remote jungle town while travelling through remote jungle. Would Papacho and I, like the novel's hero, José Arcadio Buendía, discover a Spanish galleon rooted in stone, a lushness of flowers and trees growing inside it? José Arcadio thought he had found a town surrounded by water on all sides. I was surrounded by water on all sides. Every so often Papacho called, "*Mira*," and I'd look up to see the rose-coloured fin of a *bufeo*, a pink dolphin, disappearing into brown, or a stork, its long legs hanging brokenly, cutting across the sky over the river.

We stopped for a midday lunch of piranha and hiked to a lagoon. The air was close. Papacho cut through the undergrowth with his machete until we got to the edge of the lagoon. "If a caiman attacks you," he said, "wait until it is close and then dive underneath it." Absolutely.

We stopped for an afternoon swim. "*Hay cocodrilos aquí?*" I asked. "No," Papacho said, adding that they only attack people when they're very hungry. I noticed he was in and out of the tea-coloured water in record time. I followed suit, retreating to my hammock to read my book, where Colonel Aureliano had decided to retreat from the world to become an alchemist, to fashion tiny fish out of gold.

Maybe the tent problem was just miscommunication. Papacho didn't speak English. I found his Spanish hard to understand and perhaps he found mine the same. Maybe I wasn't using the right words. The word for tent, *tienda*, also means store. The other word for tent, *carpa*, also means carp. I'd asked, "*Hay dos tiendas? Hay dos carpas?*" Are there two tents? Are there two stores? Are there two fish? Or perhaps I'd said, "*Muy necesito mi propia carpa.*" I really need my own carp. He'd answered, "*Sí, claro*," meaning, perhaps, that he'd bring his fishing rod, he'd catch me one.

Or perhaps he had expectations. Did the gringas he brought down this river come to his tienda in the middle of the night, like the women who'd silently slip into the tent of the war hero, Colonel Aureliano, to partake of his genetic bounty?

Papacho disappeared over the bank. Huddling in the dark and slapping at mosquitoes, the voices in my head resumed: *You can sleep in the boat—so can the crocodiles. You can take the boat—good luck starting the motor; it takes Papacho ten minutes. He's been nice so far—yeah, so was the man in the bus station who sold you the ticket on that Mexican bus that was hijacked.*

I shiver in the dark, slap mosquitoes, put on a sweater. What the heck is Papacho doing down there, getting into something more comfortable? Just as I decide I'll sleep in the boat, crocodiles or no crocodiles, he appears with a flashlight and a rolled-up tarp. You sure you want your own tent? he asks. *"Absoluto,"* I say. I think I'm saying "absolutely" but I could also be saying "pure alcohol." He smiles as if to say, you can't blame a guy for trying, unrolls the tarp and pulls out a second tent. As we shake it out, my shoulders and stomach muscles unclench, just as they did when the hijackers finished robbing us and left us lying on the cold ground in the middle of a field. Just as the stomachs of the women in Marquez's novel did when their husbands returned from the wars.

Outside this ring of light, a dolphin jumps, crocodiles slide in and out of the water, something snorts. A bear? A caiman? The patron saint of careless gringas? The ghost of Colonel Aureliano? Papacho himself, perhaps.

STOP TALKING ABOUT DEATH

ANN CAVLOVIC

The first things my eyes focussed on were the dried-up remains of a bug. It was just like the ones you find curled up in the corner of your room under the table where you rarely clean—belly up, with legs folded in, and hard to differentiate from the surrounding dust. This bug was a little fresher perhaps, and one of several distinct specks of dirt on the white sheet upon which I lay.

I slowly shifted my focus past those sheets to the room around me. Concrete slabs housed about ten metal beds with sheets of varying shades of white, and two smaller beds for children. An examination table to my right held a loose collection of small metal instruments of the "make-do" variety. Across the room, a young mother wearing a simple *khanga* examined her sobbing child with more fatigue than distress.

This hospital wasn't always this way. This whole country once had a higher literacy rate than Canada and decent public health care. Now, foreign items like toothpaste are available at every corner store, but the hospitals are crumbling. But I wasn't debating the impacts of globalization on Tanzania when I had arrived at the gate of this hospital—I just passed out. The strangers who had escorted me had carried me up the stairs.

It was my second day in the village of Bagamoyo, situated along the Indian Ocean north of the capital city Dar es Salaam, where I had been living as a foreigner—a *mzungu*. I had come to Bagamoyo to satiate a whim for adventure. After stepping off the bus I meandered toward an outdoor restaurant and ordered fried fish and rice. I remember the fried eyeballs of the fish and its charred grey scales. I remember

176

the local men perplexed by the sight of a woman travelling alone. I remember too the arrogance I'd feel at times like this, which I carried with me in defiance while exploring the dusty streets of the village.

The queasiness in my stomach started just after lunch the next day. Malaise set in while I tried to nurse myself with a bottle of Coke on a chair by the swooning ocean. *I'm hot, mama, I want to change my clothes. Everything's spinning so fast. I need another drink. Someone help. Someone pay attention.*

Bagamoyo used to be a collection point for slaves from Eastern Africa, before they were transported to the island of Zanzibar for final sale. The name literally translates into "Here I lay down my heart." No one knows if this refers to the cries of the slaves, or those of the slave caravan handlers. I learned this from a local teenage tour guide, the same one who sold me that bottle of Coke by extolling its medicinal properties. He walked me through the town and explained the former uses of each building, along with stories of escape attempts, abject suffering and death. I was moved but completely powerless to fully comprehend or commemorate the land on which I was standing. So when someone on the street asked if I would buy a bracelet, I did—the healing power of this action proving to be quite exaggerated.

The plan was to live in Tanzania as an outsider. I'd thus be able to comment on the injustices of global economic relations, the food, the nature of neo-colonialism and maybe some interesting facts about large insects. Specifically, I wanted to observe how people suffer under a system wounded by external forces and declare how terrible it must be for them. Yet I also wanted to live close to the people, you know, really be one with them. I expected to cross the boundaries of East Africa; I did not expect it to cross my own. I did not expect to learn that I am not too good to die.

While lying in that hospital bed and trying to understand what was happening, I tuned in to the conversation my escorts were having in the next room.

"Isn't it terrible?" said one woman. Other snippets of sounds and voices followed.

"It's never easy to deal with death," said another.

"I don't know what to do. I feel very sad."

Me, me, what's happening to me? I thought. Is this really the end? Asserting myself and my life, I used what energy I had to cry out: "Stop … talking … about … death!"

They didn't hear me.

A doctor eventually came around to perform some tests. Only after he drew blood with a razor blade did I remember to check if it had been taken from a sealed package. *Someone please take care of me.*

"Malaria," he concluded, despite the antimalarials I had been taking. In my half-dead state I was shipped home with instructions to take the prescribed yellow pills as soon as I arrived. The bus ride shot a new migraine into my head with every pothole we ran over. My housemates watched over me as the pills shocked every nerve ending in my body in their attempt to remove the malaria parasite. Sheets of pain ripped through my body whenever I moved, including blinking. Too bad these pills were only making things worse.

You are not too good to die.

No human, of course, is too good to die. Yet in East Africa, I'm treated as if I am. I could walk into any foreign clinic in the city, and the leading western medicines would be available to me. And if a mzungu is sick, total strangers will bring them to the best clinic— possibly they'll be robbed along the way, but they will arrive nonetheless. To do the same thing for a local child begging on the street would be considered a waste of time. It was in such a clinic in Dar es Salaam the next day that I learned I did not in fact have malaria; I had amoebic dysentery, a souvenir from that bug-eyed fried fish. Foreign doctors provided me with the proper medicine at an affordable mzungu rate. With bedrest and the support of my neighbours, I essentially recovered after two weeks, from both the dysentery and the damage done by the malaria treatment itself.

Just when I started feeling better, I attended a funeral for a three-month-old Tanzanian baby girl. She probably had had pneumonia but was misdiagnosed with malaria and treated for it until she could no

longer breathe. She died within two days. The default malaria diagnosis seems to be a favourite for many doctors when they don't really
know what's wrong. So this little girl and I had had similar experiences, but I survived, and she didn't.

*I am vulnerable. I am small and insignificant, but I am privileged be-
yond imagination.*

———

What I had actually been overhearing in that village hospital was not,
as I had perceived, a conversation about my own impending doom.
My escorts were discussing the weight of the deaths that are still
felt in this town like one feels the cold in my hometown. From the
miseries of being confined and transported like cargo, the majority
of captured Africans who arrived here were already dead. Those who
were sold into slavery were the survivors. *Me* ... ? Little old *me*? Well,
I was close to touching death, and yet I never really was. And I've
come home with an exotic little story to tell, just as I expected. The
hardships I thought I was facing proved to be quite exaggerated.

Awkward & Broken

MONI BRAR

O i!" he yells, followed by a string of Dhari that I fail to comprehend. His words are fittingly rapid-fire, a *rat-a-tat-tat* that come directly at me, matched by a hard gaze that unapologetically bores into me. I instantly feel small and afraid.

I try to shuffle past, head low, eyes averted, as I quickly but gingerly pick my way through the rubble-filled street that seems to be in an endless cycle of construction-destruction-construction. Over time the holes in the street only seem to get deeper, the gaps bigger and the piles of debris larger.

This time he tries English. "You! STOP!"

I come to an abrupt halt, both the distance between my friend Simon and I and the panic in my chest growing. I try to pull my headscarf forward to cover any bit of me that may have escaped and shouldn't be exposed. It's a habit that becomes more ingrained with each successive trip to Kabul. All that remain un-swathed are my face and my hands, and even these feel like a glaring taboo in this context.

"Where are you from?" he shouts at me as he moves in closer, the gun hanging over his shoulder swinging menacingly.

Looking down at his dust-covered army boots, I stammer "Canada." I feel tiny and imagine those big, dusty boots squashing me like a fly, grinding me into nothing but an ugly stain on the ground.

I glance up to sneak a quick peek at Simon and he seems to not have noticed that I've been left behind as he ambles casually toward the gate of Le Bistro. This worries me. I look over my left shoulder and both the car and driver that dropped us off have vanished as well. This worries me even more.

"Pah!"The man snickers and spits hard on the cracked, dry earth. "Where are you *really* from?"

And there it is.The eternal question, with emphasis on the *really*. As if on autopilot, I launch into my rehearsed and often-repeated response. "Well, I was born in India and my family moved to Canada when I was three…"

I'm cut off by his quick retort of "Aha! I knew it! You're not really Canadian!"There's a new smugness in his voice that makes me uncomfortable. I feel like I've been called out. I feel like a fraud. I feel that the rest of my response is not important, as he's successfully extracted the information that means the most to him.

"What part of India you from?" he continues.

"Punjab."

"Hmm. Indian-Punjabi," he muses. I'm familiar with the an-imosity toward Pakistani-Punjabis in Afghanistan and the fine line I'm riding. He seems satisfied with the answer for the moment and continues on. "What are you doing here in Afghanistan?"

I mumble something about working for a Canadian NGO, but my answer seems to matter little to him as he waves me past him before I even finish. I quicken my pace to reach Simon. He's waiting for me at the gate, gazing up at the bright sky and seems unperturbed by my delay.Without a word, we hurry in through the layers of heavy, battered gates topped with tangles of razor-wire and glinting shards of glass from broken bottles.We go through the procession of searches of body and bags, each with its own group of sinister-looking guards with guns. My time in Kabul is often a blur of gates/men/guns/repeat.

At last, we enter the courtyard of Le Bistro and breathe a mutual sigh of relief.

"Well, what was that about?" asks Simon as he scopes the court-yard of the restaurant for a free table. As usual, it's nearly full even though we've arrived earlier than usual this Saturday morning. The sizable and popular restaurant, set in the Shahre Naw district of Kabul, serves up decent French food amidst lulling music in a garden setting. The weekend draws out the expats from the insular world of their compounds to feast on crepes and lattes while they imagine being elsewhere. It is escapism at its finest in Kabul.

I look blankly at Simon, barely comprehending what he's asked me.

"What happened back there?" he asks again. "Why do you look so awkward and broken?"

"Oh, just a misunderstanding," I answer and quickly change the subject.

———

That night Simon's question gnaws at me, but that's not what keeps me up. The nights feel endless in Kabul. The busyness of work gets me through most days, but it's nights that I dread.

My work focuses on bridging the efforts of a Canadian NGO with that of an international NGO that has pressed on with its work in Afghanistan for over thirty long years. Over the course of these thirty years, the capacity they have built and the impact they have had on rural areas throughout Afghanistan is laudable. The bulk of the staff I work with are local Afghans. While their warmth and hospitality is unwavering, they seem to approach our collaboration with more and more ambivalence. Increasingly, I find myself turning toward a few expat colleagues who are from different places around the globe. On days when the safety situation is most unstable, I turn to Simon, who is becoming more and more like my human wall of protection. Between his bulking size, magnanimous smile and Dutch humour, he exudes confidence and stability, which is fitting given that he's a safety and security expert in conflict zones. He is in Kabul conducting a safety audit for the international NGO we're working with, and the employees, expats and locals alike are grateful for the contributions Simon makes.

Every night, however, I find myself alone with my thoughts. I often sit on the edge of my lumpy bed with a frayed duvet wrapped tightly around me, staring at the ancient *bukhari* stove in the corner as it spits and spews noxious fumes. It barely keeps the room warm, and its rusty exhaust pipe is held together with filthy old rags. The pipe exits the room through a rough-cut hole in the wall, which I've stuffed with old, yellowing newspapers I can't bear to look at. I'm convinced that these newspapers hold images that once seen will not easily be forgotten. The paper keeps the birds and insects out, but

more importantly, the act of using it to block out things that are unwanted gives me a sense of control in a place where I have absolutely
no control.

I sit through the better part of most nights listening to aircraft
flying overhead. Some nights they fly so low the walls shudder and
the thin windowpanes rattle. The shatterproof film on my windows
does little to reassure me, despite Simon's warnings that if I do die
in Kabul, chances are it will be as part of "collateral damage" rather
than a targeted approach, so the film may be my best bet at ensuring
safety. I hear loud booms and bangs, unsure if the source is something
as innocuous as construction or something more ominous. I feel
suffocated, not from the kerosene-scented plumes that escape from
the bukhari but from my own loneliness. This isn't the momentary
loneliness that has washed over me in other countries, but rather, it's
rooted in the undeniable fact that I feel utterly alone in this place. Of
the thirty countries I have travelled to, none is more heart-wrenching
and isolating than Afghanistan. I travel through this country as if in a
bubble—insulated, exposed, adrift, and fragile. I'm always ill at ease,
unsure and frightened. I am unwilling to let my guard down, unable
to breathe.

What broke for me in that brief encounter near Le Bistro was
the false sense of belonging and how intricately this is connected to
my loneliness. My Canadian colleagues and I had naïvely thought
that in comparison to my white-skinned peers, I was the best choice
for Afghanistan. That the combination of a head scarf, appropriate
clothing and brown skin would shield me from danger and aid me
in blending in with the Afghan landscape. It did the exact opposite.
It only highlighted the fact that I was different and positioned me as
an imposter. My broken Urdu that allowed me some communication,
my brown skin, my natural deference to men, my understanding of
a cultural sub-text—these were all superficial commonalities that we
had convinced ourselves meant more than they actually did. That day,
the guard had been successful in removing my cloak and I had been
exposed. I was just as vulnerable as anyone else.

Amongst my Afghan colleagues, I am an outsider in an endless
stream of outsiders, a temporary nuisance with unrealistic demands, a

foreigner who has come unbidden, always held at arm's length, apart and mistrusted. In the compound, the other expats don't know what to make of me. I look Afghan, but I'm not. Even in my rushed trips to Finest Supermarket to buy imported and out-of-place bright yellow lemons and Twining's tea, I feel ill-at-ease amongst the other shoppers as we avoid making eye-contact due to a heady combination of indulgence and privilege. I imagine that like me, they all rush back to consume their coveted luxury items in silence, alone with their guilt.

———

The loneliness that seeps into my bones overnight and makes them feel so heavy and brittle is alleviated each morning with the sound of the initial crackle of the loudspeaker. I've come to look forward to the prayer call that is a predictable and welcome start to the day.

Allah hu Akbar, La ilhaha illullah, wall ah hu akbar…

For these few moments, as both the sun and the sound of prayer rise on a new day, I feel some reassurance that while I may feel alone in Afghanistan, I need not feel broken.

The prayers wash over me while I lay curled up and reluctant to step out of the bed that it's taken me the entire night to warm. I bury my head further under the musty duvet. As I close my eyes and listen to the prayers warbling through the loudspeaker, they remind me of the prayers I would hear each morning in our dusty village in Punjab. There as well, the loudspeaker would crackle to life before dawn, announcing the start of a new day. The women in our household would busy themselves in the dark with starting the fire for cooking and milking the water buffaloes, and the Japji Sahib prayers from the Sikh temple, the epicentre of the village, would rouse us all awake.

In Kabul, I know that the feeling the prayers evoke is momentary and will quickly evaporate as soon as I step out. Part of this morning ritual is telling myself that while I may be in a place where much is broken, I do not need to be broken. I lie there, conjuring the courage to get up and get on with it. What awaits me today is the same every day: unpredictability, hostility and ceaseless nerve-wracking fear, yet also hospitality that is generous, and beauty in the most surprising places.

This morning, my momentary reprieve is dashed before I step outside. As my mobile phone buzzes, I glance down at the incoming text message. There's a security alert: a white Toyota Corolla has entered Kabul with explosives and a bomb threat is imminent. I carefully take note of the licence plate number and target buildings, not missing the irony of being in a city where 80 percent of the vehicles are Toyota Corollas. This is the first of many text messages I'll receive today from the local Safety and Security Advisor, Naseem. He is my source for safety intel and I rely on him to keep me informed. Upon arriving at the office each morning, my first stop is to receive security updates over a cup of green tea with cardamom in Naseem's cramped office. We start our daily conversation by politely asking each other about the welfare of our families. The conversation then shifts to suicide bombers, insider attacks and high-value targets, but is always casual and lacking the urgency or intensity one would expect for such topics. Little of what Naseem communicates to me is fed back to my colleagues in Canada. Their focus is more on the work that needs to get done and less so on the details of security. This reinforces my feeling of isolation as well as my colleagues' complacency. Over the course of two years, with each successive trip to Kabul, I feel less and less safe, and more and more alone.

I place my mobile on the three-legged stool beside my bed, take a deep breath, slough off the duvet and last night's dreams, and step out of bed to face what awaits me.

TRAVEL BLOWS THE MIND: CAUTIONARY TALES

TRYSH ASHBY-ROLLS

1960 PARIS

Waiting for takeoff at Heathrow, a fly lands on a curtain high up by the flight deck. Rubs its face with its front legs. Carries bits of shit, spreads disease from London to Paris. If that fly, so tiny and confident, can manage this terrifying journey, so can I.

"Mother birds push their babies from the nest so they learn to fly on their own," according to my mother.

Block my ears.

"It's time you ..."

By myself? I'm only seventeen.

"I never had advantages like you. My childhood was ..."

Ya ya ya. Stomp up to my bedroom.

Madame Cunin meets me at Orly Airport. Reeking of class, money and Dior perfume, hair coiffed, nails manicured and polished. Cigarette in hand, its cork tip ringed with scarlet lipstick, she drives a Citroën DS, known for its futuristic body design, along the auto route into Paris. We follow the River Seine on Voie Georges-Pompidou, turn off onto a small side street, Rue Beethoven.

The doorman takes my luggage, rings for *l'ascenseur*, a cage that grinds and clanks its way from ground to second floor. Madame shows me to my room with ensuite bath and toilet.

The view is to die for from the balcony. If I open *les portes fenêtres* and step outside, the roar of traffic almost knocks me over. Across the river is the Eiffel Tower. To left and right are bridges: Pont d'Iéna and Pont de l'Alma. Madame says my nearest *métro* station is Trocadéro. *Les jardins du Trocadéro* and the Palais de Chaillot are almost next door. Palaces and gardens are my mother's domain to which I pay scant attention except to say "been there." I don't even bother taking photos. During this initiation into solo travel I form a revulsion for the Tourist and his [*sic*] trappings: photographic equipment, maps; loud and noxious comments in English; British food with French names such as *le fish et chips*.

After breakfast (which a maid brings to my room), Madame's daughter, Marie-Christine, and I speak English for two hours in the salon, furnished with antiques similar to those in my mother's drawing room. Except ours are Chippendale and these are Louis whatever. Stuffy, claustrophobic.

At meals I watch carefully, eyes down, seeing how things are done. "In Rome do as the Romans" is one of my mother's lessons. God forbid I should do otherwise. Lunch is served in *la salle à manger* soon after Monsieur arrives from his office at French Shell. When Madame is not about he tells me to call him Jean.

Beginning explorations are of the surrounding neighbourhood. Sit in a café first, order *café au lait, crème glacée, bière* by week's end. Venturing forth I take the métro, sign up for courses at the Alliance Française, sharpen the dull edges of my spoken French and meet boys. Hang out. Cough on Gauloises cigarettes. Drink wine in sidewalk cafés on *la Rive Gauche*, the bohemian Left Bank.

The Cunin family spends weekends at a stone cottage in a hamlet halfway between Compiègne and Soissons on the River Aisne, Picardy. Sometimes Jean comes with us, sometimes not. Madame's particular interest is medieval churches. She points out elemental symbols of the old goddess religions—many of them erotic—carved into corners. We visit Maréchal Foch's railway carriage in the forest of Compiègne, where the Armistice was signed at the end of World War I. We visit Jeanne d'Arc's birthplace at Domrémy and where she died at Rouen. We see Notre Dame de Reims where French kings were crowned, and the labyrinth at Chartres—covered in chairs, apparently the only place to store them. One weekend we swim in the river at a picnic; on another I get drunk at a shoot (pheasant not film) at the Rothschild Estate. Madame is furious next day but all I remember is a Rothschild son pushing up my skirt behind a barn. I should have worn male clothes like Joan of Arc. Imprisoned, she believed pants prevented rape.

I turn my face hard against the world, keep my metaphorical radar spinning, refuse the Cunins' weekend jaunts and go off on my own. Especially after Jean propositions me, offering a fee for service.

On the Champs Elysées I make eye contact with a Black older man. He follows me into a cinema, sits behind me. Removes the pins from my Brigitte Bardot topknot. Caresses my long blond hair. I don't stop him. I don't know how.

When I leave the cinema, he follows, catches up, takes my arm. "My place?" he says. Saying no is impolite.

The room, lit by a naked bulb over the bed, contains a desk and chair, nightstand and the bed. Papers cover the desk. Piles of typewritten pages spill onto the floor. I look at the man, who says to sit down. Perched on the edge of the bed, its sheets rumpled and dirty, I watch him. He takes a white clay pipe from the nightstand. White powder from a plastic bag. Scoops some into the pipe. Strikes a match, lights it. Smokes.

"Helps me write," he says, handing me the pipe.

I smoke cigarettes. Have done regularly since my sixteenth birthday. Pipes are different. He teaches me what to do.

Feel weird. Sleepy. Cold. Lie back on the bed. Under the sheets, blanket on top. The man is next to me. I stare at the ceiling, pockmarked and slashed. I'm flush with heat as if I have a fever. Rush of adrenaline perhaps. Stand up on the bed. Snatch a knife off the nightstand. Observe myself from outside myself jab the ceiling. Stab it. Kill it. Snow flutters onto the bed, the desk, the floor. Snow drifts in a tiny room in Paris where I have come to spread my wings. Broaden my mind.

The man calls next day. Madame answers. "*C'est pour vous*," she says. "*Un homme.*"

"Tell him I'm not here," I say in French. I crave from my lips to the back of my throat whatever he put in that pipe. But I won a scholarship to drama school—against all odds. And the passion to become a classically trained actress burns deeper than that man's white powder.

1961 ROME

No seats on the train taking me to au pair in Rome this summer. Have to stand from London to the Italian border. Day and night merge except for Passport Control. The European Union and high-speed rail are years away. Half-awake in Milan station, the stink of garbage overwhelms. Passengers get out to buy snacks and coffee. I don't, in case the train leaves me behind. At the last minute I muster the courage to haul my ass from the seat, shamble down the platform to buy a *caffè con leche* and return before departure.

Dawn breaks as we roll into Roma Termini. The advertising blurb calls it "a great station to spend time in." Presumably not with feet swollen into fat puff pastries. Dispensing with my leather flip-flops, I walk barefoot along the platform into the main concourse, where I am to meet the father of the family for whom I am to … what? Look after children? Speak English? I can't remember the precise nature of the job.

Making my way to a *ristorante* decorated with plastic grape vines, I order *un gelato, spaghetti alla bolognaise e un caffè.* Then wander about looking for "a father." Without photograph, description of any sort or even a father at home since I was three years old, I don't know what, or whom, I'm looking for.

A man, eyes staring at each other across the top of his mountainous nose, comes up to me, his voice filled with concern. "What are you doing here? Who are you waiting for?"

Rome Railway Station is familiar now. I've been here six hours, found a restaurant where people make me welcome. I explain the situation to Signor Squinty. He thinks I should call home.

"Absolutely not. Tell my mother I failed? No way."

Squinty says I can't stay in the railway station. I must call somebody, do something, get help.

I remember Mummy has a friend in Rome: Betty, who works at the embassy. Squinty finds the number in the phone directory. Dials. Hands me the receiver. When I explain my predicament she surprises me. "I'll call the police," she says. "And you must catch the train home."

"After coming all this way?" Don't say it but why call the police?

She fetches me at six o'clock. Takes me to her flat. Scolds me. Scolds my mother when she gets her on the telephone, a complicated "trunk call" overseas. "Waited in Rome station over twelve hours," I hear Betty say. Mummy calls the au pair agency.

Rome police are familiar with the "father of the family." Mummy says later something about the "white slave trade and a lucky escape."

While I wait for a new placement, I take in the sights. Followed everywhere by silly young men I try to ignore. They embarrass me. I walk along the Via Appia, where crucifixions and a slave revolt occurred in a previous century. The Appian Way is cobbled, dusty, solitary. Trees point toward an indigo sky. Reaching the *Domine Quo Vadis* or Church of Santa Maria in Palmis, I go inside. Wondering whether they're fakes or not, I stare at the imprints of Jesus' feet. Then explore behind the church for what I'm told is a sanctuary dedicated to Rediculus, "Roman god of the return." Before my return to the Coliseum and Betty's place near the Spanish Steps, I rest in the shade. My feet hurt, swollen still.

The au pair job is in Reggio Calabria, the father, a gynecologist, tells me at the interview. He gives me a train ticket. Says his wife and children are there already; he will come later.

On the train I see a map, discover where I'm going—down to Italy's toe where you get the boat across to Sicily. The other passengers are all men. Not one speaks English or French. I watch Italy pass by through the window, enjoying myself. Unmolested by persons or language.

It's like a prison, the gynecologist's summer house. I sleep in an attic without amenities. A maid sleeps on a straw pallet outside my door at the top of steep wooden stairs. The family sleeps on the next floor down, with access to the main floor via a gracious marble staircase that it is my duty to clean every day. My other job is washing dishes after breakfast. There is no pot scourer or brush to strip the scummy residue off the milk pan. I scrape it off with my fingernails. Rinse it under a tap. There is no hot water.

Nobody tells me not to drink the water. That edict, I think, is only for France.

I am not allowed to go out of the house without a chaperone, even to mail a postcard. If we go to the beach I must stay on "our" side. The people "over there" look the same as us, except they laugh and play. They are not "our class" but lesser mortals, yet infinitely freer and more interesting. I wish I could live in a classless society.

At dinner, when *il dottore* is home, he bangs on his plate with a ring he sports on one of his fingers. Staff hurry into the dining room: serve food, clear dishes, fill glasses. One day everything fades to blank. I am taken to my room sweating, shivering; dozens of tiny alligators scurry across the walls and ceiling. I retreat inside myself. Sometimes it's good being ill; a way in to solitude and peace. I am sent back to England by train. Sleeper this time, my lullaby clackety clack. Clackety clack. Clickety click. Clickety click.

"Darling, you really ought to know better. No water is fit to drink from the tap except in England," my mother says.

Not sure how the water plays into an illness that, in spring, means surgery to remove a cyst the size of a grapefruit from an ovary. Drama school waits another year.

1962 FRANCE AND SPAIN

The meeting with my father is the first in eight years since those awful visitations ended. He summons me to explain why I need money to go to Paris. We eat strawberries and cream, drink chilled white wine. Not knowing how to behave with him except flirtatiously, I ask for an allowance so I may study French.

"The French lingo? Or French men?" he scowls. "You marry a frog, or such nonsense, I cut you off. Toot sweet." Haw-haws. Tee-hees. He's an embarrassment.

I stay with the Cunins again, just for the first month. Marie-Christine is away at school and I am free to do as I wish.

Spring in Paris and the cafés bustle with life. Chestnut trees burst into leaf, their flowers bloom like candelabra. I walk everywhere, take the métro as little as possible. The stink of garlic and urine and the crush of people scare me. With reason. I see a man rubbing himself against a woman. She grabs his hand. Holds it in the air. Yells, "*À qui la main?*" I can't believe she dare ask whose hand.

The worst station is Montparnasse. Miles of white-tiled passages and the same advertisement posted every few feet as far as the eye can see. Reminds me of a horror flick. Especially late at night when footsteps behind me stop when I stop, run when I run.

The area has the best cafés where artists of every stripe once hung out: Le Dôme and Le Select, La Rotonde and the Dingo Bar. I like imagining sharing wine and conversation with Man Ray's Dadaist friend, Marcel Duchamp, Morley Callaghan, Hemingway—my list is inexhaustible. Bigger than my list of jazz clubs.

What I really want is to visit the jazz clubs but I'm shy to do so on my own. I trim my list: Caveau de la Huchette, Caveau des Légendes, Chez Georges, La Palette, Le Blue Note, Le Bar Dix. I visit by degrees. First, Le Chat Noir. Frequented by students, its entrance fees low, the dance floor big enough to get lost on.

I stand outside. Listen to a clarinet wail, piano riff, drum beat.

Breathe deep. Hold my head up high. March inside.

A red light swirls from the ceiling. The place is loud and thumping. Jumping. Rocking. Buy a drink. Get on the floor, boogie on down until the trio plays "Georgia on my Mind" as the lights lower, signalling the end of the evening. Pianist George plays the *Moonlight Sonata*. A few stragglers hum along. I howl like a wolf in heat along with the music.

"Christ, where did you learn that?" The drummer turns toward me.

"Picked it up on my travels."

"It is awful," he says. "Stop it."

I rarely do anything I am told. Yet, to my astonishment, I stop. Look into his green eyes. Notice his slim hips, broad shoulders. I soften. Go all melty like the heroines in romances I read by Danielle Steele. There is even a full moon as he walks me home.

He takes my arm. "So, babe, what were ya doing in a place like Le Chat Noir?" His American accent is cultured.

I fall in love.

Thomas Arne Berge takes his time romancing me. On the evening of my *rite de passage* from girl to woman it rains. Trees drip. The earth smells musky. We creep past the concierge, climb innumerable stairs to the top of the building, stifling giggles. It is a night for the Memory Bank—even the date is never forgotten.

Creeping upstairs to the Cunins' apartment is a pain. Half an hour after I climb into my own bed, the maid brings my breakfast. Living in the posh sixteenth arrondissement so far from Tom and the Quartier Latin is a pain. I confide in two guys I know at the Alliance Française. They ask if I want to move into their flat in the thirteenth arrondissement, near Glacière métro. It's an easy walk along Rue Mouffetard to the Latin quarter. My allowance stretches to a third of the rent, food and wine. Dancing on street corners and playing extras in movies takes care of sundries, entrance fees to jazz clubs and La Piscine Deligny, where I swim every day.

By the end of July, Tom is restless, wants sea spray on his face, seabirds' cries and the smell of engine-room oil. Explains it's nothing to do with me. Says something about a merchant seaman's certificate. Something about avoiding the draft to Vietnam.

On the final day we breakfast at Les Deux Magots. He takes hold of my hand. Whispers, "I love you." Slips the green jade ring I wear on my index finger onto my engagement finger.

"I'm going to drama school next semester."

We say au revoir at the Gare du Nord, promising to write, meet in London, New York, Paris again, until the train to Genoa starts moving. We throw our cigarettes onto the platform. Last kiss. Jump down, the train gathering momentum.

I run blindly along the platform until I find our cigarette butts fallen parallel, their smoke curling upward, entwined.

"The first week is the worst," my roommates say. I am inconsolable. Stay in bed, head under the sheet. They bring food, get me drunk, do everything they can to cheer me up. Without Tom it's lonely. On the street people hurry about their business, expressions serious.

The City of Light is the City of Gloom.

Signs of political unrest I thought nothing of before are every-where. The letters OAS—synonym for a right-wing Secret Army Or-ganization that wants Algeria to continue as a French colony—are daubed onto billboards, scratched into walls. Cars honk in time to people chanting O-A-S. O-A-S. Parisians opposing the OAS find bombs in their mail slots, delivered by terrorists known as *les plastiqueurs*. Injuring or killing the recipients. August 1962, an attempt is made by an OAS officer to assassinate Charles de Gaulle in a Paris suburb. By then I'm on a motorcycle trip with a friend of my roommates.

Riding pillion with my arms round Hugh, hair flying from be-neath my crash helmet, is a tonic. We travel through Normandy and Brittany, cut across the Dordogne into the Massif Central sleeping in barns or under the stars. In Avignon we take a room with bath. Hugh wants to bed me. I am not ready yet, I say. In Perpignan he tries again. Same response. Across the border into Spain, we make for a fishing village, Cadaqués. I give in.

We go to a bullfight in Barcelona. I love the roar of the crowd, the smell of sawdust, the picadors and matadors in their brilliant-coloured garb. When the bull thunders in I seize Hugh's hand, scared. But when the contest starts I take the bull's side. Silently, I urge him to run even though that's the sign of a weak, bad animal. The matador sticks him in the neck. The bull coughs up blood. I groan, sick to my stomach. The crowd yells. The matador strikes the death blow. Sweat breaks out on my face. "He's killing him," I shriek.

"That's the whole point, silly."

The bull keels over, writhes in the sawdust. I push my way out of the stadium. At dinner Hugh says you don't cry when the bull is slaughtered. You cheer. He's annoyed.

After Barcelona, we head to Madrid, stopping for a couple of nights at Zaragoza. Hugh wants to buy things for his mother and sisters. Neither city interests me. I'm angry about the bullfight. Resent Hugh's lovemaking. Pretending he is Tom no longer works. How do I tell Hugh? Suppose he dumps me in the middle of this strange country where I don't speak a word of its language? Then what?

Avila is not a good place to run away. Its crenelated fortifications are built on top of a craggy outcrop, surrounded by brown, scrubby desert. It's hotter than Hades and I'm exhausted. Hugh insists we traipse around looking at the walls, the cathedral, the basilica, the convent, a gazillion churches … on and on until I want to scream. He even takes a firm stand over eating the local specialty for dinner: T-bone steak, grilled rare, which comes from the local *Avileña-Negra ibérica*—an indigenous black cow. Clapping my hand over my mouth I rush to the toilet and puke.

We stop next in Pamplona, famous for its bull run. Mercifully, we missed it. While Hugh plays tourist, I fall asleep over a café table. Wake up. Puke again. The smell of coffee is nauseating. Order bottled Evian water.

"*Vous êtes enceinte, Madame,*" the proprietor says in French. Brings dry toast. More Evian. "*Trois mois, je pense.*" She says she ought to know, she's had seven.

Pregnant? Three months pregnant?

Tomorrow we'll ride fifty-seven miles (ninety-two kilometres) to San Sebastián. Cross the border. Stay a night in St. Jean de Luz in a charming pension. The following morning I sunbathe naked on the beach and swim in the ocean before we ride eleven miles into Biarritz. After that it's only 480 miles (775 km) to Paris.

En route I miscarry.

1963 FRANCE, ANDORRA, SPAIN

Julia's father sends us to the airport in a chauffeur-driven Rolls Royce. He allows my best friend to travel through France to Spain because my mother says I can. My mother consents only because Julia's father says Julia can. Julia and I cooked up these agreements between us. At Orly Airport, we stick out our thumbs and hitchhike across France, stopping as little as possible. We're heading for Andorra, an independent country in the Pyrenees between France and Spain.

Some eleven thousand people live in the Principat d'Andorra in an area of 181 square miles (468 sq km) of mountainous terrain, narrow passes and hand-built stone houses. We squat in one of these for a night.

Without electricity, running water or plumbing. Up a rickety staircase we find bunk beds equipped with ancient, thick, grey blankets. During the night, rain lashes the windows; peeing outside in the dark is no joke. Our food stores dwindled, we hurry to the nearest café shivering in the early morning mist. Bread dipped in hot milk revives us.

On the first ride of the day the driver pinches Julia's nipple. She shouts at him in Spanish to stop. He brakes. We get out. Two men offer our second ride. We both get fondled. We yell, get out, find a third ride. Negotiating the coast road, we want to admire the view but must keep our wits about us, staving off unwanted touch. When we stop, men whistle at our short skirts and long hair. Women stare disapprovingly. We're considered prostitutes apparently, and no self-respecting innkeeper gives us a room. We sleep on the beach until the *Guardia Civil* arrest us. We pay a fine (read bribe) only to be arrested again further south for entering a church without our upper arms covered. The police threaten jail unless we cough up more money than Julia offers.

By Malaga we're pissed off with men, our travels and each other. We try the local youth hostel, which accepts us. The price includes breakfast. A porter carries our bags to the dormitory. Apologizing for bitching at each other, we decide to stay a few days. Being best friends doesn't necessarily make for good travelling companions.

One morning we're out exploring when a car pulls alongside.

"Julia?" asks the driver in an upper-crusty English accent.

"John!" she exults. "Tony!"

She introduces two fellow Oxford students. We hop in the car, go for lunch with lots of wine. While we eat, an enormous rat skitters along the tiled roof. That afternoon we drive to Benidorm, where we stay in John and Tony's rented apartment. From the balcony there's a view of sparkling blue sea and an expanse of sandy beach. It's a quiet place, probably once a fishing village, on the verge of an upwardly mobile tourist industry. "Cuando Calienta el Sol" plays somewhere.

I'm out of my depth, lonely and alone. Tony is not my type; John is obnoxious. It worries me Julia seems so attracted to him. I am the proverbial spare prick at a wedding.

A few nights later, we go to an open-air cabaret and bar set up in a field in the countryside. John buys the drinks. "Bet you can get any man you want," he taunts, leering at me. "When the dancing starts, I'll pick you a man. You show me your stuff. Dare you."

Drunk on wine, excited by the eroticism of strippers, fire-eating muscle men in loincloths, tigers led by women morphing into men, I rise to the challenge. Saying no is still an unknown concept.

"Time to dance," John orders.

"Who with?"

"The man in the white suit."

Pierre-Antoine reminds me of a bird of prey. Sinister yet exciting. Dark eyes under heavy lids. Olive skin. Tall. Toned, sexy body. I invite him to dance. Easy peazy. I chit-chat, ask questions. In French.

"What's your occupation?"

"Army."

"Where?"

"French Algeria."

"Lot of OAS in Paris."

"Not slogans and chanting. Prisoner information."

"D'you ever torture them?"

Shakes a finger at me. "Never ask such things."

"Sorry." Shame envelops me.

He smiles disarmingly. "I invite you and your friends to my villa."

The others are enthusiastic. They pile into John's car; I ride with Pierre-Antoine. He says we're going thirty miles—I don't catch in which direction. It's inky black outside. When he slows down, the car bumps over a railroad crossing onto a rutted driveway.

The villa has several bedrooms leading off a central hallway with a table and chairs down the middle. A couch and armchairs form a sitting area at the end, where a huge flag depicting a Nazi swastika covers the wall.

"Heil Hitler!" John says.

"Sieg Heil!" Pierre-Antoine salutes, arm straight out.

We party until our host announces time for bed. He organizes where each guest is to sleep; who will sleep with whom. Taking me by the hand he leads me into a bedroom. Locks the door. Pushes me onto the bed. Pins me down with his body. Says women who pick up men in clubs are whores. Rolls over. Falls onto the floor.

I laugh.

He stands up. Bellows, "Cunt." Grabs me, pins my wrists behind my back. Drags me to my feet.

"Let me go."

Strikes me hard across my face. Throws me on the bed. Tears off my clothes.

"I'm sorry, sorry." I burst into tears.

Thrashes me with his belt. Rapes me.

In the morning, he lies to Julia and John—and I suppose Tony too—that I want to stay. They leave. I hear them drive away.

Six weeks he keeps me under lock and key. Beats, rapes, tortures me. If I need the bathroom he ties me like an animal, leads me to the courtyard, watches. Ties my hands and feet when we drive to the beach—a deserted, rocky place. Unties me, pushes me into the water. Pelts me with stones when I swim away. Shows me to a French Algerian pal who gives us lunch. Locks me in a room while they talk. More men join them, talking in low voices. I lie down and sleep.

What triggers my anger into planning escape I don't know. I plead illness. "My kidney's acting up again. Could be serious."

He takes me to a hospital. Sits outside the door. The doctor takes him for my husband. Tells him he finds nothing wrong. Takes me back to the villa where I pay for my backfired plan.

Demoralized and broken, I overdose on pills I find in his dresser drawer. Fall unconscious.

Twenty-four hours pass. Maybe thirty-six or forty-eight. When I wake, the door is open wide. I'm not pleased to be alive but Pierre-Antoine is, as is his cousin Marc. The rule of law in Spain, 1963, is that if someone commits suicide, police throw all members of the household in jail. These men are from a well-known aristocratic family. Marc tells me later they carry me with them wherever they go.

I am told to get up and dress, am given my passport and wallet but not my return plane ticket, Paris to London.

Outside there's a thunderstorm, pelting rain. Pierre-Antoine opens the front door and is about to turf me into the street. But not before I tear at his face with fingernails grown long and dirty. I hear later the gouges become infected. He puts it about that a cat scratched him.

He kicks me down the steps, shouting, "I'm keeping your clothes to use as toilet paper." I fall into rivulets of mud. A few minutes later Marc says he'll drive me as far as Benidorm.

Somehow I make my way back to France. In Paris my money runs to either bed and breakfast, or dinner. I choose the safety of a room.

I return to drama school for Second Year but leave in spring 1964 under a cloud. Addicted to Valium, I'm unable to retain lines, which prompts the principal to expel me. As soon as a suitable man comes along, I ask him to marry me. In 1967 we emigrate to Canada.

———

Julia and I don't ever mention Spain until she's in a London hospice, dying of an inoperable brain tumour. Saying the last goodbye in 1994, I remind her how young we were; how, under John's thrall, my rescue was impossible. Her relief is obvious. A week after I return home she dies peacefully in her husband's arms.

Except for the odd trip to London and once to Seattle, I don't travel alone again until 2003.

WHERE LIFE LEADS

JOEI CARLTON HOSSACK

The country and western music sweeping through the Walmart parking lot perked my ears up like a dog listening to a faraway ambulance siren. I couldn't imagine anyone other than a kid with his gang of followers being so bold to blast the car radio loud enough for me, half a parking lot away, and the world to hear. My sixty-plus years, the last ten of which I'd spent living in a camper full-time and frequently availing myself of free camping in Walmart lots, have turned me into a cautious but still curious soul. I want to be where the action is, but not at the expense of my safety.

The tip of my index finger separated the kitchen curtains less than an inch and I peeked through the slit. My eyes gravitated toward two wagging, bushy tails pacing back and forth in the bed of a pickup truck.

I sang along to Willie Nelson's "On the Road Again" while I climbed down the steps of my truck camper. I approached rather boldly, considering there were three men, scruffy-looking and well past middle age, standing around talking and eating wieners that the short, dark-haired guy was handing out. When I got close, he offered me the last shrivelled meat tube wrapped in an unadorned bun.

"Thank you, no," I said. "I just finished eating."

The music was coming from a relatively new red minivan belonging to the heavyset one standing between the other two. He introduced himself as Bruce and asked if the music was bothering me.

I had to smile. "No, I love this kind of music. I just didn't want to miss the party. What's going on?" I asked.

It was a man who introduced himself as Charlie who answered.

He was sitting on the open tailgate of a battered 1973 blue and white GMC pickup truck with a crack in the windshield the length of a good-sized snake and the two dogs I'd seen from my camper window. "We're all just living here in the parking lot," he said with a smile.

The other man, who had been handing out the somewhat charred food, voiced his opinion about the music, preceded by and followed with a string of foul language that had me momentarily intimidated. I had no idea what he was ranting and raving about.

"Stop it, Max," said Charlie with authority. "We have a lady here." To me, he whispered, "Max is adjusting to life without alcohol. He has no idea what he's saying when he starts to swear, so please just ignore him."

"These are beautiful dogs," I said, and the two border collies came over to sniff me, lick my face and, I assume, check for anything that might be edible.

"They used to be really good dogs and they used to listen to me," Charlie said. "They were recruited and trained by the Federal Emergency Management Agency as cadaver dogs and since we've come back from New Orleans they don't listen to me anymore. It's most annoying."

"Are you really homeless?"

"Yes," he said. "I'm waiting for my cheque from the government to come through. It'll be put into a bank account next Wednesday, the first of the month. I have an appointment with the VA hospital on that day. I've been told that I have a tumor on my liver," he confided. "They're going to take care of it."

"Don't you have any family you can turn to?" I asked.

"I have two daughters, but they don't know that I'm homeless and I don't want to tell them."

"Don't you think they would want to know?" I asked.

"Yes," he said, "but I don't want to leave this area. I'm looking for my wife. Are you travelling alone?" he asked, and I knew that part of our conversation was closed.

"My husband died fourteen years ago and I've been travelling alone ever since," I responded. "I'm on a bit of a book-signing tour."

"How long did it take before you stopped missing him?"

"I'll let you know when it happens," I answered.

"That's what I thought," he said.

—·—

We talked for an hour or so—about his dogs, about spending some of his cheque money on camping equipment so he could move into a campground with showers and flush toilets, about needing to get his teeth pulled because of an accident where his face hit the windshield. I never pried; I let him choose the topics. It was late when I returned to my camper.

The next morning started with an hour's drive, then an extraordinarily long book-signing for my series of adventure travel books, finished with another hour's drive back to the Walmart. I went over to the guys just to say hello and see how their day had been. Max was feeding them wieners again. I was tired and didn't stay long after the swearing started.

A free day followed. The library, I learned, was within a short driving distance. With Charlie's self-imposed isolation weighing heavily on my mind, I needed to answer my e-mails and update my website so my friends and family would know where I was and that I was okay. When I got back, mid-afternoon, Bruce and Charlie had moved from the middle of the lot and were parked against the curb in the back row.

I went over to say hi. "I don't cook very much, but would you guys be interested in beef stew for dinner tonight?" I asked. A verbal answer was unnecessary. Their smiles said it all.

That afternoon I picked up some stewing beef, two of the largest potatoes in the box on the display table, an onion, a couple of big, fat carrots, a handful of mushrooms and a box of onion soup mix. Just before heading to the cash register I grabbed a yard-long crusty French bread in case the gravy needed to be mopped up. The rest of the afternoon was spent in my camper with the stew bubbling in my pressure cooker. At around seven I grabbed a shopping cart that had been abandoned near my camper, loaded it with all my goodies and delivered my meals on wheels still in the pot, along with bowls, spoons, a ladle, and a roll of paper towels that I always refer to as my "Irish linen on a roll."

Bruce had set out his only deck chair for me, and an empty food chest that he kept in the back of the van was placed between the two vehicles to be used as a table. With the doors open, they sat in their vehicles.

Under normal circumstances there would have been enough food for a small army on manoeuvres but both men were ravenous. I had one bowl and was delighted that it was flavourful despite the lack of celery, green onions or anything to thicken it. Bruce had a couple of bowls along with a chunk of bread and Charlie, after asking if anyone wanted more, finished everything else, including mopping up the gravy that was left in the pot with the last of the crusty loaf. It wouldn't have mattered how much food I prepared. It would have all been gone.

We spoke little while we ate, but afterward Bruce was the first to offer his story. He admitted that he had worked long hours for not much money most of his adult life, but when he slipped into a deep, dark depression and things went from hard to impossible he just drove away one day leaving his wife, grown children, a house, a mortgage and a pile of bills. He couldn't stand the stress anymore and turned left instead of right at the end of his street. He never looked back.

Then Charlie told me more about his wife. "She had some mental problems. She was a little slow. We were visiting friends near the mountains," he said as he turned his head west and pointed to the hills. "She went for a walk after dinner one day and I never saw her again." His voice softened and trailed off. "In the last few years sixty-one women have disappeared in the area. The police and everyone living nearby, including me, looked for her. We found nothing. I want to stay around here until I find her. I know she would never stop looking for me. I need to find her. I have lost everything looking for her."

We talked until dark and the mosquitoes came out for their dinner.

Sleep did not come easily to me that night and my mind replayed a conversation I had had with my brother years earlier. It was at a time that he was feeling overwhelmed with depression and was lashing out at anyone who would listen. "People don't die in alpha-betical order," he said. "I could just walk away from everything and everyone and no one would be the wiser. No one would know if I was dead or alive."

I had become angry with him and screamed, "Don't you dare do that to your family. Don't even think about it. We won't survive not knowing where you are."

When I finally fell asleep, I relived the conversation with my brother but instead of ranting and raving back at him I listened with-out saying a word. I felt only sympathy for him and Charlie and the others I had met along the way.

The next two days were busy ones for me. I had signings both days and would be leaving the morning after the second one because I was due in Coeur d'Alene, Idaho, about twenty miles east.

The morning I left I walked every food aisle in the Walmart. I purchased a gallon of water, a soft bread, a box of crackers, indi-vidually wrapped cheese, some sliced meats, a couple of bananas—everything Charlie would need to sustain himself for one day since the weather was unbearably hot and anything left over would spoil by the end of the day. I didn't see Bruce, but if he returned there would be enough food for him as well. I bought a small bag of dog food and some milk bones.

I wished Charlie luck. "What are you going to do for the next few days?" I asked, knowing it would be two more days before the money would be put into his account and he would be admitted to the hospital.

"I'll just sit here and watch. I've learned to wait," he said with a sad smile.

I smiled back as best I could. I said goodbye quickly and turned so he wouldn't see the tears filling my eyes.

RETREAT

KELLY PITMAN

I spend the first few days walking Boston, speaking only to waiters and ticket sellers. The best day begins at the Isabella Stewart Gardner Museum and ends at Harvard. The first moves me as a testament to what one woman can accomplish on her own: a palazzo filled with paintings and *objets d'arte*, and at its heart a sun-drenched courtyard. The other moves me because, well, it's *Harvard,* but also because it decided a young Sylvia Plath was not promising enough for even a summer workshop and thus, perhaps, played a role in her first suicide attempt.

The hotel offers breakfast, and on my last day in the city, I am the first to spear melon slices in the cocktail lounge. Eventually, three other tables are occupied, all by couples: a pair of Francophone scruffians in hip-hanging jeans who get double value from the breakfast buffet by assembling a lunch for later; an elderly German couple talking quietly over bowls of granola; a middle-aged gay couple with matching tans and paunches, who compare maps on their respective cell phones. I sit by the window, smiling vaguely when a young woman comes round to replenish my coffee. She too is half of a couple—she snatches a kiss from a young man in kitchen scrubs when she thinks no one is looking. I am the no one who is looking. Unless she is very rich or very beautiful, a middle-aged woman alone in a hotel can be made visible only by an act of collaborative will. I let myself fade into the furnishings, pull my notebook from my bag and write down what I see.

The bus fills quickly. I nab a window seat and take out my book. The tourist season is just beginning, and many of the passengers, their chatter reveals, are locals heading to the cape for business, or after business, or to visit relatives. I am on my way to ten days alone at a borrowed house near the beach. The plan is to retreat, to drop all the cares of my day-to-day life and have nothing to do but eat, walk, read and write. Especially write.

At each stop, the driver calls out the destination, leaps from the bus, swings the hold open and proceeds to hurl luggage onto the concrete. I am glad I have my laptop with me. It might not survive his enthusiasm, and it's the most important thing I carry. "Hy-AHN-is!" he finally yells. "Lahst staup!"

The cab smells like vanilla, somehow at odds with the driver, one of those men who can't keep his shirt tucked in or his shoes tied up or his hair flat on his head. Attached to the dashboard is a picture of him with a large woman and three chubby kids posed in order of height. They smile in front of a bucolic meadow scene that looks like a paint-by-number scheme, the kind of picture taken in a department-store photography studio. He has the same accent as the bus driver, broad nasally vowels and dropped r's. "No bautha," he calls over his shoulder when I thank him for the ride.

The house has four bedrooms, two bathrooms, cupboards full of dishes and closets full of hangers. Much more than I need. I open all the windows and try all the beds. Outside, leaves droop in the afternoon heat, but the house gets a cross breeze that smells of baking asphalt and salt water. I take the laptop out of its case and set it on the dining-room table. In the morning, I will scroll through the poems I have written over many months. I will try to discern what's okay, what's shit, and what's pretty close to shit but could become okay. And in the time I am here, I will try to write the missing poems, if I can figure out what they are.

I wander from room to room, then drift to a stop on the glassed-in porch, where slatted windows let the sea air in. I can see the metallic green swell of the Atlantic from here. I have travelled five thousand kilometres from my very own ground zero. I have come a long way to write about death.

I sleep heavily and wake to a symphony of birdsong. Shower, dress, breakfast, tea, look out the window, another cup of tea, another look out the window. I wash my bowl, plate and cup, dry them, put them back in the cupboard, flick at a crumb on the counter. I am stalling. I can hear the gulls singing their hard songs, and somewhere among the scrub pines beside the house, a dove calls oooh, woo, ooh-ooh. The house itself is silent. This is what I came for. I turn the computer on.

Once I sit down, it's easier, but not easy. Sometimes, persistence will loosen my inner tongue, but sometimes it won't. I turn to revision. It's hard work, wrestling a poem to the mat, but it has its satisfactions. Slashing adjectives and recutting lines is one step removed from the messy business of bleeding onto the keyboard, but it's still writing. After two hours, words are starting to break into random syllables, and I know it's time to stop. I stretch and stare at the screen. Then I take a long time eating a nectarine, standing at the kitchen sink and looking out the window at a rope of ivy twined so tightly around a rhododendron that it's a wonder it doesn't choke it to death. I consider whether this spectacle might find its way into a poem. Nothing. Time for a walk.

I head downtown and along Main Street. Hyannis is the least quaint town on Cape Cod. It's got a mall and a cineplex. It's got Walmart. But except for one trip to an enormous grocery store, I spend my time in the historic town centre and the picturesque residential area around it. It has a small-town feel with a touch of greasy boardwalk. There's a tiny library in a rustic brick building. A candy store and a second-hand bookshop. The JFK Memorial Museum. Bistros, pubs, ice cream parlours, clothing stores catering to wealthy women on boats. Souvenir shops selling Hyannis T-shirts and Red Sox caps. A diner called the Daily Paper. And sunburnt tourists in hats and sandals, strolling, smiling, peering into store windows.

You are never more anonymous than when you walk alone in a strange town, especially one used to tourists, where the locals have grown tired of observing strangers and the visitors are caught up in their own adventures. I have always been a solitary walker, but this is different. No one stops me on the street. No storekeeper recognizes me. No neighbour says hello or asks me about work. This is freedom. Or loneliness. It's hard to tell the difference.

I turn into the Compound Bar and Grille, which offers authentic Irish fare and the inevitable burgers. It's the perfect time for the solo patron, late afternoon, between lunch and dinner. Business is slow, so I'm more likely to be noticed. In a busy establishment, the lone diner can sometimes become all but invisible, less a person than the memory of a person.

The cook writes the dinner specials on a whiteboard. I order a spinach salad and a glass of wine, which I consume while reading. I am the only customer.

The waiter brings the bill. He doesn't have the Massachusetts accent. Probably a student working for the summer. He is wearing cargo pants and a Nirvana T-shirt. He must have been a toddler when Kurt Cobain died.

"So, where you from?" he says.

"Canada. Near Vancouver."

He nods uncertainly.

"You on vacation?" he asks.

"Sort of."

"Cool. You sail?"

"Actually, I came here to do some writing."

"Writing!" He busies himself with the credit card machine. "What do you write?"

"Poetry," I say.

"Poetry. Huh. Cool. What's it about?"

What *is* it about? It's about the sorrow at the centre of existence, it's about ineffable beauty. To be more specific, I broke up with my lover and he killed himself. I am writing poems about that.

"Oh, you know," I say. "Just ... life."

"Right on, right on."

Only after I emerge, blinking in the sunlight, does the name of the pub click. Compound, as in Kennedy Compound, the holy ground of Cape Cod. The Kennedys—glamour, riches, death, murders and tragic accidents. And recently, a suicide. A Kennedy wife, embroiled in what the papers always call "a bitter divorce," hanged herself in a barn on her New York estate. Dead, she was brought back into the fold, and she is buried in Hyannis, not far from where I'm staying.

I walk down Sea Street and see that on my return to the house, I will always pass the curiously named Oak Neck Cemetery. I have always liked cemeteries. The quietness. The rolling turf, kept lush and green by hidden sprinklers. The carefully spaced graves with their bundles of carnations and baby's breath. The trees, oak and dogwood here, so graceful, as if feeding on the dead gives them a particularly delicate beauty. I toy with using this in a poem, but the symbolism seems too obvious.

I bypass the house and head to Keyes Memorial Beach. Keyes, the plaque tells me, died in World War II. The beach he left behind is quiet but for the ocean, which falls upon the sand with a plosive sigh, withdraws, then falls again. The tide is coming in. I pace along the surf and then back, thinking of that other sea where I put the ashes. I wonder how far he has drifted. Was he gobbled up by fish right away, or is some remnant of his body even now floating in the Pacific? Or maybe even the Atlantic? Are the seas really separate, or all one? Perhaps a small part of him, even one dead cell, has ended up here, far from home.

I go back to the house and carry the laptop into the living room, but I know there's no point. I won't write anything new today. I go upstairs to bed and read for hours. Once it's dark, even the clamorous gulls are asleep, and the only sound is the pages turning under my hand.

Over the next few days, I fall into a routine. In the late afternoon, a walk, usually to the beach or along the mostly empty streets of the neighbourhood, and then into town for my salad and glass of wine, never in the same restaurant. And every morning and every night, I manoeuvre words from my head to the computer, delete half of them, get up and stretch, do a couple of laps around the room, look out the window at the water, then go back to my chair. Occasionally, I hear people on their way to the beach, a father telling his daughters to stop at the curb, the singsong murmur of lovers. On the third night, two new poems. The next morning, one of them still has potential. I am communing with the dead.

In contrast, the people I encounter in town seem particularly alive. The Irish girl, here on a work exchange, who serves me at Pizza Barbone. Her skin is so fair and thin, I can see her pulse jumping in her throat. The raven-haired taxi driver from Bulgaria, who moved here to live with his uncle and make money. The red-faced woman selling strawberries at a tiny farmers' market, who wears denim overalls and a checked shirt without a hint of irony. The pair of parking attendants at the ferry dock, both young, both black, both wearing regulation yellow jackets. The owner of the convenience store where I get my milk and wine, who talks to me in brusque English and to his indolent daughter in voluminous Russian, his *e*'s and *v*'s wrapped around each other like tangled wire.

And the tourists. They cluster around the menus posted in restaurant windows. They order fish and chips and beer. They settle on benches like flocks of pigeons. They shriek with laughter. They consult maps and debate the best way to go. They are never alone. They scatter without looking at me when I approach, and I don't have to turn back to know that they reassemble like drops of mercury, chemically drawn together. I weave through the crowd, seemingly unnoticed, though I feel exposed. My wound is so deep that I am surprised it has not left a visible sign, like a limp or a livid purple scar. But the figure I catch sight of in store windows and restroom mirrors is just an ordinary woman in walking shoes.

We lived together two years. I can count it up in days, or I can count it up in gestures. The dinners we cooked. The dishes we washed. The times we made love, gasping in the dark. The arguments. It was a heady romance at first, the kind, I see now, I shouldn't have trusted. There were good times. But there were bad times too. And then the bad times added up to more than the good times. Sometimes, he was happy, all baritone laugh and gleeful proclamations. He had a way of filling space, of seeming more alive, somehow, than the people around him. But his anger was big too, and he was angry more and more. Angry at friends, who gave up and stopped talking to him. Angry at bosses, who lost patience and fired him. And angry at me. I said the wrong thing. I worked too much. I didn't understand him. I made a mess of toothpaste tubes and left cupboard doors open and forgot to fill the water jug. I took things too seriously, or not seriously enough. I didn't know about the drugs then. If I had been a different person, I might have suspected, but I had survived my early years by tiptoeing carefully around a furious father. I was conditioned to expect rage. I was conditioned to placate. Even when he didn't come home at night and didn't call, I kept trying. Even when I found out about the drugs and suffered with him through the hell of withdrawal—a temporary one, as it turned out—I kept trying. Even on my knees sweeping up broken glass, I kept trying. And even that could make him angry, as if my tenacity were an accusation. We went to counselling, where he talked a lot and I said little, and in the safer space of the counsellor's office, we'd approach something almost like progress, but we always fell apart before the next session. One day, vacuuming drywall from the carpet beneath a fist-shaped hole, I found myself thinking, have I become one of those women?

We can't keep doing this, I said. I'm sorry, he said, you're the best thing that ever happened to me. Please, I said, you have to leave. I have never loved anyone like I love you, he said. I love you, too, I said, but this is killing me. Then he jumped off the top of the Yates Street Parkade, as if to say, killing *you?* It's killing *me.*

Now I drag him around like a spirit limb, one that aches or itches even though it's altogether gone. Our conversation continues in my head, though I do the talking now, which is why the poems are relentlessly second person. You, you, you—just what the counsellor told us not to say. Writers should issue a formal warning when a relationship ends, maybe even when it begins: I will set this down, I will have the last word. Except the last word never comes. There are always more words.

Now, though, there aren't enough words, or not the right words. I draft and redraft, but as the days pass, I walk more and more too. Half the day, sometimes, under an unvarying blue sky. Into Hyannis Port, with its sturdy great homes on flawless lawns. Along shaded streets. To beaches, which all offer the same postcard view of shell-strewn sand and wide sea reflecting the sun in a million points of light. At the beaches, parents help their children fill buckets with sand, saying "good job, good *job,*" mothers and fathers exchanging grins in perfect complicity. Teenagers sprawl on striped towels, the girls heavy-lidded and glistening with holy oils, the boys saying things like "yeah, that's so dope" while eying the girls' supple bodies. An elderly couple sits shoulder to shoulder, sharing a Thermos and gazing out at the water, their sparse white hair ruffled like feathers. At the end of Sea Street, a great nest is built round a utility pole. Two ospreys poke their heads over the edge and eye me as I pass.

In town, I make conversation with the locals. I meet the young man who runs the vintage clothing store, which seems out of place in a world of nautically themed leisure wear and overpriced boat shoes. He is going away to study communications in the fall, taking his girlfriend with him. They've never lived off the cape before. I talk about the pleasures of paper with the owner of the bookstore, who doesn't know how long he and his wife can keep their enterprise going in the age of Amazon and Kobo. I hear about the trials of last winter, its snow and punishing winds, from Robin, the woman who runs the café on the corner. Her twin boys are off to summer camp for a week in July. She loves her kids but is looking forward to a week without them. She and her husband might go camping by themselves. They haven't done that since they were first married. I tell her my own children are grown. "But they're always your babies, right?" says Robin. She suggests a cinnamon bun or a Danish to go with the coffee. "We need to fatten you up, sweetie," she says.

The streets at home are haunted. The streets here are just streets. They have neat gardens and pots of geraniums and quaint mailboxes. At dusk, televisions glow blue through picture windows. Sometimes, I glimpse the people inside the houses. A woman holding a baby looks out at the traffic, then turns to speak to someone behind her. A family gathers around a dining-room table. They are talking. I cannot hear what they say, but I see their mouths moving, their hands waving. The mother throws back her head, mouth open in what might be a hearty laugh or a howl of frustration. It's all nothing to do with me and him. But then I think, this is something he didn't see and never will. That is the way of the dead, creeping even into the new, which is defined primarily by their absence, and so is haunted too, in its way.

I imagine saying it to someone, to Robin maybe, sipping bad American coffee while she leans against the pastry case, arms folded. My lover smashed himself on the concrete. And I am writing about it.

It's been over a year and I am still writing about it. Actually, Robin, I spend a lot of time with a dead man. Is that healthy? It doesn't seem healthy. It doesn't seem sound.

And maybe Robin would tell me it's okay. Maybe Robin would say that writing is a way to put things in perspective. Maybe Robin would say that you can't make sense of suicide, but you might make sense of sorrow. Or maybe Robin would shake her head and say, sweetie, stop this nonsense! You've got your whole life ahead of you! Today is the first day of the rest of your life!

The last time I saw him, on the last day he lived, I got ready for work just like I did every other day. He hadn't moved out yet, but we contrived to encounter each other as little as possible. Every night, he came in late, long after I was in bed, and slept on the couch. He lay there that morning under the spare blanket, radiating misery. I almost put my hand on his bare shoulder, then pulled back. What are you doing today? I asked. The trouble with you, he said, is that you don't know how to live with another person. Do you really think that, I said, do you really think that about me? I don't know, he said, maybe I don't know you at all, maybe I never did. I looked at him. Then I turned and walked away, closing the door gently, coldly, behind me. Fog softened the gold-leafed oaks. Crows were busy in the gutter. Someone had a fire going. That early autumn smell of damp earth and wood smoke. I could feel my future coming toward me.

On my last day at the cape, I walk down a different part of Main Street, where the tourist shops peter out and the road widens to allow for more purposeful traffic. In the triangle where South Street angles toward Main, I come upon another graveyard, as different from Oak Neck Cemetery as can be. It is small and flat. The grass is not green, but yellow, brittle looking where it grows tall around the tombstones. The markers are pockmarked, worn round at the edges. They lean against each other, or against nothing. There are no flowers, no paths worn in the parched ground. A few thirsty pines mark the boundaries, and beyond them, the passing cars sound like gusts of wind. A weathered wooden sign says this is Ancient Cemetery. I wonder if there are any suicides in this scattering of neglected graves. There must be, life being what it is. Although it is a ragged, lonesome place, it is peaceful. Whatever they had and lost, it was a long time ago. It doesn't matter anymore.

That night, I write the poem I need to write. The poem about loving and hating, the poem about tearing free. I drink half a bottle of merlot and listen to jazz, swaying around the room. He sits on the couch. I love to watch you dance, he says. A little drunk, I step out onto the grass between the house and the sea. In the dark, everything is leached of colour. Even the hydrangea flowers, violently purple under the midday sun, are reduced to an ashy grey. I cannot see the water, but I hear it, scraping away at the land. Tomorrow I will erase all traces of my presence, and it will be as if I have not been here at all. I will go home, taking from this place only what I have written. Surely, it is almost done.

TOUTE SEULE? (ALL ALONE?)

JULIE PAUL

Dear Younger Self,

You are lucky. Really lucky. It might sound corny, but you're living the dream. The dream you've planned into reality, the typical trip the young Canadian takes to Europe, but you're not so young, and the trip's not so typical. You are a little unconventional, at least that's what some people tell you, and you cling to this identity because you've begun to call yourself a writer, and that's what a writer is supposed to be.

You are taking this trip on your own, as a woman, not on a package tour, but on a bicycle, alone. In France, where you will spend two of your four months in the saddle, they say *en velo*. There, men on the ancient back roads will call out *Ah! Canada! Quebec?* when they see your flagged panniers. After a couple of *Nons* and their disappointed faces, you start saying *Oui*.

You do not want to disappoint anyone. You've always been the good girl, the rule follower, the sensible one (minus the six free and easy months you lived in Mexico, writing and learning about tequila and surfer boys), which is why you feel okay about taking this trip. Your maturity will get you through—your common sense; your alertness to danger.

It is 1997. You're nearly twenty-seven. You have already been working as a health professional for six years, taking care of people, making them feel better one therapeutic massage at a time. After that break in the Baja, you were ready for more. More adventure. More challenges to the norm. More reasons to love the world.

But before you leave, and even once you're on the journey, people don't get it when you tell them about your plan, mainly because of the alone part. They ask hard questions: Why? Aren't you afraid? Won't you be lonely?

You don't really know why you're doing it. And yes, you are a little bit afraid. You think they're right, that you might be lonely, now and then, but you've been lonely before. It hasn't felt great, but you know it won't kill you. And you'll be able to use it, later, in your writing. You're filling your memory banks.

———

What does a person remember about a trip? The endless miles, the lovely sunsets, the clear water, the nice weather? Or does a person remember, more fully, the trouble?

You will remember the roads. You begin in Ireland, continue via England to France, then Spain, with a plan to head south to Portugal. The narrow, curving roads of Ireland—left-side cycling instead of right—past ruined castles and sheep and fuchsia hedgerows. The quiet French roads along rivers, canals, fields, hundreds of gorgeous villages. The winding roads in the Spanish Pyrenees, where you pass horses laden with gathered sticks, red-roofed houses tucked into the hills, olive trees.

You will remember your thick stacks of Michelin maps, region by region. But a map does not give traffic information. In Ireland and France, there are few days when the road feels dangerous; you stick to quiet back roads when you can. On your first day in Spain, it is a different story. You take the coastal road and head south, alongside transport trucks and insanely fast drivers, and end up fearing for your life. After only one day on that route you change your whole plan to keep going south to Portugal. Instead you turn around and stay in the Pyrenees, amid Basque farmers, then head back into the welcoming French countryside.

You will remember less-than-tranquil encounters in Ireland. The day in County Kerry when you cycle, uphill, faster than you've ever pedalled, because a man is calling for help as he's jerking off beside his open car door. The one truly horrible day of Irish weather, cycling sixty kilometres through driving rain to arrive at the remote hostel and find it full, which means cycling twenty-five more kilometres to get to a town where you splurge on a B & B and attempt to dry out your gear (it doesn't work). The days you spend at a hostel in Waterville hanging out with a Kiwi who shows you a good enough time in his tent. The afternoon you hitchhike with him to donate blood because they reward everyone with Guinness and a biscuit. The anger he displays when you rest a pop bottle between your thighs in between sips, because he thinks it's dirty. The impetigo he gives you that takes way too long to go away.

You will want to forget parts of your months in France. The day of cycling along the Loire when you can't stop crying from loneliness. You call a friend back home from a payphone at a campground resort, but you can't hear much of what she says because everyone around you is whooping it up, having the time of their lives. The days you have to keep going past castles, churches, museums, because you can't leave your loaded bike by itself: your whole existence is on that frame. The evenings spent not drinking wonderful wine or eating at restaurants because you are on a budget and it somehow seems lonelier to drink or dine alone.

You will certainly remember the night you arrive in Marseilles by train from Paris and cannot find your hostel, one of the only times you booked ahead. You cycle through the city, known to be a rough port town, late on a Sunday night, looking at a map that doesn't help, and begin to panic. Most businesses are closed up tight but you eventually find a bar—also closed—filled with drunk men. You have no choice but to ask them for help, and while they look at your heaving chest, it is partly to assess your panicked breathing. When they bring you a glass of cold water, once you are calm enough to drink it, you begin to cry. Yes, they know where the hostel is. After a few of them argue over which way is the best for you to go, one fellow tells you he will escort you there on his moped. He sees your Canadian flag and breaks into a grin. *Quebec!* he shouts. You follow his weaving tail lights through streets you have not been on, praying to a nebulous god that he is not leading you anywhere but to the bed you have paid for. He isn't. Your knight in rusted armour rides away, waving, tooting his little horn.

The day you spend lost, trying to leave Marseilles, because no matter how many people try to help you, you seem to be going in circles. Then, finally, you realize that *à droite* and *aller tout droit* do not mean the same thing; instead they mean turn right and go straight, respectively.

Then there is the day you cycle through the Camargue in the south of France and a group of black, sharp-horned bulls block your path, stare you down, move closer, until a Peugeot comes along to your rescue. And that night in the south of France when you camp alone in a private campground at the end of September, no one around but a barking dog and all the murderers and rapists in your imagination; at first light, you pack up and head back into peopled villages, grateful for noise and company.

And then, you'll always keep this long-lasting memory: the day in the fourth month of your trip when you wake up and cannot muster enough strength to cut your fingernails or tie your shoes. You have carpal tunnel syndrome from so much braking, and you must cut your trip, and your dream, a little short. You throw your cycling shoes into a garbage can and continue in sandals up the coast of France to Nantes, where you catch a train back to Normandy, then across the sea once more to England, and eventually, back home to the BC coast.

But there are other days. Days when you feel the magic. Walks in the Irish countryside, this landscape both in your ancestral blood (you cry when your plane touches down in Cork) and your heart (it's so much like the coast where you live, other than the lack of trees). Despite mourning for those trees, taken long ago by the British to make boats, you rejoice when you happen upon standing stones, cows rubbing their flanks against them. Or a ring fort in a farmer's field, unmarked, untouristed. There is the day you help one such farmer clear stones from his field, then meet him in the pub for your pint of payment. He is waiting there for you, clean-shaven, in a tweed jacket, hope in his eyes as he tells you, *All the girls have gone to Dublin.* You've adopted an Irish accent in no time and even as you let him down gently, he calls you a lovely wee colleen, a blue-eyed, dark-haired Irish girl. It feels like a kind of baptism.

You'll remember the beach made of coral and a warm ocean to swim in, real Irish music in a Doolin pub with new friends from around the globe who make you laugh like you haven't in weeks.

You love every small French village you enter, especially if you can find a cold Orangina, a bakery and a campground not directly under the church bells. You meet a woman at the store who spies your Canadian flags; she invites you to dinner at her house because you're the parallel version of her son, who's in Canada, on a bike trip. You end up staying over, sleeping in a real bed in her three-hundred-year-old house, swimming in a fancy pool.

You swim topless in the bathtub that is the Mediterranean. You, just a girl from a small village in the middle of Canada, in the ancient azure sea.

You fry up local mushrooms and eggs from the market, eat a round of Camembert and a baguette nearly every day and work it off on your steel horse, past fields of drowsy sunflowers and salt marshes and lavender and for many days at a time, off-road altogether, along the Canal du Midi and the Atlantic coast. You swim and cycle and hike and your body is fit and strong and you fall asleep in minutes, at least when you feel safe.

And you do feel safe, nearly all of the time. Alone, as a woman, without the safety nets of cell phone, email, Google or GPS, you spend days at a time when no one knows where you are, offline before there was an online, happy with the autonomy.

It reminds you of the swims you take in the early mornings back on Vancouver Island: no one but you and the bald eagles at the lake, the feeling of risk right alongside the high of freedom and independence, cushioned by the incredible luck and good fortune you possess by simply being a Canadian, a healthy person with myriad choices.

You'll want to remember this feeling, recreate it often, and keep this balance of risk and security. Right now, you are living it. And because you are alone, you reach out more often to others. If you had a travelling companion, you would be less likely to talk to strangers, to reach out, to feel. You have only your own resources to draw upon, your own courage, and mostly, your own company.

Although your trip will end months before you intend it to, the truth is, you will still have had an amazing adventure. You find out something important: you're easy to hang out with.

———

You do not know where the rest of your life will go after this journey. And despite the setback of injury, you know you have still met the goal you set out to reach, of travelling by bike through Europe. Younger self, you are setting yourself up for success, long past the days cycling in forty degrees Celsius, the mirthless miles in the mountains, the weakened wrists, the aching loneliness. You will take this accomplishment into the future, remember it when you're birthing your daughter, when you are sleep-deprived, ill or simply in desperate need of a break. You will crave alone time, and every moment you spend by yourself turns precious; your journeys will become page-bound, geography-bound, but your imagination will still roam wide and free.

After this trip, you will rarely cycle anywhere; those five thousand kilometres you covered in Europe haunt your wrists and arms whenever you lean onto your handlebars. In fact, the year your daughter turns three, pain will begin to shoot from your hand to your wrist, then all the way up to your shoulder. It is so bad that at times you will not be able to hold your daughter's little hand.

For two years, you will go into temporary retirement from practising massage, seeking every kind of treatment from physiotherapy to electro-crystal light therapy (in which the male therapist concludes your arm pain is repressed sexual energy and wants to help you get in touch with the divine feminine; you decline the offer). Often, during long days of mothering and the struggle to stay hopeful, you will draw strength from the memory of your journey by bicycle. Even if it might be a contributing factor, the rigours of that trip will have made you stronger, able to keep on going. Eventually, as it is on the trip, rest is the solution, and you are able to return to your profession.

So yes, you are lucky. So lucky! You are no longer alone, and rarely lonely, and when you return from your first solo trip as a mother, two weeks in Banff when your daughter is seven, you will be greeted not only by the beautiful girl and husband you've missed so much while away, but also by the new bicycle they've bought for you.

This bike is not built for hauling camping gear, nor is it built for speed: this bright red bike will have a bell and a basket—perfect for baguettes—and will sit you up nice and tall so your wrists don't bear any weight. Eight years later, you will still ride this bike all over town and, on a hot summer day, end up *toute seule* at the beach. Then, after wading in the chilly Pacific, with warm sand coating your wet feet like silk stockings, you will find a hospitable log to rest upon, crack open a cold Orangina and begin to write all of this down.

The Contributors

Trysh Ashby-Rolls is an award-winning journalist and the author of *Triumph: A Journey of Healing from Incest*. Forthcoming is *Left Behind Dad*, about international parent-child abduction. She is currently researching and writing her third book.

Victoria's 2014 poet laureate, Yvonne Blomer's most recent collection of poems is *As if a Raven* (Palimpsest Press, 2014). Her first book, *a broken mirror, fallen leaf*, was shortlisted for the Gerald Lampert Memorial Award.

Moni Brar is a freelancer, editor and educator. She was born in India and moved to Canada at the age of three and has explored over thirty countries and worked in nine. When she is not travelling or writing, she can be found coaxing things to grow in her garden in Calgary, AB.

Ann Cavlovic's writing has appeared in *Alternatives, Event, Room, Sub-Terrain, The Centennial Reader* and the *Globe and Mail*. She is this year's second runner-up in the PRISM International Creative Non-Fiction Contest. Her play *Emissions: A Climate Comedy* was the "Best in Fest" of the 2013 Ottawa Fringe Festival.

Yamuna Flaherty is a writer, photographer and addict of nomadism. Her quest for soul-stirring experiences led her on a fifteen year global pilgrimage that has filled thirty diaries, broken as many hearts and made having a regular life impossible.

Lori Garrison is a writer and a poet. She has worked as a ranch hand, a waitress, a bartender, a nanny and a door-to-door salesperson. She currently lives in Whitehorse, YT, and whenever possible she sneaks off to go salmon fishing and drink beer in Haines, Alaska.

Jane Eaton Hamilton is the author of eight books, including *Love Will Burst into a Thousand Shapes*. She is the two-time winner of the CBC Literary Prize in fiction (2003/2014) and the two-time winner of the PRISM International Short Fiction Contest. She has been published in *Salon, Full Grown People*, the *New York Times, Seventeen, Macleans* and the *Globe and Mail*.

Elizabeth Haynes' writing has appeared in many pubications including *Shy* (University of Alberta Press) and *Walk Myself Home* (Caitlin Press).

She has won numerous awards including the Western Magazine Award for fiction and the James H. Gray Award for non-fiction. Her short fiction collection, *Speak Mandarin Not Dialect* (Thistledown Press), was nominated for an Alberta Book Award.

Joei Carlton Hossack is a solo RV-er. She started travel writing at the age of fifty and has been writing, publishing, photographing, teaching and storytelling for the past twenty years, transforming her old age into an exciting adventure.

Vici Johnstone has worked in theatre, radio, television, film and digital media. She entered the publishing industry in 2006 when she was hired by Harbour Publishing as the production manager, and later the managing editor and general manager. She purchased Caitlin Press in 2008.

Desirée Jung is a Canadian-Brazilian writer with a background in film, journalism, creative writing and comparative literature. Her work has been published in periodicals across North America and Europe.

Kami Kanetsuka was born in England. She spent time in Israel and Italy. In the mid-sixties she went on the overland trail to Kathmandu, where she lived for several years. Now residing on Bowen Island, BC, she is writing a memoir about Kathmandu in the sixties.

Karen J Lee writes memoir, humour, and personal essay—sometimes simultaneously. Her work has appeared in *PRISM International* and the *Globe and Mail*. Karen is a graduate of The Writer's Studio at Simon Fraser University and Humber School of Writing.

Miriam Matejova is a PhD student of Political Science at the University of British Columbia in Vancouver. Her creative writing has appeared in the *Globe and Mail*, *Her Circle* and several travel magazines. She volunteers as a translator and reviewer for the TED Open Translation Project.

Kim Melton is an ardent naturalist who explores life from her tiny cabin on wheels, currently parked in the Hamlet of Mount Lorne, Yukon. She enjoys farming, playing the banjo and occasionally combining coffee and yoga.

Catherine Owen lives in BC. She is the author of ten collections of poetry and one of prose essays and memoirs. Her upcoming book is a compilation of interviews with fifty-seven Canadian poets on writing in the world practices called *The Other 23 and a Half Hours* (Wolsak & Wynn, 2015).

Julie Paul has published two collections of short stories, *The Jealousy Bone* (Emdash, 2008) and *The Pull of the Moon* (Brindle & Glass, 2014). She writes, massages and bikes to the beach in Victoria, BC.

Sarah Paynter lived in Ottawa, Geneva, Bangkok, New Delhi and Toronto before settling in Vancouver. She is a geography instructor and globetrotter. Her academic work focuses on geographies of identity, difference and belonging.

Nancy Pincombe has an MFA in Creative Writing from UBC and lives in Roberts Creek, BC. She is a community arts writer for the *Local* newspaper. Nancy worked for years selling bonds at an investment bank, but now spends her time keeping up with her small daughter on a rural property, riding horses, encouraging tiny apple trees and counting hens. She is working on a short story collection called *En Rose*.

Kelly Pitman grew up in Calgary, AB, on the traditional territories of the Tsuu T'ina people. She now lives with much gratitude on the traditional territories of the Lkwungen and W'SÁNEĆ peoples in Victoria, BC. She teaches English at Camosun College

Julia Selinger is an award-winning graphic designer and multimedia artist, with a passion for writing, travel, art and singing. A mother of two, she has resided in various countries around the world and now makes her home by Rattray Marsh on the shore of Lake Ontario.

Waaseyaa'sin Christine Sy is Anishinaabe of mixed ancestry. Her poetry, prose, short stories, literary essays and interviews appear in various journals, anthologies, and magazines such as *Rampike, Matrix, Kimewon, Briarpatch, Lemonhound, Muskrat*, the *Conversant* and *EVENT*. She is presently completing a pre-doctoral dissertation in Indigenous Studies/ American Indian Studies at Michigan State University.

Shannon Webb-Campbell is an award-winning poet, writer and journalist of mixed Aboriginal ancestry. She is the inaugural winner of Egale Canada's Out in Print Award and was the Canadian Women in the Literary Arts 2014 critic-in-residence. *Still No Word* (Breakwater Books 2015) is her first collection of poems. She lives in Halifax.